D1457407

Labor Markets under
Trade Unionism

To Louise

Labor Markets under Trade Unionism

Employment, Wages, and Hours

John Pencavel

BLACKWELL
Oxford UK & Cambridge USA

Copyright © John Pencavel 1991

First published 1991

Basil Blackwell, Inc.
3 Cambridge Center
Cambridge, Massachusetts 02142, USA

Basil Blackwell Ltd
108 Cowley Road, Oxford, OX4 1JF, UK

Library of Congress Cataloging in Publication Data

Pencavel, John H.
  Labor markets under trade unionism: employment, wages, and hours
John Pencavel.
    p.   cm.
  Includes bibliographical references and index.
  ISBN 1-55786-077-7 (hardback)
    1. Labor market.   2. Hours of labor.   3. Wages.   4. Trade-unions.
I. Title.
HD5707.P45   1991
331.12 – dc20   90-44349
                                                                        CIP

British Library Cataloguing in Publication Data

A CIP catalogue record for this book is available from the British
Library.

Typeset in 10 on 12 pt Times
by Colset Private Limited, Singapore
Printed in Great Britain by T.J. Press Ltd, Padstow, Cornwall

Contents

Preface

The purpose of this book is to bring together some of my thoughts on economists' research on the determination of wages, employment, and hours of work in markets where workers are represented by trade unions. This topic has been the subject of a good deal of research in the past 15 years or so and there have been some notable contributions to the literature. However, to an unfortunate extent, this literature is split into a theoretical branch and an empirical branch and only occasionally have there been efforts to bring these two branches closer together.

For instance, there is a very large body of research attempting to compute the effects of unions on wages and there is another class of work proposing models of union wage objectives and union–management wage bargaining. For the most part, researchers in these two areas have gone their separate ways with little attempt to relate their work to that in the other branch. This is curious and also regrettable because ultimately a satisfactory understanding of the role of unionism and collective bargaining in the economy requires a fusion of this research: empirically relevant behavioral models of trade unions and collective bargaining.

This book is an attempt to relate and bring a little closer these two branches of the literature on unionism. This reflects my underlying view of the purpose of research in economics. That is, I do not see economics as a subdivision of applied mathematics where little essential recourse is made to empirical phenomena. I view economics as a science which requires, therefore, a meaningful interdependence between theoretical models and real world experiences. And this interdependence is better achieved not by invoking evidence in a cursory and casual fashion, but by closely relating aspects of the theory to the facts in an organized manner. Of course, we seek not total explanations of empirical phenomena, something that would replicate the complexity of the world, but rather key components of explanations. In fact, we are so far from understanding the behavior of unionized labor markets that we are still at the stage of trying to identify these key components.

This book is by no means an encyclopedic review of the literature on wages, employment, and hours of work in unionized labor markets. No doubt I have overlooked a number of important contributions to research. What I have attempted here is to write an essay on the themes that I find most pertinent and promising. In so doing I draw upon the literature selectively.

This selection is most obvious in the fact that I address these issues as they relate to only two economies, the United States of America and Britain. I am aware of some of the corresponding literature describing the Canadian, Australian, Scandinavian, and other economies, but my knowledge here is more irregular and I find it convenient in exposition not to range across many different countries' experiences. This was a difficult decision because I believe that international comparisons of the way labor markets operate represent a most useful and somewhat unexploited dimension of labor economics research. (Fortunately, a recent paper by Holmlund (1989) has brought together much of the literature as it bears on the Scandinavian economies.) Though it is restricted to two countries, I hope the analysis herein is enhanced by drawing upon the experience of more than one economy.

I have attempted to write this book so that it is accessible to an audience wider than that encompassing only specialists in this field. Thus I have eschewed a certain amount of the formality that is the fashion in much of economics today. In particular, I have tried to reach out to specialists in industrial relations in the belief that there is little separating a good economic approach from an industrial relations approach to the questions addressed in this book. I am well aware of differences in methods of inquiry between the economist and the industrial relations scholar, but I see these methods as largely complementing – not competing with – one another.

Work on this book started during the academic year 1988–89 when I was awarded a Guggenheim Fellowship. I am most grateful to the Guggenheim Foundation for this opportunity to embark on this research. Though actual writing began at this time, in fact portions of this book have appeared in my graduate labor economics class at Stanford University for many years, in a few instances for over a decade. By their questions, many students have helped me clarify and improve upon my arguments and I thank them for their skepticism and challenges. A number of scholars and friends have read portions of the manuscript and their reactions have greatly improved it. The detailed comments of Robert Elliott, Henry Farber, Robert Flanagan, Andrew Oswald, and Melvin

Reder were especially helpful. Other useful comments were provided by Paul Chen, David Green, Julie Lee, and Fernando Salas. The manuscript (in all its drafts) was typed extremely professionally by David Criswell. I thank them all very much. Most of all I have been fortunate in my family – for being there.

John Pencavel

1 The Context of Unionism

1.1 Introduction

The primary focus of this book is on the determination of wages, employment, and hours of work in labor markets where employees are organized into trade unions. There are several reasons why such a study commends itself. First, as we shall see, there appear to be differences (and sometimes substantial differences) in the values of these variables between unionized and nonunionized labor markets and this calls for some sort of explanation. Second, though in some instances the unionized labor market operates differently from its nonunion counterpart, in other cases unorganized workers bear formal resemblance to a union and therefore the analysis of such nonunion markets may be enhanced by a better understanding of unionism. As shown later in this chapter, many labor markets are characterized by a bargaining relationship between management and workers whether employees are organized into a trade union or not. An improved understanding of the workings of labor markets characterized by explicit contracts between unions and managements may help an understanding of markets with implicit contracts.

There has been a great deal of economics research on unionized labor markets in the past decade or so and this book is an attempt to take stock of some of it and to assess what we know and what more needs to be known. In my view, this should mean paying attention both to the empirical regularities associated with the operation of unionized labor markets and to theoretical models that are designed to provide structural explanations for these empirical regularities. An evaluation that confines itself to empirical work or that outlines models seriatim with only casual reference to the facts is seriously deficient. This book aims to weld the empirical and theoretical literature on these topics so that economists' models are assessed not in terms of their conformity with models in other areas of economics, but in terms of their correspondence with the facts appropriately organized.

This book is not a comprehensive analysis of unionism, but only covers that part closely bearing on wages, employment, and hours. In so doing, it focuses on what have been major goals of trade unions, namely, to raise the level of wages, to increase the worker's security in his employment, and to reduce and regularize the level of hours worked. Because questions relating to the quality of the work environment, the internal administration of the union, the effectiveness of grievance machinery, and other issues are not addressed, I do not pretend to offer a treatise on unionism that might claim to be a comprehensive analysis. Even with the perspective so narrowed to wages, employment, and hours, the larger context of unionism needs to be recognized and, I believe, this context cannot be appreciated without some idea of how labor markets operate in the absence of trade unions. So, first, consider some factors that make the market for labor services distinctive and, perhaps, singular.

1.2 The Exchange of Labor Services Absent Unions

With respect to its dealings with its employees, the primary goal of the firm is to convert disparate, inchoate, and perhaps grudging individuals into an integrated, productive, team. This conversion of raw, uninformed, labor into an organized force is effected by the operation of various rules and conventions regulating the nature of employment contracts. These contracts specify the terms and conditions of the exchange of labor services. Such transactions in the market for labor tend to have distinct characteristics that are not well described by analogies to the market for most commodities. There are several reasons for this.

The first derives from the fact that, as Alfred Marshall expressed it, the seller of labor services must deliver these services himself. This means that, in specifying the terms and conditions of the exchange, the worker cares not only about the price (the hourly wage rate or the piece-rate), but also about other factors that affect his welfare: how hard is he expected to work?; with whom is he supposed to work?; what orders may he legitimately refuse to follow?; and so on. Where the product of the worker's efforts can be measured without much difficulty and the product can be stored with little cost to the organization of production, the task may be "contracted out" and the worker may become an independent contractor selling his output to the firm. But when the worker's product is not measured so easily or when the worker's immediate proximity to other workers is important to production, the labor force is organized as a team within a firm. Under these circumstances, work assumes social aspects that affect the value placed by the employee on the labor transaction.[1]

The second reason for the distinctive nature of transactions in the labor market is that there are several dimensions to the exchange of labor services. Obviously employees supply their time and, indeed, time is usually used as the accounting device to apportion payments among employees. Also, employees supply their effort and skills to work activities, including effort in the form of cooperation with fellow employees and with management. In such team work, the contribution to output made by each employee cannot be identified (Alchian and Demsetz, 1972). Moreover, as Coase (1937) emphasized, the employee grants management the authority to direct him to a range of tasks, the limits of which are often poorly specified. In short, the employment contract involves the employee delivering his time, effort, skills, cooperation, and a subset of his liberties to management.

Even when the employee's input of time is easily observable, the effort he applies to his work, his willingness to obey orders, and the ingenuity with which he handles unforeseen problems are not clearly defined. These problems pertaining to the measurement of the labor input explain why the delineation of the labor contract – to what tasks may the worker be directed, with what effort should the employee work, under what conditions may the exchange be terminated – is so difficult. Even if a statement of the terms of the exchange could be written down, the parties would be likely to have ample room for disputing whether the terms had been broken. Hence the very nature of the commodity, labor services, tends to exclude simple contracts where a well-defined good is exchanged on unequivocal terms.

The third distinctive feature of the labor exchange is that labor services have "experience characteristics" (Nelson, 1970): the quality of the exchange is difficult to assess prior to the transaction and, indeed, as experience of the exchange accumulates, so the parties are better able to estimate its value. Much labor turnover can be understood as a consequence of these experience characteristics: workers and employers sample one another, workers shopping among jobs and employers sorting

---

[1] Cf. "[T]he labour market is – by nature, and quite independently of Trade Union organization – a very special kind of market, a market which is likely to develop 'social' as well as purely economic aspects. . . . The conditions for this to happen are: (1) that the worker should be free to change his employer, not being bound down by any form of quasi-serfdom; (2) that employment should be regular, i.e., non-casual, so that there is a presumption that the relation between the employer and at least a major part of his employees will be a continuing relation. When these conditions are satisfied, there is a strong presumption that the 'social' characteristics will appear" (Hicks, 1963, p. 317).

through workers. When a promising match has been made, an accumulation of labor market transactions between an employee and an employer makes subsequent contracting much easier; in other words, the cost of transacting falls with the duration of the employment relation and long-term contracts tend to develop. Under these circumstances, the contract is inclined to become singular: management believes a new employee is only an imperfect substitute for an existing employee while the worker's alternative job opportunities are distinctly inferior to his present job. A "good working relationship" becomes a resource that cannot be perfectly and immediately replicated by hiring a new employee or working for a new employer. Therefore, the value of the match between a current employer and current employee is surrounded with much less uncertainty than if either contracted with a new party. In any event, because of the experience characteristics of labor services, part of the costs of transacting may include employment for a trial period with the attendant costs of turnover if the outcome of the experiment is unsatisfactory.

A fourth feature of transactions for labor services arises whenever the worker accumulates skills specific to the employer or the job.[2] In this case, the employment contract takes on the appearance of a bargaining relationship: there are terms of employment defining the employee's minimum utility such that, at any terms below this minimum, the employee will choose to quit and look for work elsewhere; there are terms of employment corresponding to management's maximum cost such that, at terms above this maximum, management will replace a worker with a new hire. Where the terms of the contract will settle within this range set by the employee's minimum utility and management's maximum cost is an issue for bargaining theory though it is in the interests of both parties to minimize the costs of bargaining themselves. These costs include not only the resources consumed in negotiations and the expenses borne by each party in the event of disagreement, but also the potential morale

---

[2] The terminology of specific training or specific skills stems from Becker (1964). A closely related concept is Williamson's "task idiosyncracies" (Williamson, 1975). "Almost every job involves some specific skills. Even the simplest custodial tasks are facilitated by familiarity with the physical environment specific to the workplace in which they are performed. The apparently routine operation of standard machines can be importantly aided by familiarity with a particular piece of operating equipment. Even mass-produced machines have individual operating characteristics which can markedly affect work performance. In some cases workers are able to anticipate trouble and diagnose its source by subtle changes in the sound or smell of the equipment. Moreover, performance in some production and most managerial jobs involves a team element, and a critical skill is the ability to operate effectively with the given members of the team. This ability is dependent upon the interaction of the personalities of the members, and the individual's work 'skills' are specific in the sense that skills necessary to work on one team are never quite the same as those required on another," (Doeringer and Piore, 1971, pp. 15–16).

problems when equally productive individuals are employed on terms that vary with their bargaining skills.[3] Thus the pervasiveness of specific skills implies the presence of bargaining costs in very many labor market transactions.

Hence, because labor services cannot be disembodied from the worker, because of difficulties in measuring the input of labor services, because labor services possess experience characteristics making experimental exchanges worthwhile though costly, and because specific skills introduce bargaining costs into the exchange, the market for labor is characterized by much greater costs of transacting than is the case in many consumer goods markets. It is prohibitively expensive of time, effort, and money to draw up and enforce detailed contracts. An efficient market should be expected to develop means to economize on these transaction costs and it has been suggested[4] that this drive for efficiency accounts for the extent and nature of the rules, procedures, and institutions that have developed to mediate between "raw" labor and the application of "effective" labor input in production.[5]

For example, consider the widespread practice of attaching wages not to individuals but to jobs and of constructing a cardinal index to each job that allows for comparisons to be made across jobs and, therefore, for wage differentials to be determined within the organization. This procedure of job evaluation is followed primarily because, in a bargaining setting so common in labor market exchanges, it is a relatively inexpensive method of arriving at agreeable prices. Though disputes arise over its operation, by and large the process is viewed as a fair one and, when it works well, it has the effect of removing from the province of bar-

---

[3] Hicks (1963, p. 317) writes that the technically efficient input of labor services requires that "there should not be strong feelings of injustice about the relative treatment of different employees (since these would diminish the efficiency of the *team*), and there should be some confidence about fair treatment over time (which is necessary in order that the individual worker should give of his best)."

[4] See, for example, Doeringer and Piore (1971, pp. 29–32, 57–9) and Williamson (1985, pp. 240–72).

[5] Evidence that transaction costs constitute an important feature of labor markets is provided by the fact that sometimes firms are willing to pay someone else to discharge some of the exchange functions. Examples are provided by labor contractors in New York's garment industry and in California agriculture, the Italian *padrone* operating usually in the construction and railroad industries, the *jamadar* in the Indian construction industry, and the temporary help agencies supplying workers at short notice for brief periods. For information on the services provided by labor contractors, see Epstein and Monat (1973). The classical analysis of the contractor in California agriculture is, of course, that of Lloyd Fisher (1953) who writes of the contract system, "It depends finally for its persistence on the fact that it is one of the few organizing influences in a disorganized market. It continues to bring workers and jobs together, to provide an element of stability and regularity in a chaotic market" (p. 21).

gaining the potentially factious issue of wage differentials within the organization.[6]

A second example of procedures designed to conserve resources used in labor market exchanges concerns the heavy reliance in some firms on internal promotion to fill vacancies rather than hiring new employees. This preference arises in situations in which an employee's skills are partly specific to the firm rather than specific to a particular task. Even though he has been working at a different job, an existing employee's productivity in a higher ranking job is estimated with less uncertainty than is normally the case for a new employee. At the same time, even working at a different task, the employee will have a better understanding of the firm's "way of doing things" than he would have if he took an equivalent job in a new firm. Especially when employees are not compensated by some variant of piece-rate methods, promotion may also represent a device for rewarding continuous and cooperative work effort. In other words, the extensive use of internal promotion and career ladders within the organization is an incentive system that avoids the uncertain costs of contracting with new and untried employees.

Because labor transactions do not follow clear, explicit, specifications, much contractual behavior is governed by convention. That is, largely unwritten rules prescribe what may be expected of each party to the labor market transaction. Some rules are specific to a particular job, others to a firm, others common to an industry, and still others will describe the entire society. These conventions relate to how hard employees are expected to work, the scheduling of work, the allocation of workers to tasks, the payment of compensation, and so on. These are items that usually have the characteristics of public goods within the firm. That is, the rules and conventions of the working environment affect the welfare of all employees so that, for instance, the "consumption" of safety regulations by one worker does not prevent other workers from benefiting from them.[7] These rules are best thought of not as impeding market processes, but rather as means of effecting transactions where the terms of the contract are not being continually negotiated and where the attempt to specify these terms precisely would be impossible.

[6] Writing of job evaluation procedures, Doeringer and Piore (1971, pp. 84, 90) observe, "Their quasi-ethical character and the laborious process through which they are applied lends a certain aura of legitimacy to them and makes them appear as 'natural' a manner of wage determination as competition and bargaining. . . . The institutional wage setting procedures are to be understood as a less expensive means of arriving at a determinate set of wage rates."

[7] A number of writers have argued that unions are especially well placed to represent workers' demands for workplace public goods. See Olson (1965), Duncan and Stafford (1980), and Flanagan (1983).

The firm- or job-specific conventions operate best when the parties have contracted together for a long time. Then there is a better understanding of the class of behavior expected of the worker and that expected of management. With repeated transactions, the employment relationship is nourished by mutual trust and confidence. Although elements of trust are present in most transactions where exchanges are not simultaneous and inspection not costless, they assume special importance in contracts of long duration where honesty and rectitude can substitute for resources allocated to monitoring contractual behavior.

1.3 Labor Transactions with Unions

The previous section has argued that transaction costs tend to assume greater importance in labor markets than in most commodity markets and, consequently, rules and conventions have evolved to economize on these costs. Many of these rules and conventions exist quite independently of unionism. The important feature introduced by unionism is the manner in which these rules are determined.

In nonunion markets, the form of these rules is determined largely by management who announce "take it or leave it" terms. Of course, in setting these "take it or leave it" conditions, management are themselves conveying influences from the market, but nevertheless the initiative rests with management. They establish rules or institute practices regulating the responsibilities and rights of workers and management, including measures for dealing with situations in which the responsibilities have not been met and rights have been infringed. It is true there are occasions of explicit individual bargaining in nonunion markets and, indeed, it may well be a useful analytical device to characterize nonunion markets as if they also had their terms of employment settled by bargaining. As noted in the previous section, a bargaining situation is endemic in labor markets whether unionized or not. Viewed in this way, in many markets the union does not supplant a wage-taking competitive labor market with a monopolistic combination of workers, but rather it supersedes single worker bargaining with bargaining by a single agent who represents many workers.[8] In most nonunion bargaining contexts, a single worker

[8] This was well expressed by Sidney and Beatrice Webb: "In unorganized trades the individual workman, applying for a job, accepts or refuses the terms offered by the employer without communication with his fellow-workmen, and without any other consideration than the exigencies of his own position. For the sale of his labour he makes, with the employer, a strictly individual bargain. But if a group of workmen concert together, and send representatives to conduct the bargaining on behalf of the whole body, the position is

negotiates in isolation from other workers and usually in ignorance of the terms of employment other workers have secured. What is distinctive about unionism is not the fact of bargaining, but that this bargaining is explicit and manifest and that the workers collaborate.

This procedural difference is of genuine importance to individuals. That is, even if the outcomes were the same, it is of some consequence to employees to have the sense that they or their agents contribute to determining their work environment. Thus trade unions give greater opportunities for individuals to *participate* in the joint determination of the terms and conditions of their employment. This participation is known as collective bargaining, which is both a legislative exercise (i.e., the specification of rules which the parties agree to follow) and a process of constructing administrative procedures for implementing these decisions including a role for judicial review. In this way, by involving workers in determining the terms and conditions of employment, scholars have often conjectured that there were efficiency gains from participation. As Slichter (1941, p. 575) expressed it: "The very fact that the workers have had an opportunity to participate in determining their working conditions is in itself favorable to efficiency. . . . [E]fficiency depends upon consent. Even though the specific rules and policies adopted in particular instances may not be ideal, the process of joint determination of working conditions at least offers the possibility of achieving greater efficiency than could be obtained under rules and conditions dictated by one side."[9]

Not only is the process of determining the rules different in unionized markets, but the form and content of these rules also differs: grievance procedures work more effectively in resolving disputes in unionized firms where employees have their own agent to represent their interests; work assignment and jurisdictional rules are likely to be codified more fully in unionized firms; the activities of the middleman are drastically reduced, if not eliminated, upon unionization.[10] If the rules of the work-

---

at once changed. Instead of the employer making a series of separate contracts with isolated individuals, he meets with a collective will, and settles, in a single agreement, the principles upon which, for the time being, all workmen of a particular group, or class, or grade, will be engaged" (Webb and Webb, 1902, p. 178).

[9] Slichter's arguments about the efficiency improvements from employee participation have been reiterated by Freeman and Medoff who maintain that collective bargaining provides employees with an effective voice at the workplace: "If management uses the collective bargaining process to learn about and improve the operation of the workplace and the production process, unionism can be a significant plus to enterprise efficiency" (1984, p. 12).

[10] Writing in 1953, Fisher observes, "The trade union and the labor contractor are implicit competitors. . . . [S]uccessful unionization of seasonal workers would either destroy the contract system or transfer its functions to the trade union in which the seasonal workers

ing environment mediate between "raw" labor and "effective" labor (as the previous section argued) and if these rules tend to differ between union and nonunion firms, then we should expect the effective input of labor services to be different in union and nonunion firms. Expressed differently, unionism introduces a different production technology, where technology is understood to include the rules, procedures, and institutions relating to the use and application of labor.[11] Unionism represents one element in a firm's organizational structure which defines its maximum attainable output from its inputs.

If the union affects the production technology in this way by changing the manner in which raw labor is converted into an effective work force, then the obvious question is whether unionized firms are more or less efficient in this regard. The answer is not evident. If the union is better able to defend or enforce make-work practices than an unorganized workforce, then the production frontier for the union firm will lie inside that of the nonunion firm. On the other hand, scholars emphasizing the rule-making activities of unions are sometimes impressed with the potential of unionized markets to contribute to a productive employment relationship and economize on transaction costs. Indeed, this was the dominant view in nineteenth century Britain where both professional and lay opinion held that usually unions promoted the smooth operation of labor markets. In Phelps Brown's (1983) words, "In the experience of Victorian employers it was the most skilled, responsible, and steady workmen who took the lead in the unions and unionism had an uplifting influence on the weaker brethren. Industrial relations were found to be at their best when strongly organized unions entered into voluntary negotiations with stable associations of employers" (p. 19).[12]

If there is scope for the union to develop rules and procedures that result in a more efficient transformation of "raw" labor into "effective"

---

were organized. There might be either a contract between producer and contractor, or a contract between producer and trade union; there would not, however, be both at the same time. . . . [T]he services rendered [by the contractor] are important and even necessary services, and it is conceivable that a responsible trade union could perform these functions more efficiently than does the labor contractor at present. . . . [I]f unionism is to develop among seasonal agricultural workers, it will have to borrow many of the characteristics of the contract system, performing many of the same functions for both producer and worker which the contract system now performs" (Fisher, 1953, pp. 87–90).

[11] This justifies the inclusion of indicators of the performance of the personnel management system as inputs into fitted production functions. See, for instance, Ichniowski (1986) and Pencavel (1977). A similar argument appears in Jensen and Meckling's (1979) analysis of labor-managed firms.

[12] The predominantly sympathetic view of union activities at this time is reflected in Alfred Marshall's writings. See Petridis (1973).

labor, why doesn't management institute them without the existence of the union? The reason is that usually management cannot exploit these opportunities without at the same time bringing into being an organization that engineers wage increases for workers and reduces the incomes of the owners of capital. In other words, it is doubtful whether the union can be an effective agent for the worker and act as a rule-making authority unless it also has the clout to push up wages.

For example, normally each employee has a better estimate of his actual and potential work effort than his supervisor, but the employee may be reluctant to reveal that information because of the concern that management might use it to further their interests at the expense of the worker. Indeed, a long line of industrial relations research has documented the presence of restrictions in work effort and output among nonunion workers that are the product of worker distrust of management.[13] A union can provide the worker with some assurance that he would enjoy some of the returns from revealing his actual and potential work effort, thereby providing an incentive for the employee to disclose it. The processing of more and better information enables the firm to generate rents whose division is the subject of bargaining.[14] This example is one of a number of instances in which the worker has superior information about work effort and the organization of production at the shop floor level and which he has little incentive to reveal unless he is confident it is in his interests to do so. Of course, management could spend resources to try and acquire this information, but it conserves resources if the worker truthfully volunteers what he knows. Where these issues of asymmetric information are important, transaction economies cannot be exploited without the workers having the confidence that they have an agent representing their interests.

The argument in the previous paragraph also bears on the issue of the compatibility of unionism with competitive labor markets. Lewis (1959) argued that many of the procedures governing the exchange of labor services in unionized firms were fully consistent with the operation of competitive labor markets.[15] In setting up and operating a system of industrial jurisprudence and acting as an employee's agent, the union offers services that, in principle, are of value to a worker who pays for

---

[13] The classic study is Mathewson (1931). Other examples are provided in Lupton (1963) and Roy (1952).

[14] Also see Aoki (1988).

[15] Note, however, that the argument above has reasoned that these procedures affect the output obtained from a given number of employees (i.e., these procedures affect the firm's production function) whereas Lewis (1959, p. 183) assumes no effect on production functions.

them directly through union dues and initiation fees and indirectly by supplying his labor to unionized firms at lower wages than to nonunion firms. These activities of competitive unionism are contrasted with the wage-making activities of unions: in effecting a wage increase for their members, unions are said to behave as monopolists, driving up the price of labor by fabricating or threatening a shortage through entry restrictions, coordinated malfeasance, or strike action. The *analytical* distinction between competitive and monopoly unionism is evident, but there must be some doubt whether, in practice, the activities of competitive unionism can be undertaken without the union also exhibiting its monopoly-wage features. For the ability of the union to act as the worker's agent and to provide an effective system of industrial jurisprudence almost certainly requires an organization that, by the same token, can extract monopoly wage gains.

To summarize, in altering the rules and procedures by which raw labor is transformed into effective labor, a trade union changes the production technology. Whether these changes result in enhanced or diminished efficiency cannot be determined *a priori*. Moreover, as we shall see in the following chapter, the empirical examination of this issue is frustrated by the fact that the union also changes wages. Indeed, it is the wage-making activities of unions that economists have tended to emphasize in the past few decades. Like most economists' analyses of unions, this book stresses their role in the determination of wages, employment, and hours of work. Their other activities in modifying the employment relationship will receive only tangential treatment. Hence I offer no pretense of providing a full evaluation of unionism in the economy of the sort required for recommendations regarding public policy toward collective bargaining and trade unions. No doubt, an informed public policy would take account of what has been learned about the effects of unions on wages, employment, and hours of work, but these considerations would not form the exclusive basis for any policy.

1.4   An Overview

In reviewing and evaluating what is known about unionized labor markets, I turn first to a statement of the basic empirical regularities regarding the relationship between wages, employment, and hours of work on the one hand and unionism on the other. Any satisfactory model must be consonant with these basic facts. So in chapter 2 I describe and assess this research. In one important respect, it is a curious literature: there is a voluminous amount of work trying to quantify the effect of unions on wages, but comparatively little on measuring the union impact on work hours and employment. The result is that certain, widely held beliefs about the effects of unions – for instance, that unions reduce both employment and work hours – rest on little sound evidence. Though much more is known about the association between wages and unionism, even here there are commonly accepted notions that lack a firm empirical basis: an example is the belief that union wages are less responsive than nonunion wages to business cycle shocks. Chapter 2 reviews the evidence on these and other matters.

In chapter 3, I discuss the goals of a trade union. I argue that, at this stage in our understanding, it is best to think in terms of "the" union leader's objectives. No doubt, in unions complying with some sort of democratic processes, the leader's objectives are related to the rank-and-file's values and wants, but at the same time it would be remarkable if the union leader were no more than a cipher. First, the rank-and-file do not speak with one voice and the leader's task is to reconcile different preferences and to ensure they do not manifest themselves as a weakness in bargaining. In most organizations, the information available to the leadership endows it with a different perspective from its rank-and-file. Thus it is the leadership that retains the institutional memory to explain how current practices emerged from past decisions and that looks beyond current circumstances to the future position of the association. The union leader is in touch with the leaders of other organizations and often sees his own union as a part of a broader movement to advance the welfare of the working class. This gives the leader a less parochial outlook than his rank-and-file and makes him sensitive to the preservation and expansion of the organization.

The rank-and-file have the problem of monitoring the performance of the leader and, in particular, of preventing the leader from pursuing his own goals at their expense. This monitoring function is effected by using various rules of thumb by which the rank-and-file may compare their welfare with those of some other workers. The most common rule of thumb is a union's *relative* wage position, the rank-and-file being more likely to extend support to their leader when their wages have risen relative to another group of workers. The evidence surveyed in chapter 3 reveals a good deal of ambiguity about union objectives, but at the same time there is reason for optimism that the determination of union goals is amenable to empirical investigation.

Chapters 4 and 5 turn to the subject of bargaining. Chapter 4 outlines the simple model of contract efficiency and shows existing tests of contract efficiency to be quite unsatisfactory. Indeed, without augmenting models of contract efficiency with particular assumptions regarding the solution to the bargaining problem, I am skeptical that tests of contract efficiency can ever be persuasive.

The work reviewed in chapter 5 concerns those models that, for one reason or another, place the variables constituting the bargaining set in a particular order such that the value of one variable is determined prior to that of another. I dub the contracts resulting from these models as recursive contracts. They include models where the mechanism for resolving disputes (such as strikes or compulsory arbitration) is specified explicitly. Although, in principle, there is no reason why dispute resolution mechanisms cannot be grafted onto efficient contract models, in practice most attempts to incorporate strikes and arbitration into bargaining have focused exclusively on bargaining over wages and tacitly have characterized employment as determined unilaterally by management. In such cases, the profit-maximizing condition for employment provides an operational test for determining the relevance of such models, as discussed in chapter 5.

The material in chapter 6 looks beyond union–management bargaining in a single labor market and discusses interactions among several markets. First wage interactions among unionized markets are analyzed and then wage interactions between unionized and nonunionized markets are considered. To understand the distribution of employment in a partially unionized economy, a three sector model is outlined: there is a union sector, an administered-wage nonunion sector, and a competitive, employment-absorbing, nonunion sector. Models such as these are relevant for ascertaining the degree to which decentralized unions in a partially unionized economy affect aggregate wages and employment.

In chapter 7, I bring together some of the major conclusions from this study and identify areas where future research is warranted.

2 Empirical Regularities

2.1 Introduction

The purpose of this chapter is to review the empirical regularities with respect to union–nonunion differentials in wages, employment, and hours of work in the United States and Britain. There is a large literature concerning unionism and wages, but a small one concerning hours of work. The research on unionism and employment is of two types: there is an older, non-analytical, literature consisting of case studies of particular firms or industries; and there is a more recent, analytical, literature in which the effects on employment may be inferred indirectly from the estimates of the parameters of production functions. The shortcomings with the non-analytical research are that, while sometimes it is highly suggestive, it often fails to distinguish the effects of unions from the effects of other variables on employment and also it is difficult to extract information of a quantitative kind about unionism's effects. As we shall see, the production function research does not yield clear implications for the employment effects of unions partly because information about production function parameters may not be sufficient to infer something about employment and partly because of ambiguities in the studies themselves. Consequently, the quality of our knowledge of the employment effects of unions is difficult to assess: that such effects have existed is in little doubt, but their magnitude is in question, as is their generalizability.

Most of the information about union–nonunion differentials reviewed in this chapter derives from empirical work that, reduced to its essentials, compares the values taken by a certain variable in unionized firms (or among individuals covered by collective bargaining contracts) with the values taken by the same variable in nonunionized firms (or among individuals not covered by collective bargaining contracts). Usually, where information is available, account is also taken of differences between unionized and nonunionized observations in the values taken by other variables. The conceptual experiment in these studies is to compute the difference in the values of a given variable when a nonunion observation is converted into a union observation holding the values of all other measured characteristics constant.

Needless to say, this is not how the world works: the process by which firms are unionized does not conform to the controlled experiment whereby randomly chosen establishments or individuals are selected for coverage by collective bargaining contracts and the consequences for wages, hours, and employment are observed. On the contrary, there is a substantial literature documenting systematic determinants of unionization: why some individuals join unions and others do not and why some firms are unionized and others not. For instance, large establishments seem more likely to be unionized and black workers seem more disposed than white workers to join trade unions. (See, respectively, Hirsch (1982) and Farber (1983).) This and other work implies that an x percent union–nonunion differential in the values of certain variables does not necessarily mean unions have given rise to this x percent differential. The direction of causation may run in part from the variable of interest to the incidence of unionism instead of the other way round. Or, more likely, there are some other variables, unobserved to the researcher, that help to determine both the incidence of unionism and union–nonunion differentials in labor market outcomes, in which case the effects attributed to unionism are in truth the consequence of these omitted variables.

Expressed differently, the discussion in this chapter infers the effects of unions from estimates of the coefficient β in the equation $y_i = \alpha X_i + \beta U_i + \epsilon_i$ where y_i measures (the level of or the change in) wages, employment, or hours, U_i indicates union status, X_i are exogenous determinants of y_i, and ϵ_i is a stochastic disturbance. If U_i is distributed independently of ϵ_i, then ordinary least-squares procedures will compute β consistently. However, the arguments above suggest ϵ_i and U_i might be correlated, in which case conventional least-squares is an inconsistent estimator. Alternative methods are available which (explicitly or implicitly) require specifying an equation describing the incidence of U_i. The problem now becomes one of providing a convincing and robust account of U_i, a problem often manifesting itself in terms of finding genuine instrumental variables for U_i or in terms of alternative assumptions about the distribution of the error term in the equation for U_i. While I am in no doubt about the importance and potential relevance of these issues, the practical value of these alternative estimators for this problem is in dispute at the moment[1] and will probably remain so until there is a better understanding of the determinants of U_i.

To illustrate the point, Duncan and Stafford (1980) have argued that the trade union is a particularly useful mechanism for expressing workers' preferences when work conditions have the characteristics of public goods, that is, goods whose consumption is shared by all workers and one individual's consumption does not reduce the amount available for consumption by others. Such conditions occur when the production process requires interdependencies among workers (as on an assembly line) so that all employees work in the same place, at the same pace, and on the same schedules. Even in the absence of unions these working conditions may give rise to compensating wage differentials. Therefore, both the incidence of unionism and the level of wages are correlated with these working conditions and a failure to control for these working conditions variables will exaggerate the partial association between unionism and wages.

For these reasons, the effects of unionism may well diverge from the magnitude of the union–nonunion differentials reported below. The satisfactory resolution of this problem requires the specification and computation of behavioral models that describe both the process of unionization and the determination of outcomes in unionized firms. This is an important literature, but it is still very much in its nonage and so the construction of models in chapters 3, 4, and 5 below leans heavily on the interpretation of the estimated union–nonunion differentials as unionism's effects. This is a crucial qualification and it bears keeping in mind.

2.2   Wages

Procedure

There are several different concepts of the effect of trade unions on relative wages. These differences arise because the presence of trade unions is likely to affect the wages paid to nonunion workers. In other words, the wages of nonunion workers diverge from what these workers would have received in the complete absence of trade unions. To be precise, define W_i^o as the wage prevailing in labor market i prior to the organization of a trade union. Now suppose a part of this market becomes

---

[1] For instance, Lewis (1986, chapter 4) takes a rather skeptical view of what has been learned from the application of these methods while Robinson (1989) adopts a more upbeat position.

unionized so that W_i^u is the wage obtaining in the union sector and W_i^n is the wage obtaining in the nonunion sector. The effect of unions on the wages of nonunion workers may be measured by k_i,

$$k_i = \frac{W_i^n - W_i^o}{W_i^o} \; .$$

There are several reasons why k_i may be nonzero. If wages in the union sector differ from those in the absence of unionism (i.e., if $W_i^u \neq W_i^o$), then employment in the union and nonunion sectors may be affected. For instance, if employment in the union sector falls and this induces a movement of workers into the nonunion sector, the nonunion wage might be reduced to a level below that prevailing in the absence of unionism. In this case, $k_i < 0$.

Alternatively, the presence of unionism may induce a nonunion employer to pay a higher than market-clearing wage and, with a sufficiently higher value of W_i^n, k_i will be positive. The personnel policies of nonunion companies frequently involve paying close attention to the wages paid to comparable or related unionized plants in part because of a belief that morale problems would arise among their workers if a large union–nonunion wage differential emerged and in part as a device to discourage the unionization of their employees. Increasing nonunion wages to forestall unionization is known as the threat effect of unionism and this is discussed in chapter 6.

Consider now the effect of unions on the wages of unionized workers. By analogy with k_i above, this may be measured by

$$q_i = \frac{W_i^u - W_i^o}{W_i^o},$$

the proportionate difference between what union workers in market i currently receive and what they would have earned in the complete absence of unionism. q_i is sometimes called the *wage gain* of unionism. Unfortunately, because W_i^o cannot be computed without a string of highly implausible assumptions (such as those under which $W_i^o = W_i^n$), I know of no way to measure q_i. What can be measured is the union *wage gap*, the proportionate difference between the wages of union and nonunion workers both computed in the presence of trade unions:

$$r_i = \frac{W_i^u - W_i^n}{W_i^n} \; .$$

Of course, either W_i^u or W_i^n is observed, not both: we do not observe what a given worker or group of workers would be paid with and without a union contract. Hence, r_i must be estimated and the usual procedure starts from the identity[2]

$$\ln W_i = [\ln(1 + r_i)]U_i + \ln W_i^n = B_i U_i + \ln W_i^n. \tag{2.1}$$

If the observations relate to average values in market i, then W_i represents some measure of average wages and U_i is the fraction of workers in market i covered by a collective bargaining contract. If the observations relate to individual workers, then W_i is each worker's wage rate and U_i is a dichotomous variable taking the value of unity for a worker covered by a collective bargaining contract and of zero otherwise. Suppose the nonunion wage depends linearly on the set of variables X_i and on an unobserved component u_{1i}, $\ln W_i^n = \delta X_i + u_{1i}$, and suppose the relative wage effect of unionism also may be specified as a linear function of observed variables Z_i and an unobserved component u_{2i}, $B_i = bZ_i + u_{2i}$. Variables in X_i may be included in Z_i and, if the elements of X_i and Z_i are the same, then this implies that the estimating equation below allows for an entirely different wage structure in the union and nonunion sectors. These assumptions imply that equation (2.1) may be written

$$\ln W_i = bZ_i U_i + \delta X_i + u_i, \tag{2.2}$$

where the stochastic term, u_i, incorporates both u_{1i} and u_{2i} and has heteroskedastic properties (that is, $u_i = u_{1i} + u_{2i}U_i$). An estimate of the union wage gap is usually recovered by the transformation $\hat{r} = \exp \cdot (\hat{b}\bar{Z}_i) - 1$ where the hats denote values computed by some procedure and the bar over Z_i denotes mean values.

Cross-Section Estimates

An excellent application of this procedure is Ashenfelter's (1978) research that draws upon data collected in the United States Survey of Economic Opportunity in 1967 and in the Current Population Surveys in 1973 and 1975 to fit equation (2.2) to samples of all workers as well as to white men, black men, white women, and black women separately. Table 2.1 presents ordinary least-squares estimates of B (not of r) for these groups of workers in each of these years. Estimated standard errors are usually many times smaller than the point estimates reported in the table. On average, the union wage gap was 12 percent in 1967, 16 percent in 1973, and 18 percent in 1975. Ashenfelter's results suggest a slightly higher union wage gap for black men compared with the other groups. For

---

[2] Equation (2.1) is a straightforward rearrangement of

$$\ln W_i = U_i \ln W_i^u + (1 - U_i)\ln W_i^n = (\ln W_i^u - \ln W_i^n)U_i + \ln W_i^n.$$

Table 2.1 Proportionate union–nonunion wage differentials in the United States by race, sex, and year

		Male workers		Female workers	
Year	All workers	White	Black	White	Black
1967	0.116	0.096	0.215	0.144	0.056
1973	0.148	0.155	0.225	0.127	0.132
1975	0.168	0.163	0.225	0.166	0.171

For white men, the sample size is 6,593 in 1967, 20,069 in 1973, and 19,070 in 1975. For white women, the sample sizes are 3,757, 13,318, and 13,400. For black men, the sample sizes are 2,977, 2,095, and 1,987. For black women, the sample sizes are 1,629, 1,649, and 1,726. Other variables in the regression equation are years of schooling completed and its square, estimated labor market experience and its square, marital status, region, size of SMSA, occupation, industry, and part-time worker status. The dependent variable is usual hourly earnings defined as the ratio of normal weekly earnings to normal weekly hours. For the years 1967 and 1973, U_j takes the value of unity for workers who are union members whereas for 1975 U_j is unity for workers covered by a collective bargaining contract. The 1967 data exclude public sector workers. Otherwise, the data do not include the self-employed, farm workers, and private household workers.
Source: Ashenfelter, 1978, table 2.1

Table 2.2 Proportionate union–nonunion wage differentials in the United States for white men by industry, occupation, and year

Industry	Occupation	1967	1973	1975
Construction	Craftsmen	0.30	0.42	0.40
	Operatives	0.34	0.49	0.51
	Laborers	0.40	0.45	0.48
Durable manufacturing	Craftsmen	− 0.01	0.04	0.06
	Operatives	0.11	0.13	0.19
	Laborers	0.16	0.14	0.22
Nondurable manufacturing	Craftsmen	0.05	0.10	0.07
	Operatives	0.12	0.14	0.16
	Laborers	0.16	0.24	0.15
Transport, communications, and public utilities	Craftsmen	0.02	0.09	0.08
	Operatives	0.11	0.23	0.24
	Laborers	0.21	0.26	0.25

Source: Ashenfelter, 1978, table 2.3

the large sample of white male blue collar workers, Ashenfelter fitted equation (2.2) allowing for different union wage gaps by industry and occupation and these estimates of B are contained in table 2.2. Evidently the wage gaps in the construction industry are many times greater than those in the other industries in table 2.2: on average, the union wage gap in construction in 1973 and 1975 was 54 percent, a plausible estimate for these years given the collective bargaining structure in the industry. With respect to occupation, Ashenfelter's estimates in table 2.2 indicate union wage gaps that are inversely related to skill, being highest for laborers and lowest for craftsmen.

There is by now a very large literature estimating union wage gaps for US workers for the past 20 years or so. Fortunately, Lewis (1986) has meticulously surveyed this work and we are able to draw upon his remarkable evaluation. Table 2.3 is a summary of my own reading of Lewis's compilation of various estimates of union wage gaps (again estimates of B, not r) by certain labor force characteristics. He contends that the computation of union wage gaps from ordinary least-squares estimates

Table 2.3   Summary of variations across the labor force in estimates of union wage gaps, B, from Lewis's survey of US studies

Variables	Sign	Magnitude
Continuous variables		
Partial derivative of B with respect to:		
Years of schooling	Negative	From −0.015 to −0.030
Years of labor market experience	U-shaped	Minimum at 28 years with a slope of −0.08 per decade at zero years
Years of seniority	Negative	About −0.05 per decade
Extent of unionism	Sensitive to choice of variable	
Discrete variables		
Difference in B for:		
Male–female	Ambiguous	Close to zero
Black–white	Inconsistent[a]	
Married–other marital status	Negative	About −0.10
Manufacturing–nonmanufacturing	Negative	About −0.10
Manufacturing–construction	Negative	−0.26
White collar–blue collar	Negative	−0.10
Laborers–operatives	Positive	0.04
Private–public	Positive	0.13
South–other	Positive	0.05

[a] The estimates based on Current Population Survey data indicate a black–white wage gap difference of about zero. On the other hand, estimates using other data are usually positive with a central tendency of from 0.05 to 0.10.
Source: Lewis, 1986, chapter 7

of equation (2.2) is inclined to overstate the true gap. This is because firms respond to higher union wages by upgrading the quality of their employees and the quality and skills of workers as perceived by employers are measured incompletely by the set of variables in X_i in equation (2.2). Accordingly, indicators of labor quality that are correlated with unionism are omitted from equation (2.2) and as a result the estimates of B attribute to unionism what really should be credited to labor quality.[3] By adjusting estimates for the incompleteness in the set of variables included in X_i and Z_i and by omitting certain estimates designated as outliers, Lewis calculates that, on average, over the years 1967–79 an upper bound for the union wage gap in the US work force as a whole was 14 percent.

If management responds to higher union wages by upgrading the quality of their work force, then the effect of unions on wages *holding constant worker quality* understates the full impact of unions on wages. In other words, this argument suggests the presence of unionism affects both the distribution of employees across firms in the economy and the incentives for employees to acquire skills. This illustrates the point that what is *not* being measured by estimates of B in equation (2.2) is the difference in wages between unionized workers and what these workers would have received in the absence of unionism in the economy. The effect of unionism on the characteristics of employees has been one of those issues receiving much less careful attention than that concerning wages.[4]

By comparison with US research, the work on union–nonunion wage differentials in Britain is an infant industry. Nevertheless, a careful study by Stewart (1983) reports estimates of wage gaps for full-time manual male employees in UK manufacturing in 1975 and these are reproduced in table 2.4. The estimates measure differences in weekly earnings associated with union membership, not differences associated with coverage by a collective bargaining agreement. The difference between union membership and coverage wage differentials is very small in the United States, but this is less likely to be the case in Britain where the coverage of collective bargaining agreements is greater than union membership.

[3] Lewis's argument considers the behavior of union employers only. As Robinson (1989) points out, there is also the supply of workers to the union sector. Those workers standing to gain most from employment in the union sector are those whose nonunion wages (adjusted for X_i) are relatively low. If these workers move out of the nonunion sector and queue up in the union sector, this will tend to remove the low wage observations from the nonunion wage distribution thereby raising average nonunion wages and reducing the least-squares computed union wage gap.

[4] A theoretical analysis of labor quality, wages, and unionism is offered by Pettengill (1980).

Table 2.4   Variations in estimates of union wage gaps, *r*, among full-time manual male employees in manufacturing in Britain

	Percent
Average differential	7.7
Man with the reference characteristics[a]	7.0
Deviations from the reference category, each considered singly:	
10 years of labor market experience	10.2
40 years of labor market experience	6.4
Left school at 16 years or after	7.7
Neither household head nor primary wage earner	11.0
Married	6.0
Undertaken a trade apprenticeship	9.3
Training received for current job	12.7
Works in plant with 25–99 employees	6.9
Works in plant with 100–499 employees	4.2
Works in plant with 500 or more employees	8.3
Resident in East Anglia	1.0
Resident in Wales	20.0
Industry with collective bargaining coverage of 70 per cent	6.4
Industry with union membership of 90 per cent	9.7
Industry with concentration ratio of 80 per cent	4.7

[a] A man with reference characteristics has 25 years of experience, left school before age 16, is the primary wage earner in the household, is not married, lives in Greater London, is not responsible for the work of others in the firm, has not undertaken any further education or special training, and works in a plant with less than 25 employees. This man is employed in a hypothetical industry which has the union members' mean values for all industry-level variables (namely, the proportion of workers in the industry whose pay is covered by a collective bargaining agreement, the proportion of workers who are members of a trade union, and a five firm concentration ratio). The results are based on maximum likelihood estimates of earnings equations fitted separately to 3,903 union members and 1,449 non-union members working in the United Kingdom in late 1975.
Source: Stewart, 1983, table 2 and appendix

Stewart estimates a 7.7 percent average union–nonunion wage gap in Britain which is close to Ashenfelter's (1978) estimate of 9.4 percent for white male blue-collar workers in US durable goods manufacturing in 1975. While the average wage gap in Britain resembles that in the USA, variations in the wage gap do not appear to be qualitatively the same. In Britain, the wage gap declines with labor market experience whereas in the USA it is U-shaped. However, measures of firm-specific experience are not available in Stewart's data and one wonders whether the labor market experience variables are absorbing an influence that should be attributed to job- or firm-specific human capital. Unlike the US results, in Britain the wage gap rises with skill level among blue-collar workers. The regional variations within Britain in the wage gap are considerable.

Aggregation

The estimates of the union–nonunion wage gap presented above all exploit observations on individual workers and, on the few occasions where the question of the appropriate unit of observation is discussed, a presumption in favor of such data for these purposes is often expressed. For instance, Geroski and Stewart (1986) show how estimates of union wage gaps from industry-level data are very sensitive to the precise specification of the fitted equation, thereby casting doubt on all such estimates that do not explicitly demonstrate their robustness. Lewis (1986) believes that wages, unionized or nonunionized, will depend on the extent of unionism in the industry or occupation or local labor market in which the individual works and, for this reason, he strongly prefers estimates of equation (2.2) fitted to observations on individual workers where each worker's union status can be distinguished from the fraction of workers unionized in each individual's industry or occupation or area. Equations aggregated over individuals to the level of industry or occupation averages will not permit the identification of the union wage gap separately from the dependence of both unionized and nonunionized workers' wages on the extent of unionism.

This is a sound argument and Lewis shows how union–nonunion wage differentials in aggregated wage equations exceed those estimated from data on individual workers.[5] The argument would be conclusive if the estimates attached to the extent of unionism variable were measured precisely and reliably, but they are not. (See Lewis, 1986, pp. 146–53.) Therefore, while fitting equation (2.2) to observations on industry or occupation aggregates risks overestimating union wage gaps, the inclusion or exclusion of the extent of unionism variable from Z_i and X_i in equations fitted to data on individual workers seems to be an issue of second-order importance. The higher union wage gaps typically estimated with industry-level data may well be the consequence of a smaller number of variables included in Z_i and X_i in the aggregated equations, not the consequence of confounding two different effects of unionism on wages.

Moreover, one should not presume that the "right" level of disaggregation is invariably the individual worker. Wages in most unionized settings and for most nonunion workers in large private firms and in the public sector are not tailored to all measured characteristics of each worker. For instance, unions do not negotiate wages by personal characteristics such as race and gender so that any measured race and gender

---

[5] This also seems to be true of the British estimates where use of industry-level data usually (not invariably) produces higher union wage gaps than Stewart's (1983) estimates from individual data.

union wage effects must be artifacts, in part, of union policies such as those designed to reduce wage differentials or to codify promotion procedures.

But one would never recognize that these wage effects were the consequence of such policies nor learn anything about bargaining goals from this literature that, almost entirely, excludes all reference to the actual unions and employers engaged in bargaining. One would never know from this literature whether, for the past 70 years, the United Mine Workers have followed different wage policies from the Amalgamated Clothing and Textile Workers Union. There have been no attempts to relate the measured wage effects of unions to the goals of the union and management and to the constraints under which the parties operate. In other words, not only has the literature been one of measurement without much underlying theory, it has also been one of measurement with little reference to the institutions associated with the observed wage effects.

In most medium-sized and large firms, the typical procedure is for a certain base or key wage to be determined by some procedure for a reference worker or a reference job. A small set of worker attributes (such as years of seniority and age) or job attributes (such as indexes of skill and responsibility) is identified and the wages of workers or of jobs with values of the attributes different from the reference worker or the reference job are adjusted to conform to some given relationship with the base wage. Earnings equations such as (2.2) that are fitted to large numbers of individual workers in many different firms cannot be expected to duplicate exactly the establishment-specific wage algorithms that describe pay differentials. Such equations should be regarded as convenient approximations to the wage algorithms operating in different firms. But once equations such as (2.2) are recognized as approximations, it is not obvious that the inferences from fitting such an approximation to data on individual workers are to be preferred to those from an equation fitted to observations on the base wage where the level of observation is the bargaining unit or establishment. In fact, in the few studies using establishment data as the level of observation, union-nonunion wage gaps have tended to be close to or lower than those estimated from data on individual workers.[6] These questions relating to

---

[6] For instance, Freeman (1982) calculates an average gap of 0.06 (see his tables 8 and B) for production workers in a group of manufacturing industries while for manual employees in British manufacturing industry (that is, for workers similar to, although not quite the same as, those studied in Stewart's research) in 1980, Blanchflower (1984) claims to have measured union wage gaps of 2.0 percent for semi-skilled workers and − 0.7 percent for skilled workers, neither estimate being significantly different from zero by conventional criteria.

the appropriate unit of observation have received scant attention in a literature otherwise thorough and prolific.

A rare example of the use of establishment data is provided by Stewart's (1987) measurement of union wage gaps for British manual employees in 1980. He computes an average gap of 8 percent for semiskilled workers and 3 percent for skilled workers, the latter figure not being significantly different from zero.[7] The establishment data allow Stewart to examine the association between union wage gaps and bargaining structures and, contrary to some previous research using industry-level aggregates, he finds no significant differences according to whether the parties bargain at the national or industry level or at the level of the individual establishment or firm. On the other hand, the presence of a pre-entry closed shop approximately doubles the union wage gap to 15 percent for semiskilled workers and 9 percent for skilled workers. Simulating the estimated equations at the mean values of the variables for the unionized establishments, he ascertains that only 19 percent of the unionized establishments pay semiskilled wages significantly greater than those paid by nonunion establishments and only 12 percent pay skilled wages above those paid by nonunion establishments. In other words, union–nonunion wage gaps are insignificantly different from zero in some 81 to 88 percent of all unionized establishments so the distribution of union wage gaps is heavily concentrated in a few plants. In general, Stewart's results raise the question of whether the US literature has overlooked some important variations in the union–nonunion wage gap. Most US research has exploited data sets describing the attributes of individual employees and information on certain institutional characteristics (such as bargaining structures and the presence of a closed shop) is usually lacking.[8] Data at the level of the establishment or bargaining unit could be usefully examined to determine whether inferences about the variation of union wage gaps across workers with different personal characteristics are unaffected by institutional features of union and firm structures and of bargaining.

---

[7] Not too much should be made of the fact that this 8 percent average union–nonunion wage gap for semiskilled workers is the same as that estimated in his previous study computed from observations on individual workers. The two samples cover a somewhat different population: this analysis of establishments covers all industries in 1980 and provides no information on characteristics such as the fraction of the establishment's work force who are male or who are full-time workers; the previous analysis was restricted to full-time, male employees in manufacturing industry in 1975. Also note that the observation on the wage rate in Stewart's establishment analysis is not the base wage, but the weekly pay of a "typical employee" within a given skill class. Stewart's results regarding the average union–nonunion wage differential are very similar to Blanchflower's (1984) earlier analysis of the same data.

[8] Such information is sometimes available for manufacturing industry and has been usefully exploited by Hendricks (1977) and Hendricks and Kahn (1984).

Time-Series Estimates

The union wage gaps reported above have been calculated from disaggregated data and relate to the years from the late 1960s to early 1980s. If the US estimates are arranged by year, they suggest a rise in the economy-wide wage gap, B, from about 11 percent in 1967 to 18 percent in 1976 and then a fall to 13 percent in 1979.[9] Data from the Current Population Survey suggest an unchanged union wage premium in the early 1980s until about 1984, when it may have risen a little. (See Edwards and Swaim, 1986; Freeman, 1986b; Linneman and Wachter, 1986; Moore and Raisian, 1987.) To calculate such wage gaps for earlier years requires the use of more aggregated data. For this purpose, in his earlier book, Lewis (1963) divided the economy into two sectors and, in essence, determined the partial association over time between the relative wage in the two sectors and the difference in the extent of unionism between the sectors. Sector a consists of the mining, construction, manufacturing, transportation, communications, and public utilities industries and most of the economy's unionized workers have been employed in this sector; sector b consists of wholesale and retail trade, finance, insurance, and real estate, services, public administration, and agriculture, forestry, and fisheries.

Write equation (2.2) for sector j ($j = a,b$) in year t and subtract the equation for sector b from that for sector a:

$$Dln W_t = \gamma X_t + B^a U_t^a - B^b U_t^b + u_t \tag{2.3}$$

where $Dln W_t \equiv \ln W_t^a - \ln W_t^b$, $(\ln W_t^n)^a - (\ln W_t^n)^b = \gamma X_t + u_t$, and for the moment the B^j coefficients have been assumed constants. Here X_t represents measured variables affecting the relative movement of union–nonunion wages over time and u_t is an unobserved stochastic component. Estimating this equation with annual data over the years 1920–80 yields point estimates of B^b that are very sensitive to equation specification and estimated standard errors attached to B^b that are consistent with a wide variety of different hypotheses.[10] In fact, in his original study, Lewis (1963) reported the consequences of fitting

$$Dln W_t = \gamma X_t + \bar{B}(DU)_t + u_t^* \tag{2.4}$$

where $(DU)_t = (U^a - U^b)_t$. $\bar{B}$ is a weighted sum of B^a and B^b, the weights being the fraction of all unionized workers employed in each sector, and u_t^* incorporates errors in approximating (2.3) by (2.4). The

[9] I am reporting here Lewis's (1986) tentative upper bound in his table 9.7.
[10] See Pencavel and Hartsog (1984), table 3. Usually, the hypothesis that $B^a = B^b$ could not be rejected nor the hypothesis that B^b was zero.

error of this approximation depends on the degree to which B^a diverges from B^b or on the partial correlation between the arithmetic difference in unionism in the two sectors and the level of unionism in each.[11]

Fitting equation (2.4) by ordinary least-squares to the years 1920–80 suggests estimates of $\bar{B}$ of between 0.17 and 0.24. When $\bar{B}$ is permitted to vary as a function of the unemployment rate, $(UN)_t$, and of the ratio of the price level in year t to its level in years immediately prior to year t, $(P/\bar{P})_t$, the results are as follows:

$$\hat{\bar{B}}_t = \underset{(0.13)}{0.41} - \underset{(1.03)}{1.41}(UN)_t - \underset{(0.98)}{2.18}\ln(P/\bar{P})_t \qquad (2.5)$$

where the figures in parentheses are estimated standard errors. The hypotheses that $\bar{B}_t$ is independent of the unemployment rate is always consistent with the estimates. By contrast, $\bar{B}_t$ falls when the price level rises above its level in immediately preceding years, suggesting perhaps that unionism tends to reduce the responsiveness of money wages to transitory changes in the price level. When five-year average values of $(UN)_t$ and $\ln(P/\bar{P})_t$ are inserted into the previous equation, the implied values of $\bar{B}_t$ are those given in table 2.5. The point estimates imply large swings in the union wage gap with a low of 0.07 in the late 1970s and a high of 0.39 in the early 1930s. However, the estimated standard errors signal that not too much should be made of the differences among the point estimates: thus, the estimates of $\bar{B}_t$ in table 2.5 for the years 1965–80 are not significantly different from the range of 11–18 percent offered by Lewis (1986) as his best guess from the analysis of highly disaggregated data.

An alternative procedure used to compute movements in the union wage gap over time has been to fit a wage equation of the form

$$\ln W_i = BU_i + \gamma X_i + u_i$$

to a cross-section of industries in a number of different years, thereby deriving a sequence of estimates of B. Johnson (1984) applied this method to US production workers' average hourly earnings in one- and two-digit industries between 1958 and 1979 and he linked up the estimates of B to conform to Lewis's (1963) estimate of 15 percent in 1955–58. Johnson's estimates are 22 percent in 1960–64, 17 percent in 1965–74, and 26 percent in 1975–79. If standard errors had been computed, I wager Johnson's

---

[11] That is, equation (2.3) may be written

$$D\ln W_t = \gamma X_t + \bar{B}(DU)_t + (B^a - \bar{B})U_t^a + (\bar{B} - B^b)U_t^b + u_t$$

and u_t^* in equation (2.4) is given by the final three terms on the right-hand side of this equation.

Table 2.5   Estimates of the US economy-wide union–nonunion wage differential, $\bar{B}$, 1920–80

Period	$\hat{\bar{B}}_t$	Period	$\hat{\bar{B}}_t$
1920–24	0.273 (0.082)	1950–54	0.235 (0.085)
1925–29	0.375 (0.109)	1955–59	0.269 (0.085)
1930–34	0.393 (0.120)	1960–64	0.275 (0.084)
1935–39	0.210 (0.113)	1965–69	0.258 (0.087)
1940–44	0.150 (0.090)	1970–74	0.160 (0.088)
1945–49	0.136 (0.094)	1975–80	0.071 (0.110)
1920–80	0.231 (0.080)		

Estimated standard errors are in parentheses beneath estimated coefficients. The estimates are derived from a generalized least-squares procedure that allows for first-order serial correlation of the residuals. The variables representing X_t are the ratio of national income in sector a to that in sector b, the lagged value of manhours worked in sector a relative to that in sector b, the unemployment rate, and the ratio of prices in year t to prices in previous years. The estimates are found in equation (7d) of table 5 and column (2) of table 6 of Pencavel and Hartsog (1984).

point estimates would not be significantly different from the values of $\hat{\bar{B}}_t$ for these years in table 2.5. Layard, Metcalf and Nickell (1978) applied the same procedure to 91 manufacturing industries in Britain between 1961 and 1975. In their case, W_i measures the hourly earnings of male manual employees and U_i is the fraction of workers covered by collective bargaining agreements. Their estimates imply a value of B that rises from 0.17 in the early 1960s to about 0.28 a decade later. Their estimate of B of 0.31 in 1975 using aggregated data compares with Stewart's (1983) of 0.08 in the same year for the same type of workers using observations on individual employees.[12] A shortcoming with both studies is that the same values of U_i are used in each of the regression equations fitted to different years. This is particularly unfortunate in the British study, which covers a period that witnessed a remarkable increase in union membership

---

[12] Layard, Metcalf, and Nickell (1978) report other estimates of B corresponding to different measures of the coverage rate. The others suggest values of B in the early 1970s of 0.19 and 0.11 (the latter reported in footnote 24 of their paper). It appears the authors want to stress the tendency of all these estimates to be higher in the 1970s and they are less confident about the level of B in any year.

(though perhaps not in the coverage rate).[13]

All these point estimates of the union wage gap over time – those in table 2.5 as well as those described in the previous paragraph – provide only a very rough indication of the economy-wide influence of unionism on relative wages. Less emphasis should be placed on any single point estimate and more on the general movement of these estimates over time – the tendency for the union wage gap in the United States to be higher in the 1930s and lower in the late 1940s and in Britain for it to be higher in the early 1970s than in the 1960s. In the case of the United States, unanticipated changes in prices have been identified as the only significant influence on the union wage gap, but the role of other factors affecting the wage gap has not been quantified. These factors include changes in the legal and social climate surrounding union organization and collective bargaining, which surely helped unionism in the 1930s and hindered it in the early 1980s. Because these other factors are correlated with price changes, I suspect that the estimates in table 2.5 overstate the degree to which unions temper the responsiveness of many wages to transitory changes in prices and that the movements in the union wage gap are not quite as volatile as these estimates suggest. Nevertheless I would be surprised if it were discovered that the *qualitative* pattern in table 2.5 is quite wrong.

What is interesting about the variation over time in the union wage gap estimated for the United States is how its economy-wide movement is not highly correlated with the general health which observers have ascribed to the trade union movement. It is true that the union wage gap is highest in the 1930s, a period when union membership surged forward. But the union movement grew in the 1940s too, yet this was a time when the union wage premium fell to relatively low levels. The 1920s and 1980s were difficult periods for new union organizing activity yet the union wage premium seems quite robust during these years. Insofar as a relatively large union wage premium discourages the growth of employment in the union sector and incites greater management resistance to union organizing efforts,[14] the weak association over time between union growth and the wage premium should not occasion surprise.[15] This does

---

[13] In Layard, Metcalf and Nickell's (1978) study, X_i includes a constant term, two indicators of workers' skills, two measures of the age distribution of employees, and two location variables. The values of these variables also remain the same in each regression equation in different years. In Johnson (1984), X_i is simply a constant.

[14] With respect to management resistance, Freeman (1986a) reports a positive association over the years 1950–80 between a measure of the union wage premium and an indicator of management opposition to union organizing efforts, namely, the number of unfair labor practices per worker in National Labor Relations Board elections.

[15] Analogously, across 42 major cities (SMSAs) in the United States in 1983, the correlation coefficient between the union wage gap and the fraction of employees unionized was virtually zero (0.020). See Montgomery (1989).

serve to show, however, that for the most part these movements in the union wage premium have not been the subject of much interpretation in the context of the times. We do not know, for instance, the extent to which movements in the union wage premium reflect variations in the goals of unions as distinct from variations in their ability to realize fixed objectives.

2.3   Employment

Procedure

The industrial relations literature provides a number of case studies of trade unions pricing themselves out of the labor market. Usually the effects take some years to manifest themselves clearly, but their existence in some instances is indisputable. The history of bituminous coal mining in the United States affords such an example.

At the beginning of this century, coal in the Central Competitive Field (Pennsylvania, Ohio, Illinois, and Indiana) was mined almost exclusively from union districts. Unionism in Kentucky and West Virginia enjoyed bouts of organizing success when the demand for coal was rising rapidly, but trade unions languished and disappeared in times of recession. In essence, the unionized mines of the Central Competitive Field competed with the largely nonunion mines of Kentucky and West Virginia. Production in the Central Competitive Field fell from 62 percent of the US total in 1900 to 46 percent in 1929 while Kentucky and West Virginia's output rose from 13 percent to 37 percent over the same period. During the boom years accompanying and immediately following the First World War, the Central Competitive Field's shrinking share was masked by its growing total output. The less buoyant markets of the 1920s resulted in a widening union–nonunion wage differential as union wage rates held steady while nonunion rates fell markedly; output in Kentucky and West Virginia continued to expand while that in the Central Competitive Field fell.[16] This pressure on the union mines brought forth the long strike of 1927 which resulted in a large cut in union wages in some districts and the deunionization of other districts; thereafter, the Central Competitive Field's relative standing declined more gradually.

The dramatic shift in social attitudes and in legislation in the early 1930s had an immediate and profound effect on union organizing activity in the

---

[16] See Dix (1988) and Lunt (1979) for particularly vivid accounts of the experience of West Virginia, which was very much the battleground (literally) for the ebb and flow of unionism in the underground coal industry at this time.

coal industry and by the mid-1930s well over 90 percent of production was mined from union districts which now embraced Kentucky and West Virginia. The union aggressively pushed up wages and, after the Second World War, imposed a tax on each ton of coal output, the purpose of which was to finance health and welfare benefits. The unionized part of the industry has shrunk both relatively and absolutely: whereas 90 percent of total production came from United Mine Workers' mines in 1947, this had fallen to 44 percent by 1980 (Navarro, 1983). It is likely that union policies are partly responsible for the decline in the unionized sector of the coal industry.

The coal mining example is by no means singular. Other instances in which union activity is supposed to have reduced employment (or the growth of employment) in the United States are provided by the men's clothing workers,[17] the shoe workers, the hosiery workers, the carpet and upholstery workers, and others. In some of these and other cases, however, the evidence is less definitive than it seems to be for the United Mine Workers: other factors affect the growth of employment and research has not quantified the effects attributable to unionism and those attributable to these other factors.

In fact, there are reasons for believing that, in some cases, unionism will depress employment little or not at all. First, insofar as a bargaining situation exists between workers and management even in the absence of a union, the higher wage accompanying unionism may do no more than redistribute rents away from management towards labor with few or no employment repercussions. Second, as argued in the previous chapter, the unionization of a firm means more than a higher wage. In some cases it brings (explicit or implicit) work rules that raise unit costs beyond those implied by the higher wages. In other cases unionism introduces a system of industrial jurisprudence that arbitrates grievances, involves employees in the determination of their working environment, and disseminates information about current and future conditions, the consequence of which is to increase industrial morale (that is, the cooperation extended

---

[17] In his analysis of the relative wage effects of the Amalgamated Clothing Workers of America in the 1920s, Rayack (1958, p. 682) writes, "The wage differentials between the union and nonunion markets seem to have had a serious effect upon the shares of output and employment held by the union markets. Between 1923 and 1929, the shares of employment and output held by the unionized markets declined steadily from 48.8 and 63.1 percent, respectively, in 1923 to 37.9 and 52.9 percent in 1929. It is also significant to note that almost all of the decline in the union markets came in Chicago and New York, the two high-wage markets, whereas Rochester, the union market with by far the lowest wages, had practically no change in output or employment. The reverse movement occurred in the nonunion markets; in these, employment and output grew from 39.4 and 26.4 percent, respectively, in 1923 to 49.3 and 36 percent in 1929."

by the work force to management in its entrepreneurial activities). In this instance, the firm's unit costs rise less than the increase in wages and, indeed, if the productivity gains are enough, costs need not rise at all.

Instances both of productivity-impairing work rules and of enhanced industrial morale accompanying unionism are provided by the contemporary and historical industrial relations literature.[18] Thus in Britain the 1894 Report of the Royal Commission on Trade Disputes "concluded, largely on the evidence of leading employers, that industrial relations were at their best when strongly organized trade unions met stable employers' associations in voluntary negotiations. The leaders of a strong union, it was true, might sometimes bring it out on strike when its members would not have moved of themselves; and when powerful organizations on both sides did become involved in a conflict, it was often protracted. But the alternative was worse – in the absence of well-established unions there would be 'continued local bickerings, stoppages of work, and petty conflicts' " (Phelps Brown, 1983, p. 25). This implies it is not unionism *per se* that affects employment and productivity, but the form that unionism takes.

Consequently, although some case studies suggest that unionism depresses employment, it is difficult to determine from these studies the magnitude of these effects and whether these case studies are representative of unionism in general. The issue of the employment effects of unionism is one which, in principle, could benefit from the direct application of modern quantitative methods of enquiry. More often than not, the view seems to be that all we need to determine is "the" wage-elasticity of demand for labor and the effects of unionism on employment may be inferred by multiplying this elasticity by the relative wage effect of unionism. For instance, this is how Lewis (1964) proceeded to measure the effect of unionism on employment in the bituminous coal mining industry. He concluded that unionism was responsible for less than half of the employment decline in this industry between 1945 and 1962. The assumptions here are, first, that unions do not alter the labor demand function but merely change the wage on a given demand curve and, second, that the labor demand function is the relevant analytical construct to determine the effect of unionism on employment.

In other words, suppose the labor demand function of a nonunion (n) firm is

$$(\ln L)^n = a^n \ln W^n + b^n X^n$$

where X denotes variables other than wages. The corresponding union (u) firm's demand function is

---

[18] See, for instance, Slichter (1941, especially chapters 14–19).

$(\ln L)^u = a^u \ln W^u + b^u X^u$.

Of course, the elements of X^u and X^n need not be the same. Then the effect of unionism on labor input might be measured by[19]

$$C \equiv (\ln L)^u - (\ln L)^n = a^u B + (a^u - a^n)\ln W^n + b^u X^u - b^n X^n$$
(2.6)

where, as before, $B = \ln W^u - \ln W^n$. The first term on the right-hand side, $a^u B$, embodies the argument that the union effect on employment may be ascertained from the product of the relative wage effect of unionism and the wage-elasticity of demand for labor.

For the purposes of the subsequent discussion, it is useful to illustrate this with the labor demand function implied by a Cobb–Douglas production function. That is, suppose a nonunion (n) firm uses physical capital, K, and labor, L, to produce output, X, in the following manner:

$$X = A^n (q^n L)^{\alpha^n} (s^n K)^{\beta^n}$$

where A is a neutral efficiency parameter, q an index of the efficiency of each unit of labor, and s an efficiency index of each unit of physical capital. The firm employs each unit of labor at the given price W^n and each unit of capital at r. The firm faces a constant-elasticity product demand function $p = X^{\rho-1}$ where p is the price per unit of output and $0 < \rho \le 1$. The production function for the unionized firm is

$$X = A^u (q^u L)^{\alpha^u} (s^u K)^{\beta^u}.$$

Assume the unionized and nonunion firms face the same price environment except for the price of labor, W. Then, the proportionate difference in their profit-maximizing use of labor,

$$C \equiv (\ln L)^u - (\ln L)^n,$$

is

$$C = \gamma^u (\beta^u \rho - 1)(\ln W^u - \ln W^n) + [\rho(\gamma^u \beta^u - \gamma^n \beta^n) - (\gamma^u - \gamma^n)]\ln W^n$$
$$+ \rho \gamma^u \ln(A^u/A^n) + \rho(\gamma^u - \gamma^n)\ln A^n + \rho \gamma^u \alpha^u \ln(q^u/q^n)$$
$$+ \rho(\gamma^u \alpha^u - \gamma^n \alpha^n)\ln q^n + \rho \gamma^u \beta^u \ln(s^u/s^n) + \rho(\gamma^u \beta^u - \gamma^n \beta^n)\ln s^n$$
(2.7)

where $\gamma^j = (1 - \alpha^j \rho - \beta^j \rho)^{-1}$ for $j = n, u$. As is evident, the effect of unionism on the use of labor equals the product of the elasticity of

---

[19] I have not belabored the distinction between "gains" and "gaps" here because it is too much to ask that we should quantify the difference between a unionized firm's employment and what employment would have been in the total absence of unionism in the economy. What we can aspire to is the measurement of employment gaps.

demand for labor (here $\gamma^u(\beta^u\rho - 1)$) and the union–nonunion wage differential, $\ln(W^u/W^n)$, only if the production function parameters are unaffected by unionism including the values of the technical efficiency parameters, A, q, and s. In fact, some research has argued these conditions do not obtain.

Labor Productivity

As an instance of the last point made above, Freeman and Medoff (1982) argue the wage-elasticity of demand for labor is lower in unionized than in nonunionized settings. The evidence offered in support of this belief comes from the study of data aggregated to the level of two-digit manufacturing industry in 29 regions of the United States in 1972. Throughout they work with the implied first-order conditions for a price-taking cost-minimizing firm. Representative of their many estimating equations is the following:

$$\ln(V/L)_{ij} = \sum_i a_{0i} D_i + \sum_j a_{1j} R_j + a_2 \ln W_{ij} + a_3 U_{ij}$$
$$+ a_4 (\ln W \cdot U)_{ij} + \epsilon_{ij} \tag{2.8}$$

where i indexes 19 manufacturing industries and j 29 regions within the USA. D_i and R_j are 19 industry and three region dummy variables respectively. V refers to value added, L to production worker manhours, W to the hourly wage of production workers, U to the fraction of production workers who are members of unions, and ϵ denotes a stochastic disturbance. In many estimating equations, L is adjusted by an index of labor quality.[20] Freeman and Medoff interpret equation (2.8) in terms of the first-order cost-minimizing condition from a CES production function in which case a_2 equals the elasticity of substitution in the nonunion sector and a_4 indicates how this elasticity differs in the union sector. Other things being equal, an industry's wage-elasticity of demand for labor rises (in absolute value) with the elasticity of substitution.

Though they report the least-squares estimate of a_4 to be negative, suggesting reduced substitution possibilities in the union sector, usually it is insignificantly different from zero by conventional criteria. A similar absence of significant difference between the union and nonunion sector's substitution opportunities is suggested when capital–labor ratios and nonproduction–production worker ratios are used as dependent variables

---

[20] This index of labor quality is derived by fitting to the 1973–75 Current Population Survey data wage equations (for men and women separately) where age, schooling, union membership, and regional dummy variables were regressors. On the basis of the average relationship described by the regression equation, each worker's implied wage is predicted (ignoring his own union status) and used as an indicator of quality.

and when some establishment level data are examined.[21] Notwithstanding the consistent tendency for their results not to find meaningful differences between the union and nonunion sectors, the authors conclude that substitution between production labor and other inputs is lower in unionized settings. Their results do not warrant this conclusion.

It is fruitful to compare this work by Freeman and Medoff (1982) with that of Brown and Medoff (1978) who use almost the same data to fit

$$\ln(V/L)_{ij} = \sum_i b_{0i} D_i + \sum_j b_{1j} R_j + b_2 \ln(K/L)_{ij} + b_3 U_{ij}$$
$$+ b_4 [\ln(K/L) \cdot U]_{ij} + \epsilon_{ij} \qquad (2.9)$$

where the labor input (and the unionism variable) has been adjusted by the same type of quality index described earlier. In equation (2.9), K is a measure of the value of physical capital.[22] The resemblance between this equation and equation (2.8) is manifest and, as was the case with the coefficient on the interaction between $\ln W$ and U in equation (2.8), so in equation (2.9) b_4 is insignificantly different from zero. Indeed, in this case, b_3 is also estimated to be insignificantly different from zero.[23] When the interaction term, $\ln(K/L) \cdot U$, is omitted from the above regression equation, the estimate of b_3 is approximately 0.22 with a standard error of around 0.06. While Freeman and Medoff (1982) interpret equation (2.8) in terms of the first-order condition corresponding to price-taking cost-minimizing behavior, Brown and Medoff (1978) interpret equation (2.9) as a Cobb–Douglas production function with unionism's effects on productivity taking the form of labor-augmenting technical improvement. (Their specification is quite consistent, however, with unionism operating through neutral technical improvement and/or through capital-augmenting technical improvement.[24]) They infer from

[21] In this paper, Freeman and Medoff also estimate a system of input share equations from the first-order cost-minimizing conditions corresponding to a translog cost function. Their published results relate to the estimation of these equations under the constraint that the homogeneity and symmetry conditions hold. Unfortunately, standard tests indicated such conditions violated the data so it is not at all clear what to make of the reported results. For what they are worth, whenever the labor input was adjusted by the index of quality, the hypothesis that the substitution elasticity was the same in the union and nonunion sectors could not be rejected.

[22] The regression equation includes a measure of the vintage of the capital stock as well as a variable indicating establishment size. In the results reported, neither estimated coefficient on these two variables is significantly correlated with value added per manhour.

[23] The consequences of a joint test on the estimates of b_3 and b_4 are not reported.

[24] In other words, a production function of the form

$$V = (\text{constant}) (sK)^{b_1} (qL)^{1-b_1} \exp(cU + \epsilon)$$

(where s and q are quality indices that vary by union status) generates the same estimating equation preferred by Brown and Medoff.

the estimate of b_3 that "... unionized establishments are about 22 percent more productive than those that are not" (p. 368).

According to Brown and Medoff's preferred estimates (those where, in terms of equation (2.9), b_4 is constrained to zero and where the regression coefficients are supposed to be production function parameters), the implied labor demand function has a higher intercept in unionized establishments, but the wage elasticity is the same in union and nonunion settings, an implication counter to Freeman and Medoff's claims in their 1982 article. So, in terms of equation (2.7), Brown and Medoff maintain that $\beta^u = \beta^n$, $\gamma^u = \gamma^n$, $A^u = A^n$, and $s^u = s^n$, but $\ln(q^u/q^n) = 0.20$. Taking Brown and Medoff's results at face value, they suggest that the productivity-enhancing effects of unions on employment are probably not offset by their relative wage effects and so unionized employment is lower than would be the case in a nonunion market. However, this qualitative inference is not robust with respect to small changes in the estimate of the productivity-augmenting effects of unionism.[25]

Of course, maintaining that equation (2.9) is a production function does not make it so and the high partial correlation between value added per manhour and the hourly wage[26] makes one wonder whether b_3 in equation (2.9) is measuring a camouflaged relative wage effect of unionism. Indeed, Brown and Medoff report that, when $\ln(V/L)$ is replaced with $\ln W$ in equation (2.9), the coefficient on U is 0.216 with a standard error of 0.035, estimates uncannily similar to the supposed effect of unionism on labor productivity.[27] In short, the hypothesis that production function parameters in US manufacturing are different in unionized and nonunionized establishments is a plausible one, but I don't know whether the hypothesis is correct and Freeman and Medoff's (1982)

---

[25] In terms of equation (2.7), assume $\rho = 0.5$ and $\alpha = 0.70$, $\beta = 0.25$, and $\ln(W^u/W^n) = 0.15$. Then union employment is 89 percent of nonunion employment. Posit a lower value of the union–nonunion wage differential, say 10 percent. Given the same values of the other parameters, by how much does the labor efficiency parameter in unionized establishments have to exceed that in nonunionized establishments for the effect of unions on employment to be zero? The answer is that q in unionized establishments must be 1.28 its nonunion value.

[26] Freeman and Medoff (1982) report that (controlling for industry and region effects, for the extent of unionism, and for an interaction term) a 1 percent change in hourly wages is associated with about the *same* percent change in value added per manhour.

[27] If the union relative wage effect were $\Delta\ln\chi$ and the labor-augmenting effect of unionism were also $\Delta\ln\chi$, all other differences between the union and nonunion establishments being zero, the reduction in employment from unionism equals $\Delta\ln\chi$. (Check from equation (2.7).) Wessels (1985) labels this inference "an unresolved conflict" because it conflicts "... with other well-known evidence on unions. If unions did have such a substantial impact on labor productivity, they should reduce employment far more than has been commonly observed" (p. 102). Unfortunately, he doesn't cite any evidence showing "the effect of unions on employment is small", so I don't see any contradiction.

and Brown and Medoff's (1978) research does not dispel my ignorance. I do not believe their articles contain any reliable inferences about union–nonunion differentials in employment.

There have been many more studies, some of them carefully executed, of the effect of unionism on productivity. The more convincing of these are those where the analysis is restricted to a single industry for which the assumption of a common technology among firms is more plausible, where output is measured in some physical units thereby not confusing output price effects of unionism with production function effects, and where the use of panel data has allowed the researcher to control for fixed differences among producing units in labor productivity. This last condition implies that, if unionism is measured by a single dichotomous variable, the sample of observations must contain some whose union status changed otherwise the effect of unionism cannot be distinguished from firm-specific effects. I know of two studies that meet these stringent conditions:[28] one is Clark's (1980) examination of six US cement establishments that at different moments between 1953 and 1976 went from being nonunion to union; and the other is Boal's (1985) analysis of 83 coal mines in West Virginia that went from being extensively unionized immediately after the First World War to completely nonunion in the mid-1920s.

With 104 (plant-year) observations from the cement industry, Clark (1980) fitted Cobb–Douglas production functions where the logarithm of tons of finished cement per production worker manhour was regressed on a measure of physical capital capacity, manhours of production workers, manhours of supervisory workers, a linear time trend, dummy variables for each plant, and a dichotomous variable indicating union status. Exactly half the plant-year observations corresponded to a unionized status and half to nonunion status.[29] He estimated different equations corresponding to alternative assumptions about returns to scale, serial

[28] Mefford's (1986) work comes close to this and has the added advantage of a sample of 31 plants of a single multinational firm. However, he does not specify a separate intercept for each plant, but rather a separate dummy variable for each of seven regions, namely, Canada, Britain, Continental Europe, Latin America, Hong Kong, the Philippines, and Australia. With sample drawn from such diverse societies, I wonder whether cultural differences in work organization and effort are effectively accounted for by these regional dummy variables. For the years from 1975 to 1982, he fits a translog production function and controls for factors such as turnover, absenteeism and management quality and finds unionized plants have a 13 percent higher labor productivity than nonunionized plants. For only one region, Latin America, are there observations on both union and nonunion plants. When an interaction term between unionism and the Latin American dummy was introduced into the labor productivity equation, it became more difficult to determine from the data whether any union effect was present.

[29] Communication (February 1988) from Kim B. Clark.

correlation in the residuals, the role of capacity utilization, and the effects of environmental differences affecting all plants in a given region. The least-squares point estimates of the coefficient attached to the unionism variable range from 0.121 to 0.064, the central tendency being about 0.090 with a typical standard error of 0.054^{30} so a 95 percent confidence interval spans approximately the range from $+0.19$ to -0.01. Going beyond these regression estimates, Clark examined the union contracts in these plants and interviewed management and union officials to determine the nature of the organizational changes associated with unionism. He is able to identify with some assurance only one change accompanying union organization, namely, adjustments of management. These took the form of more professional managers and managerial techniques including closer monitoring of work effort and performance. In other words, these were the inputs substituting for more expensive production workers when establishments became organized. If employment in the cement industry can be appropriately determined from conventional labor demand functions, then Clark's estimates imply unionized employment is approximately 90 percent of nonunion employment.[31]

The observations in Boal's analysis consist of 83 coal mines in West Virginia in each of the four years from 1920–21 to 1925. All these mines were unionized in the first year, but all had become nonunion by 1925. Of the total 332 (mine-year) observations, 42 percent represent observations on unionized mines. Coal output in tons was specified to depend upon the number of miners, the number of other workers, the number of mine locomotives, the number of cutting machines, the number of horses, and the number of days of operation per year. Dichotomous variables for each year and for each mine were also included in estimating Cobb–Douglas and translog production functions where an entirely different form was allowed to exist in union and nonunion mines. Indeed, test

---

[30] From the nine lines of estimates reported in table 2 of Clark (1980), I have averaged the standard errors in those four lines where parameters have not been constrained to take on values estimated on some prior occasion. In the constrained estimates, the standard errors have not been adjusted to take account of the fact that the constraints are themselves estimates.

[31] Along with Clark, assume that the productivity effect of unionism comes through the neutral technology parameter. Also assume the relative wage effect of unionism in the cement industry is 15 percent, the mid-point of the range Clark reports in footnote 35 of his article. As production function parameters, take Clark's estimates in the first line of his table 2 where the coefficient on the union dummy is 0.107. Then, assuming further the price-elasticity of demand for output is -0.5, the proportionate reduction in employment arising from the wage effect of unionism is 0.204 and the proportionate increase in employment arising from the productivity augmenting effect of unionism is 0.087. On balance, unionism reduces employment by 11.7 percent or, equivalently, employment in a union establishment is 90 percent of that in an otherwise identical nonunion establishment.

statistics rejected the hypothesis of no difference between the union and nonunion production functions. The union production function appeared to cross the nonunion function with the suggestion that unions enhanced output for large mines, but hurt output at small mines. More precisely, the Cobb–Douglas production function implied about 21 percent higher output from union mines at the 90th size percentile and 13 percent lower output from union mines at the 10th size percentile.[32] Boal attributes this negative effect at small mines to "economies of scale in labor relations", managers and union officials being less cognizant of their rights and responsibilities under union contracts and, therefore, prone to damaging disputes. At the median, the effect of unionism on output was positive, 8 percent, but this estimate is barely greater than its standard error. Further analysis of unionism's positive effect among the larger mines indicates that it was present only in relatively unmechanized mines where the reduction in labor turnover resulted in smoother production with higher quality workers. At the mechanized mines, union and management often experienced difficulties in agreeing to the appropriate piece rates: incentives were damaged by long periods of negotiation and, as a bargaining tactic, miners restricted their work effort.

Boal did not compute the relative wage effect of unionism in West Virginia coal mines in the early 1920s, but if it were around 50 percent, a number within the range gauged by Lewis (1963, pp. 77–9), then Boal's production function estimates suggest a reduction of up to 50 percent in the employment of miners. This number is better described as a guess than as a crafted estimate.

However, even careful production function research has ambiguous implications for the effect of unionism on employment. There are three reasons for this. First, the relative wage effects of unionism are either not computed or are not computed with the same care so that, in terms of equation (2.6), B is not known with confidence. Second, the usual procedure of adding a union dummy (or a variable indicating fraction unionized) to a Cobb–Douglas labor productivity equation is consistent with unionism (i) affecting the production function's neutral efficiency parameter (A), (ii) modifying the efficiency with which employees work (q), and (iii) altering the efficiency of the services from physical capital (s). Yet these three possibilities have different implications for employment. Third, knowledge of the production function (and of the product market parameters) is not enough to specify the determination of employment: some assumptions are needed about the nature of bargaining in order for a labor demand function to provide the appropriate analytical

---

[32] The estimated standard error on the effect for the 90th percentile is 0.07 and that on the effect for the 10th percentile is 0.08.

framework to draw inferences about employment. If bargaining over employment takes place in the unionized or nonunionized firm, then the conventional labor demand function is not well-defined and cannot be used to infer unionism's effects on employment.

Time-Series Estimates

Time series provide a different source of evidence, one involving the comparison of relative movements in employment in two sectors over time with movements in the extent of unionism in these sectors. That is, many economists cite the relative wage effects of unionism estimated from US aggregative time-series data described earlier and so it would seem natural to determine what implications these same data harbor for the employment effects of unions. Recall that two sectors of the economy are identified, loosely, a relatively unionized sector, sector a, and a relatively nonunionized sector, sector b. By analogy with the wage equation (2.3) we might specify

$$DlnE_t = \gamma X_t + C^a U_t^a - C^b U_t^b + u_t \qquad (2.10)$$

where $DlnE_t \equiv lnE_t^a - lnE_t^b$, E_t^j being the number of full-time equivalent employees in sector j in year t, U_t^j the proportion of these employees represented by unions in sector j in year t, X_t a vector of other variables, and u_t a stochastic disturbance term. The employment equation corresponding to equation (2.4) is

$$DlnE_t = \gamma X_t + \overline{C}(DU)_t + u_t^* \qquad (2.11)$$

where $(DU)_t = (U^a - U^b)$ and $\overline{C}$ is a weighted sum of C^a and C^b.

The consequences of fitting equation (2.10) over the period 1921–80 by ordinary least-squares are shown in lines (a)–(e) of table 2.6 and the estimates of $\overline{C}$ from fitting equation (2.11) are given in lines (f)–(j).[33] The estimates of C^b vary a good deal from line to line while those of C^a

---

[33] The data used in this regression analysis are provided by Lewis (1963, chapter 6) and by Pencavel and Hartsog (1984). In the latter, E denotes not relative employment, but relative manhours. The values of E for 1919–58 are given in Lewis (1964, pp. 108–9) while for 1959–80 they are as follows:

1959	0.945	1966	0.826	1973	0.708
1960	0.868	1967	0.803	1974	0.688
1961	0.879	1968	0.790	1975	0.625
1962	0.855	1969	0.784	1976	0.626
1963	0.824	1970	0.744	1977	0.632
1964	0.829	1971	0.708	1978	0.634
1965	0.815	1972	0.703	1979	0.634
				1980	0.604

Table 2.6 Relative employment effects of unionism, 1921–80

	$\hat{C}^a$	$\hat{C}^b$	$\tilde{C}$	$DlnW_t$	$DlnW_{t-1}$	Other variables included in addition to the "base" set	R^2	see	LM
(a)	-0.050 (0.109)	1.354 (0.509)				None	0.966	0.035	10.3
(b)	0.145 (0.093)	1.578 (0.404)		-0.861 (0.151)		None	0.979	0.027	8.00
(c)	-0.017 (0.082)	0.534 (0.386)				X_{t-1}, $DlnE_{t-2}$	0.983	0.025	4.34*
(d)	0.054 (0.091)	0.811 (0.414)		-0.328 (0.196)		X_{t-1}, $DlnE_{t-2}$	0.984	0.025	4.70*
(e)	0.101 (0.114)	-0.324 (0.471)		-0.468 (0.197)	0.216 (0.160)	X_{t-1}, $DlnE_{t-2}$ T_t, T_t^2	0.988	0.022	14.67
(f)			-0.352 (0.068)			None	0.959	0.038	9.61
(g)			-0.166 (0.069)	-0.851 (0.174)		None	0.972	0.032	10.12
(h)			-0.106 (0.064)	-0.174 (0.189)		X_{t-1}, $DlnE_{t-2}$	0.982	0.025	4.40*
(i)			-0.087 (0.067)	-0.174 (0.189)		X_{t-1}, $DlnE_{t-2}$	0.982	0.025	4.58*
(j)			0.115 (0.113)	-0.475 (0.197)	0.190 (0.158)	X_{t-1}, $DlnE_{t-2}$ T_t, T_t^2	0.988	0.022	15.20

Estimated standard errors are in parentheses beneath estimated coefficients. The mean of the dependent variable is −0.123 with a standard deviation of 0.178. The variables constituting the "base" set and included as regressors in the estimates corresponding to each line in this table are as follows: the logarithm of the ratio of national income originating in sector a to that in sector b; the unemployment rate; the ratio of the actual to the "expected" price level (see Lewis, 1963, pp. 217–18); and the once lagged value of $DlnE_t$. In lines (c), (d), (e), (h), (i), and (j), X_{t-1} refers to the once lagged values of the logarithm of the ratio of national income in sector a to that in b. T_t is a linear time trend and T_t^2 a quadratic time trend. LM is Breusch and Godfrey's Lagrange multiplier test for second order serial correlation of the residuals. The asterisk denotes values of the LM statistic that do not permit rejection of the null hypothesis at the five percent level of significance.

are never measured with any precision. In other words, as was the case in measuring the relative wage effects of unionism, these data do not offer much of an opportunity to measure the employment effects of unions *within* each sector. The estimates of $\overline{C}$ in line (f) imply a logarithmic difference in employment associated with unions of -35 percent and the estimates in line (g) where relative wages are added as a regressor suggest that half of this union effect works through higher wages in the union sector, the other half operating independently of unions. But adding more variables to the X_t vector in equation (2.11) reduces the estimated absolute value of $\overline{C}$ such that a confident statement about the effect of unionism on employment becomes unwarranted. Thus the estimates in line (i) of table 2.6, perhaps the most preferred of those in the bottom half of this table in view of the smaller autocorrelation test statistics, imply a -9 percent relative employment effect of unionism holding relative wages constant, but this would not be regarded as significantly different from zero by conventional statistical criteria.

To determine whether $\overline{C}$ has varied over these 60 years, I re-estimated the specification given in line (i) of table 2.6 allowing $\overline{C}$ to differ in each decade. The estimates were as follows:

$$\hat{\overline{C}} = -0.118 + 0.270 \ (Y_2)_t + 0.230 \ (Y_3)_t + 0.201 \ (Y_4)_t$$
$$\phantom{\hat{\overline{C}} =} (0.118) \ (0.169) (0.109) (0.086)$$

$$\phantom{\hat{\overline{C}} =} + \ 0.080 \ (Y_5)_t + 0.047 \ (Y_6)_t$$
$$\phantom{\hat{\overline{C}} =} (0.077) (0.061)$$

where Y_j is a dichotomous variable taking the value of unity in any year in the jth decade and zero otherwise.[34] The point estimates imply positive effects of unionism on relative employment in the 1920s, 1930s and 1940s and negative effects in the 1950s, 1960s, and 1970s. Again, however, the standard errors in parentheses caution against any strong inferences.

Analysis of these time-series data suggests, therefore, that the effects of unionism on relative employment are not measured with any confidence. Indeed, even the direction of the effect, let alone its precise magnitude, is in real doubt. Lewis's (1964, p. 107) contrary conclusion that unionism depressed relative employment and "the order of magnitude of the relative employment effects was roughly the same as that of the relative wage effects" arises from a belief that these employment effects

---

[34] So, in terms of equation (2.11), each of these dichotomous variables is interacted with $(DU)_t$. The qualitative results discussed in the text are affected to only a small degree by changing the variables included in X_t. I also estimated equations where C_t was permitted to vary with the unemployment rate and with the ratio of the actual to the "expected" price level. The implied values of $\hat{\overline{C}}_t$ were as often positive as negative.

can be determined from the estimates of a conventional labor demand function and that the computed relative wage effects of unionism may be treated as an independent variable in measuring these effects. Certainly the latter procedure represents an unwarranted constraint on the data[35] while the former is simply a presumption.

Cross-Section Estimates

A recent British study is of a different kind in that it uses data drawn from a cross-section of establishments to infer the employment effects of unionism. With a sample of almost 1,000 establishments, Blanchflower, Millward and Oswald (1989) fit a variety of least-squares equations of the following generic form:

$$\ln E_i = \alpha X_i + \beta U_i + \gamma_1 \ln[E(t-1)]_i + \gamma_2 \ln[E(t-4)]_i + \epsilon_i.$$

The subscript i defines the establishment as the unit of observation. The left-hand side variable denotes employment in 1984. Note that employment in these same establishments in 1983 (that is, $t-1$) and in 1980 (that is, $t-4$) is included among the regressors along with U_i, the ratio of union members to employees. X_i stands for other right-hand side variables.[36] The authors report an estimate of β of about -0.056 with a

---

[35] In other words, in terms of equation (2.11), Lewis fitted

$$D\ln E_t = \gamma X_t + b\left[(DU)_t \cdot \hat{\bar{B}}_t\right] + u_{1t}$$

where X_t represents the logarithm of relative output in the two sectors and $\hat{\bar{B}}_t$ are the inferred relative wage effects of unionism from a prior wage regression in which $\bar{B}$ depended upon the unemployment rate and the expected rate of inflation in the manner of equation (2.5) above. Lewis's estimates of b were approximately minus unity so that $\partial(D\ln E_t)/\partial(DU)_t \approx -\hat{\bar{B}}_t$. However, when the constraints imbedded in the construction of $\hat{\bar{B}}_t$ are relaxed and the following equation is estimated:

$$D\ln E_t = \gamma X_t + c_1(DU)_t + c_2\left[(DU)_t \cdot (UN)_t\right]$$
$$+ c_3\left[(DU)_t \cdot \ln(P/\bar{P})_t\right] + u_{2t},$$

the predicted effects of unionism on relative employment (i.e., the implied values of $\partial(D\ln E_t)/\partial(DU)_t$) differ significantly from the (negative of the) implied values of $\hat{\bar{B}}_t$ estimated from the wage equation. This is the case whether the previous equation is fitted in levels or (following Lewis) in first differences.

[36] They also reported results in which U_i was replaced by a dichotomous variable indicating whether there were any trade unions engaged in collective bargaining with management. Among X_i were ten regional dummy variables, 183 industry dummy variables, the county unemployment rate, and indicators of capacity, sales, and financial performance. In some equations, X_i included a measure of the annual earnings of unskilled manual workers, but it appears that it neither exerts a significant effect on employment nor affects the inferences about U_i.

t-ratio of 2.4. Because the estimate of γ_1 is close to unity and that of γ_2 near zero, the authors choose to interpret their results as implying that unionism reduces the *growth* of employment: other things being equal, employment in a fully unionized firm grows at almost 6 percent per year more slowly than a nonunion firm. This implies a sizable employment difference after only a few years between union and nonunion establishments: consider a union and a nonunion establishment identical in all respects other than their union status in some initial period; after ten years, the union establishment employs only a little more than half (57 percent to be precise) the number of workers employed at the nonunion establishment. It is surprising such divergent employment dynamics have remained unnoticed until now.

There is another interpretation of Blanchflower, Millward and Oswald's results. Their sample of establishments is very diverse and, notwithstanding their worthy attempts to account for this diversity by including many different variables in X_i, it is difficult to believe that these variables remove all the variations in technology, input prices, and product demand conditions that affect employment. In these circumstances where the researcher lacks the requisite information, lagged values of employment may well serve as a good indicator of these diverse technological, price, and demand factors. In this event, the coefficient β measures, in part, the impact of unions on the *level* (and not the change) of employment, lagged employment doing little more than controlling for the string of unobserved determinants of current employment. The importance of including the lagged dependent variable among the regressors is indicated by the fact that, when it is omitted, the estimate of β is strongly positive, a reflection of the higher propensity for larger establishments to be unionized.[37] This illustrates clearly the awkward simultaneous equation problems described in the introduction to this chapter (section 2.1), namely, the problems arising from the fact that the incidence of unionism is determined jointly with the level of employment. These problems are not resolved, of course, by entering lagged dependent variables as regressors to employment equations.

At the moment, the evidence regarding the effect of unionism on employment is not only meagre, but also quite inconclusive. What is required is a number of microeconomic studies within an industry documenting the circumstances by which some units are unionized and some not and tracing the consequences for employment. It is likely to be

---

[37] I am grateful to David Blanchflower for providing me with this information (correspondence dated October 6, 1988).

only through many, industry-specific, studies that a convincing body of knowledge on this issue will be compiled.[38]

2.4 Hours of Work

Although the previous section has examined what is known about the effect of unionism on employment, in fact some of the evidence cited related not to the number of workers employed, but to manhours or mandays of work. This is true of the production function studies of Freeman and Medoff (1982), Brown and Medoff (1978), Clark (1980), and Boal (1985). Yet there is every reason to distinguish hours of work per employee from the number of employees. Management do not regard these two dimensions of the labor input as perfect substitutes for one another: fixed costs of employment encourage firms to seek adjustments in the labor input first by changing hours of work per employee rather than by hiring or firing workers; and, furthermore, the production technology may specify different roles for hours and for employment. Similarly, employees are not indifferent between various combinations of numbers employed and hours worked per worker as is evident from the history of trade unionism where disputes over the length of the workday and workweek occupy important chapters.[39] More recently, collective bargaining has been directed toward the length of the workyear with agreements covering the length of vacations, the number of holidays, and leaves of absence. So from the point of view of both management and the union, economic analysis should distinguish the number of workers employed from the hours each works.

Trade union objectives with respect to hours of work are sometimes difficult to assess because calls for hours reductions have often been combined with demands regarding wages and employment. Thus the push for a shorter workday or workweek has sometimes been accompanied by the demand that daily wages or weekly wages remain unchanged, so the goal is an increase in hourly earnings effected by working fewer hours. On

---

[38] This is not to deny the existence of the related literature examining the effects of unionism on turnover and employment variations. See, for instance, Freeman (1980), Kahn and Morimune (1979), and Leonard (1986).

[39] Of course, trade union pressure on work hours expressed itself not only in individual bargaining with employers, but also in political activity to legislate shorter working hours. Even after such legislation was introduced, the trade union was often the principal agency monitoring and determining compliance with the law. See the accounts in Montgomery (1967, pp. 230–334) and Cahill (1932).

other occasions, reductions in hours worked have been joined with a demand for higher hourly wage rates or piece rates, as was the well-known case of the British gas workers' hours reductions in 1889 (Hobsbawm, 1964). Reductions in hours of work have tended to be pursued by unions in firms and industries experiencing contractions in employment where the hours reductions are understood to be work-sharing devices. This has been true, for instance, of the railroad employees, the coal miners, and the steel workers in the United States.

Whether hours of work should be expected to be lower in unionized settings will depend on how management react to other ways in which the employment contract is affected by collective bargaining. Thus unionism has encouraged the development of less casual and more formal employment contracts which in some situations are associated with the tendency for labor to shed some of its features as a variable factor of production and to develop the characteristics of a fixed factor. For instance, the specification in the collective bargaining contract of procedures (such as advance notices, the ordering of workers by seniority, and severance pay) to avoid or reduce the impact of permanent layoffs on the welfare of workers increases the firm's fixed costs of employment. Furthermore, union–nonunion differentials with respect to fringe benefits appear to exceed those relating to hourly wages[40] and these fringes often have components more in the nature of fixed than of variable costs. In this way, unionism raises the fixed costs of employment relative to the variable costs, which encourages the firm to make greater use of hours per worker to secure a given labor input. Not only are management induced to substitute hours for numbers of employees, but cyclical variations in labor input are accomplished less in the form of additions to and subtractions from permanent employment and more in the form of variations in hours of work (through overtime in periods of expansion and short-time and temporary layoffs in periods of contraction). Therefore, with unions desiring to reduce working hours without any loss in pay or employment and with management responding to the fixity of employment by trying to extract more hours from each of their employees, the tension between management and union over working hours becomes evident.

Indeed, it seems to be the case that in the United States union–nonunion differentials in hours of work vary considerably by type of worker, by industry, and by occupation. Earle and Pencavel (1990) found that, for white men in 1978 outside of the construction industry, the union–nonunion hours differential is − 2.8 percent for craftsworkers, + 2.1 percent for operatives, + 14.3 percent for laborers, and + 3.3 percent for

[40] See Freeman (1981) and Lewis (1986, pp. 95–104).

all other occupations; and, in the construction industry, the differentials are -9.0 percent for craftsworkers, -0.7 percent for operatives, $+27.6$ percent for laborers, and $+6.8$ percent for all other occupations.[41] On average, for white men the union–nonunion differential in weekly hours is -1.1 percent, in annual weeks it is $+3.0$ percent, and in annual hours it is $+1.8$ percent;[42] for white women, the weekly hours differential in 1978 is $+9.9$ percent, the annual weeks differential is $+9.3$ percent, and the annual hours differential is $+20.2$ percent. What is noticeable about the union–nonunion hours differentials is that, for male workers, they tend to be positively correlated with union–nonunion wage differentials: where union–nonunion wage gaps are highest (in the construction industry and for laborers) so are the computed union–nonunion hours differentials. This is consistent with a positively sloped wage–hours locus such that greater hours of work are purchased with rising hourly earnings. (Lewis, 1969).[43]

However, these estimates of union–nonunion differentials in hours and weeks worked are derived from equations in which most of the interpersonal variations in hours and weeks are unaccounted for by the variables observed by the economist. Presumably, the omitted variables include measures of individuals' work preferences and work opportunities. These measures of opportunities and preferences may well be correlated with the variable indicating coverage by a collective bargaining contract: individuals with a greater attachment to or with more favorable opportunities in the labor market and working longer hours may well

---

[41] These estimates hold constant other variables associated with differences among individuals in hours of work. These variables are age, schooling, marital status, number of children, region of residence, location within metropolitan area, nonlabor and welfare income, hourly earnings, and occupational and industry dummy variables. It needs to be emphasized that several of these union–nonunion work hours differentials are computed imprecisely.

[42] These differentials in weekly hours for men are very similar to Lewis's (1986, pp. 104-6) consensus estimates, but his annual hours differentials are about -3.0 percent.

[43] A different procedure is applied by Montgomery (1989) who forms a city (SMSA) union strength variable consisting of the product of the fraction of the city's employees who are unionized and the city's union–nonunion wage differential. Its maximum is assumed by San Bernardino with a value of 0.0803 (fraction unionized being 0.290 and the union wage premium being 0.277) and its minimum is assumed by Atlanta with a value of -0.0015 (fraction unionized being 0.125 and the union wage premium being -0.012, the only negative value calculated). This union strength variable was then used as a regressor in equations fitted to individuals from the 1983 Current Population Survey to account for variations in the probability of being employed and in usual weekly hours worked. The union strength variable was found to depress both the employment probability and work hours, but the effects are small: a change in the union strength variable from its minimum (Atlanta) to its maximum (San Bernardino) values reduces the employment probability by only 1.7 percent and weekly hours by 1.2 percent.

place a higher value on the protection provided by unions from arbitrary treatment by management and, therefore, will be more disposed towards working in unionized establishments. In other words, individuals inclined to work longer hours will self-select themselves for employment in the union sector. This selection process could be especially important among groups (such as women) whose work patterns are quite diverse. This means that unobserved differences in work preferences or work opportunities are reflected in part in the values taken by the dummy variable indicating coverage by a collective bargaining agreement so that the computed union–nonunion hours differentials do not correspond to the difference between the time worked by the *same* individual in the two sectors.

Time-series evidence on union–nonunion hours differentials derives from fitting equations such as equations (2.10) and (2.11) to annual observations on annual *full-time* hours worked per employee. It is important to note that, whereas the cross-section data reported in the previous paragraphs related to the hours an individual works on his main job, the time-series data relate to hours worked by full-time employees only. On average over the years 1921–80, the union–nonunion annual hours gap is about −8.5 percent. When these hours gaps are allowed to vary over time, they assume their largest negative values in the 1930s with union–nonunion differentials of the order of −24.4 percent.[44] A larger hours gap between the two sectors in the 1930s is consistent with the well-documented efforts by unions to divide the available work equally among employees. (See Slichter, 1941, pp. 98–139.)

It needs emphasizing that, as is true of the literature on the effects of unions on employment, there is only a little research on union–nonunion hours differentials. Consequently, it would be unwise to attach much confidence to the estimates reported in the previous paragraph at least until they are corroborated with other data. As they stand, the estimates suggest that, though unions may have reduced full-time weekly hours of white men by about 1 percent in the late 1970s, there are marked variations across individuals and over time in union–nonunion hours differentials.

---

[44] The average figure of −8.5 percent corresponds to equation (6d) of table 5 in Earle and Pencavel (1990). Other estimates range from −6.8 percent to −14.7 percent. A differential of −8.5 percent implies that, if nonunion employees work 2,182 annual hours (the mean value of full-time hours in sector *b*), then other things being equal unionized employees work 1,997 hours or 185 hours less. The −24.4 percent hours differential for the 1930s is the simple average of the two estimates in equation (7d) of table 7 in Earle and Pencavel (1990). This set of estimates implies an annual full-time hours gap of −3.7 percent in the 1970s.

2.5   Cyclical Adjustments

In the discussion in section 2.2 of movements over time in the union wage premium, arguments were described suggesting that unionism tends to reduce the responsiveness of wages to business cycle changes in exogenous variables.[45] In fact, the evidence in support of this argument is not at all extensive even though it appears to be widely believed. For example, when Moore and Raisian (1980) examined the hypothesis that the union wage premium moves countercyclically, they found little evidence for it over the period from 1967 to 1974. It is true that, in the United States, the union wage premium seems to be correlated with unanticipated changes in prices. However, the fall in the wage premium in the late 1970s when inflation was accelerating indicates that more factors are at work, as does the apparent stability of the premium over the 1981–83 recession: the much-heralded union "wage concessions" seem to have been matched by wage reductions in the nonunion sector so that the union–nonunion wage differential barely changed. (See Freeman, 1986b.) Also, as argued above, other explanations for the movement in the union wage premium have scarcely been examined.

A more recent argument regarding the role of unionism in business cycle adjustments has been that unions encourage the use of layoffs. The evidence for this rests largely on research by Medoff (1979) in which, *for manufacturing industries only*, layoff rates across industries are regressed on a number of variables including the fraction of workers unionized. Interpreted most sympathetically, this specification measures the effect of unions on layoff rates *irrespective of the state of the business cycle*; to determine how unions modify the business cycle effects on layoffs requires an interaction between unionism and some cyclical indicator. Nevertheless, the positive association computed by Medoff between layoff rates and unionism lies behind the statement that "when demand for output declines, unionized establishments are more likely to reduce labor costs by placing workers on temporary layoffs than by cutting wage growth or weekly hours" (Freeman and Medoff, 1984, p. 114).[46] More

[45] Hence Lewis's conjecture that, "The relative real wage impact of a monopoly union, therefore, will tend to be greatest in the months immediately following a sharp downturn in the general level of money wages and prices, particularly when the downturn follows a period of high level employment and sustained inflation. The 1920–21 downturn is a good example. The relative wage impact will tend to be least at the bottom of a severe, prolonged depression–1933 is such a trough, and during periods of rapid inflation at high levels of employment such as occurred in both World Wars." (Lewis, 1959, p. 208).

[46] Freeman and Medoff's (1984) discussion in this section of their book does not make it clear that, whatever the validity of Medoff's (1979) results, they are restricted to manufacturing industry, representing less than half of all union members in the 1960s.

plausibly this positive association between unionism and layoff rates in manufacturing industry reflects the fact that unionism has tended to develop most in those sectors where cyclical fluctuations are greater (such as in durable goods manufacturing).

The general question remains of how unionized firms and nonunion firms differ, if at all, in their responses to cyclical shocks. The answer is not straightforward to address, partly because the incidence of unionism is not distributed independently of the cyclical volatility of different industries. Indeed, unionism is in some respects a consequence of the grievances that these fluctuations have induced. In addition, exogenous indicators of cyclical shocks are not always easy to identify[47] and what might be an appropriate indicator in one sector is inappropriate in another. A more modest task is simply to compute the cyclical fluctuations in the key labor market variables and, after accounting for the effects of variables that might be correlated with unionism, to describe the union–nonunion differences.

Fortunately, this task has recently been undertaken by Earle (1988) using annual observations on 48 industries (of which 21 are manufacturing industries) from 1949 to 1979. Using National Income and Product Accounts data, among a number of equations, he specifies the following:[48]

$$\Delta \ln y_{it} = \sum_t \alpha_{0t} T_t + \sum_i \alpha_{0i} I_i + \beta_0 \Delta \ln x_{it} + \beta_1 (Z_{it} \Delta \ln x_{it})$$
$$+ \beta_2 (U_i \Delta \ln x_{it}) + \epsilon_{it} \tag{2.12}$$

[47] This is the shortcoming of Raisian's (1983) careful analysis of annual changes in wages, weeks worked, and weekly hours worked of 3,828 men from the Michigan panel from 1967 to 1979. His cyclical indicator is the deviation of the individual's industry unemployment rate from the average unemployment rate for that industry over the entire period 1967–79. Only nine industrial groups are identified and a good deal of variation in industry shocks must be lost by use of such a broad-based indicator. He found that blue-collar union workers experienced *greater* procyclical wage variability than blue-collar nonunion workers, a result he describes as "a little puzzling."

[48] Earle (1988) rationalized his specification as follows. Suppose the difference between the proportional change in y, $\Delta \ln y$, and the trend growth in y, $(\Delta \ln y)^*$, is a constant fraction (except for an unobserved component ϵ) of the difference between the growth of output, $\Delta \ln x$, and the trend growth of output, $(\Delta \ln x)^*$:

$$\Delta \ln y - (\Delta \ln y)^* = \beta [\Delta \ln x - (\Delta \ln x)^*] + \epsilon.$$

Suppose the trends are given by their (constant) mean values over the sample period in which case they can be subsumed in α below:

$$\Delta \ln y = \alpha + \beta \Delta \ln x + \epsilon.$$

Equation (2.12) allows α to vary over time and across industries while β depends on industry characteristics including unionism.

where $\Delta \ln x_{it}$ denotes the proportional change in real gross domestic product originating in industry i, U_i the fraction of workers covered by collective bargaining agreements in 1979, and Z_{it} a vector of other regressors describing the characteristics of the employees.[49] Dummy variables for each of the 31 years, T_t, and for each of the 48 industries, I_t, are also included. In one set of regressions $\Delta \ln y_{it}$ represents the proportional change in hourly wages, in another the proportional change in employment, and in the third the proportional change in annual hours worked per employee.[50] For the change in wages, the ordinary least squares estimate of β_2 (with standard errors in parentheses) is 0.045 (0.056), for the change in employment it is -0.014 (0.092), and for the change in hours it is 0.168 (0.036). Of these estimates, only that associated with hours of work is statistically significant by conventional criteria and it suggests that the elasticity of changes in hours with respect to changes in output is 17 percent higher in a unionized industry than in a nonunion industry. This result survives different equation specifications and suggests to Earle that unions generally encourage worksharing in business cycle adjustments. This conclusion would be more persuasive if it were also shown that the cyclical employment responses were smaller in unionized firms (or if union–nonunion differences in labor hoarding were confirmed), but this result is obtained only in Earle's parsimonious equation specifications.

At present, research on the way in which unions modify cyclical adjustments to key labor market variables has not reached convincing conclusions. Though it is widely believed that the union wage premium rises in a recession, the evidence for this is not firmly based. A hypothesis that union–nonunion differences in such cyclical adjustments are of second-order importance would be broadly consistent with what we know. An alternative hypothesis might state that the responses vary so much among firms within the union sector and among firms within the nonunion sector that the unmodified union–nonunion distinction is not very meaningful. In view of the differences in the particular clauses of

---

[49] Included in Z are the proportion of employees who are female, median years of schooling, labor market experience, tenure on the current job, proportion of workers in white-collar occupations, proportion of workers in establishments employing more than 500 employees, and proportion of total compensation accounted for by fringe benefits. Observations on some of the variables are available for only a few years so their values were interpolated between these years.

[50] The hourly wage in these data is defined as the total compensation of all persons engaged in the industry divided by annual hours worked by all full-time and part-time employees. Employment is the sum of full-time and part-time employment. Average hours worked is annual hours worked by all full-time and part-time employees divided by the total number of full-time and part-time employees. Earle (1988) examined other definitions of these variables with results very similar to those reported.

collective bargaining contracts – some requiring worksharing and others silent about it, some carefully regulating the order of layoffs and others stipulating fewer conditions – it seems likely that naive, union–nonunion, differences miss the critical variations.

2.6   Conclusions

This chapter has been devoted to a discussion and evaluation of what is known and not known about union–nonunion differentials in wages, employment, and hours of work. A good deal is known about wages, especially in the United States: that union–nonunion wage differentials exist and averaged some 14 percent in the United States in the 1970s seem well documented. Some of the variations in this differential over time and across workers are estimated with less confidence, but nevertheless there is a substantial amount of evidence on these matters and the issues have clearly attracted much research effort.

The imbalance between the volume of research devoted over the last 20 years or so to the question of union–nonunion wage differentials and that applied to measuring union–nonunion differentials in employment and hours of work (and changes in these differentials over the business cycle) is remarkable. No doubt, part of this imbalance is attributable to the appearance of large data sets on magnetic tapes containing information on wages and other characteristics of individuals. But this is not a sufficient explanation; after all, these surveys often contain information on hours worked by individuals yet the computation of union–nonunion differentials in hours has been a sorely neglected topic.

I suspect a part of the relative inattention to union–nonunion differentials in employment and hours of work arises from a belief that the questions are merely derivative of the primary question of what is the wage-elasticity of demand for labor; once this question can be answered (and given the research findings with respect to wages), union–nonunion differentials in employment and hours may be inferred in a straightforward manner. The trouble with this argument is that it presumes that in both union and nonunion settings management unilaterally determines employment in a fashion described by conventional labor demand functions. This presumption may well be appropriate in certain labor markets, but little effort has been devoted to determining whether this is the case and so the reason for ignoring measurement of union–nonunion differentials in employment and work hours is a matter more of dogma than of scientific procedure. Consequently, if one purpose of behavioral models of trade unionism is to account for empirical regularities in wages, employment, and work hours in unionized markets, then there is not much to discipline the construction of these models as far as employment and hours of work are concerned.

3 Trade Union Objectives

3.1 Introduction

A model of the determination of wages, employment, and hours in a unionized labor market requires the specification of the objectives of the trade union and of management and, if these objectives conflict, of a mechanism that reconciles these objectives. The implications of any model so constructed will rest heavily, often critically, on what is assumed about the union's objectives. Unfortunately, our knowledge of these objectives is meagre. It rests on two types of information: first, on discursive accounts from the industrial relations literature where formal models are eschewed and, therefore, where analytical results are difficult, if not impossible, to discern; and, second, on some quantitative studies by economists on a few, perhaps unrepresentative, trade unions. In view of this scanty knowledge, economists have good reason to adopt a very modest posture when discussing the structural operation of unionized labor markets in that at least one crucial component of our modelling of such markets is not at all well understood.

This ignorance has been exploited by economists seeking to construct theoretical models of unionized labor markets because it has allowed them to specify very convenient forms for union objectives without having to deal with objections to the effect that these forms conflict with a heavy weight of empirical evidence. A cynic would speculate whether, notwithstanding statements to the contrary, many economists really do not want to see a lot of empirical work conducted on a topic as it is likely to reveal the irrelevance of certain hypotheses and thereby undermine economists' ability to derive sweeping implications from simple specifications. Certainly, the literature's heavy reliance on only a few specifications for union objectives indicates not that such specifications have been subject to empirical scrutiny and have been corroborated, but precisely the reverse – for the most part, these specifications have *not* been the subject of such a study and, therefore, the theorist is at liberty to choose those assumptions that will generate the most comprehensive and unequivocal results.

The purpose of this chapter is to review these specifications for union objectives and assess them in the light of analytical empirical research on this topic. It needs emphasizing, however, that the focus of this chapter is on how union objectives relate to employment, wages, and hours of work and the full range of union activities and objectives is by no means discussed. In fact, of course, unions have been as concerned with *processes* as with *ends* so that, for instance, it is not merely the level of employment that matters but also the methods by which decisions about employment are reached. Indeed, there are surely unionized labor markets in which wages, employment, and hours of work are barely, if at all, different from what would obtain in the absence of the union, but the union's presence has changed the way in which these variables have been determined so that employees believe the procedures are even-handed and they feel more involved in the process. By restricting attention to the outcomes of union activities, the analysis in this chapter is necessarily incomplete.

Even with the focus so narrowed, the analytical problems of specifying a well-defined objective function for the union are still considerable. This has been recognized by many researchers in this field and certainly by those who are routinely credited with launching the formal investigation of trade union objective functions, John Dunlop (1944) and Arthur Ross (1948). Dunlop argued that ". . . logical models of the trade union are as indispensable to analytical economics as the theory of the conditions under which an enterprise maximizes profits" (p. 32) and, on this basis, proceeded to describe a number of different maximands for the union. He concluded, "The most suitable generalized model of the trade union for analytical purposes is probably that which depicts the maximization of the wage bill for the total membership" (p. 44). This has usually been interpreted as a maximand for the union of the following form:

$$\Gamma(W, h, E) = WhE \qquad (3.1)$$

where W denotes the wage rate, h hours of work, and E total employment. However, when some members are unemployed and receiving unemployment compensation or employed at alternative activities, "the maximization of the wage bill for the total membership" implies

$$\Gamma(W, h, E; \overline{W}, M) = WhE + \overline{W}h(M - E)$$
$$= (Wh - \overline{Wh})E + \overline{Wh}M. \qquad (3.2)$$

Here $\overline{Wh}$ represents earnings in some alternative activity (or unemployment compensation) and M denotes total union membership. In this volume, I shall call equation (3.1) the wage bill maximand. Various statements in his book suggest Dunlop probably had in mind equation (3.1) rather than equation (3.2).[1] In either case, equations (3.1) and (3.2) imply, for any level of hours of work, convex to the origin indifference curves between wages and employment of the sort depicted in Figure 3.1.[2]

In explicit reaction to Dunlop's arguments, Ross (1948) denied that union objectives could be characterized by "the mechanical application of any maximization principle" (p. 8). He wrote instead that "the central objective of the union must be defined as institutional survival and growth" (p. 18). This objective is implemented through specific policies defined and pursued by the union leadership who, in so doing, must reconcile conflicting interests among union members. "In the normal state of organizational health, the officials identify their own personal aims with the institutional objectives of the union" (p. 43).

The position taken in this book draws upon both Dunlop's and Ross's arguments. From Dunlop, I accept the principle that the trade union maximizes a meaningful objective function, a methodological position that is innocuous until more structure is placed on the problem and the form of the objective function is specified. I depart from Dunlop by not requiring that objective function to be either equation (3.1) or equation (3.2) and, in so doing, I follow the work of Leontief (1946), Fellner (1947), Cartter (1959), and others.[3] From Ross, I accept the notion that the union objective function is most conveniently and appropriately viewed as "the" union leadership's. In current parlance, Ross was raising a host of social choice and principal-agent type problems that frustrate the construction of the union's objective function by means of a straightforward aggregation of the utility functions of the union members. I find his arguments on these matters persuasive and hence I prefer to envisage the union's objective function as the leadership's.

Of course, this still begs the question of who constitutes the union's

---

[1] For instance, "Probably the most generalized assumption respecting actual aims of trade unions would be the maximization of the wage bill" (Dunlop, 1944, p. 119).

[2] The convexity of the indifference curves follows, in the case of equation (3.1), from $d^2 \underline{W}/dE^2 = 2WE^{-2} > 0$ and, in the case of equation (3.2), from $d^2 W/dE^2 = 2(Wh - \overline{Wh})h^{-1}E^{-2} > 0$. Equation (3.1) is clearly a homothetic function while (3.2) is nonhomothetic. Note also that equations (3.1) and (3.2) imply, for any given employment, convex indifference curves between wages and hours of work (for both equations, along an indifference curve, $d^2 W/dh^2 = 2Wh^{-2} > 0$). There is no disutility of work in equations (3.1) and (3.2).

[3] A careful review of this literature is contained in Atherton (1973, chapter 1).

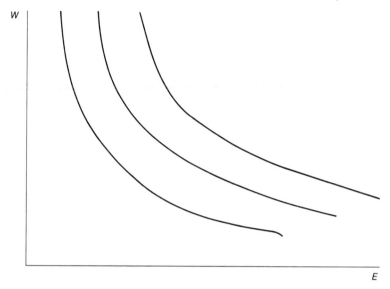

Figure 3.1   The union's indifference curves between wage rate (*W*) and employment (*E*) holding hours of work (*h*) fixed.

leadership. The answer will vary from union to union and from time to time. In some cases, effective decision-making with respect to the collective bargaining contract is in the hands of the local union officials and the regional or national officials may do little more than approve a locally negotiated agreement. In other cases, the major features of the collective bargaining contract are the result of negotiations involving the top officials of the union and the local is limited to negotiating no more than minor modifications to this master agreement. At times, such as during the shop steward movement in Britain in the 1960s and 1970s, there is some ambiguity as to where effective decision-making lies. When I maintain, therefore, that for the purpose of wage, employment, and hours determination in unionized markets it is most useful to think in terms of the union leadership's objective function, I am well aware I am side-stepping some very pertinent issues regarding the distribution of authority within unions. These are issues that may well merit analysis in terms of deriving a meaningful union objective function.

For reasons that I hope will become apparent, I think of the leadership's preferences in terms of a continuous, quasi-concave, function of earnings ($y = Wh$), hours of work (h), employment (E), the alternative or comparison wage rate ($\overline{W}$), and union membership (M):

$$\Gamma = g(y, h, E, \overline{W}, M) \qquad (3.3)$$

with g increasing in y, E and M and g decreasing in h and $\overline{W}$. Particular interest has focused in the literature on whether there exists a trade-off between W and E (as maintained by figure 3.1 and equation (3.3)) and, if so, the particular form of that trade-off. In normal circumstances, a negative wage–employment trade-off is not easy to discern because marginal changes in wages and employment are made in an environment in which other, confounding, changes are taking place. Occasionally, the trade-off is more conspicuous as in those instances in which an inter-firm or inter-plant agreement allows for a lower wage at particular, high cost, establishments where the application of the higher wage would cause reductions in employment.[4] The union's wage–employment trade-off is also unconcealed when the union agrees to open contracts for renegotiation before their expiration so that adjustments to labor costs can be made (often in the form of lower wages or deferred wage increases) to forestall layoffs. Some of these "wage concessions" have been made to prevent entire plant closings while in other instances more moderate job losses are at stake and even increases in employment have been negotiated.[5]

The empirical research directed to determining the union's trade-off between wages and employment is reviewed in section 3.6 below. I shall argue that it has delivered ambiguous conclusions because the variables actually employed in the empirical work measure something other than the wage–employment trade-off. I shall argue also that those researchers who have relied on a mixture of deduction and analogy to specify the particular form of equation (3.3) have not presented a convincing case. Nevertheless, the research on this topic has been productive and I indicate what I believe we have learned.

At the outset, it needs emphasizing how narrow is the meaning here given to trade union objectives. As stated above, we are concentrating on wages, hours, and employment outcomes, not processes. Furthermore, issues concerning the determinants of the structure of labor organizations are put aside. That is, we take as given that unions have emerged in some trades and not in others, that some unions bargain at the local level with a single firm and others bargain at a national level with many firms, that some unions embrace workers of many different types and skills and others represent workers with virtually the same skills, that some unions

---

[4] See, for instance, Greenberg (1968) and Slichter, Healy and Livernash (1960, chapter 27).

[5] See Shultz and Myers (1950), Henle (1973), and Flanagan (1984). In 1982, employees of 40 Kroger Company grocery stores in Pennsylvania agreed to $1.10 per hour reductions in wages and fringe benefits in exchange for a company promise not only to terminate its plan to sell seven stores (which would have eliminated about 365 jobs), but also to open five new stores. The employees were represented by the United Food and Commercial Workers Union.

have carefully formulated procedures for monitoring the activities of the leadership and others grant them considerable discretionary authority, and so on. These are very important issues for students of unionism and some of the classic industrial relations literature has been concerned with the effects of the characteristics of labor and product markets on the structure of labor unions.[6] In this chapter, I take this structure and its effects on union goals as given and I inquire into the nature of union preferences with emphasis on their wage, employment, and hours of work objectives. Therefore, the scope of this inquiry is necessarily restricted.

In this chapter, I first postulate a union consisting of a fixed number of identical members and in this context discuss the popular utilitarian and expected utility formulations of union objectives. I then turn to examining certain differences within the union and argue that the presence of alternative (or comparison) wages and membership size in the union objective function may emerge from principal-agent problems associated with the distinct interests and opportunities of the union leadership and rank-and-file. Finally, the empirical work on trade union objectives is reviewed and evaluated with special emphasis on the research on the coalminers and printers.

3.2   Homogeneous Membership

A natural starting point for a discussion about a group objective function is with the social welfare literature. To this end, consider a trade union consisting of a fixed number of M members. The well-behaved utility function of member i is $u_i(x_i, h_i)$ where x_i denotes consumption and h_i hours of work. Each member's utility is increasing in x_i and decreasing in h_i. One approach to defining the objective function for the union, Γ, is to aggregate the utility functions of the members and derive the classical utilitarian or Benthamite social welfare function:[7]

$$\Gamma(x_1, \ldots, x_M, h_1, \ldots, h_M; M) = \sum_{i=1}^{M} u_i(x_i, h_i). \qquad (3.4)$$

Another candidate is the Bernoulli–Nash social welfare function:

---

[6] John Commons's (1909) study of the development of various organizations of shoemakers is the venerable example of this literature.

[7] For the interpersonal comparability statements below, the members' utility functions need to be invariant with respect to affine transformations with a common positive slope. See Sen (1977).

$$\Gamma(x_1, \ldots, x_M, h_1, \ldots, h_M; M) = \prod_{i=1}^{M} u_i(x_i, h_i). \qquad (3.5)$$

which is obviously utilitarian in the logarithms of utility.

Note the important restriction here that each individual's welfare evaluation depends on his own utility only. In fact, many would maintain that this property runs counter to a cardinal element of trade unionism: an attention to the welfare of others – not merely others within the union, but also those in other trade unions and perhaps nonunion workers too – has been a consistent theme in union declarations and union behavior. It is manifested, for instance, in secondary boycotts, sympathetic strikes, the respecting of picket lines set up by other unions, and "hot cargo" clauses. Of course, one can well imagine how these actions could be rationalized in terms of purely selfish motives – union a extends help to union b in the expectation that assistance will be reciprocated when union a is in need – and it would be foolish to state this is never the case. At the same time, an insistence that utilities are always independent, that one member's evaluation of his welfare never depends on another's, seems an implausibly extreme position in view of the evidence that seems at first sight to be consonant with it.

Another defect with equation (3.4) is the tacit assumption that two individual members' utility levels are perfectly substitutable for one another in the union's evaluation of welfare, that is, the union's utility function (being simply the sum of individual utilities) is indifferent with respect to many different (and some highly unequal) distributions of utility. The consistent finding that the dispersion of wage rates in unionized establishments is narrower than that in nonunion establishments leads one to believe that unions are typically more concerned with the distribution of outcomes than is suggested by the utilitarian objective (3.4). For instance, suppose the union's objective function takes the Bernoulli–Nash form, equation (3.5), then the union's indifference curves are convex to the origin implying the union prefers an equal distribution of outcomes.[8]

Notwithstanding its denial of interdependence of members' utility functions and its negation of the distribution of members' utilities as a relevant concern, the utilitarian objective function (3.4) has formed the basis of a good deal of work in the literature. Its popularity derives not from success in the empirical domain, but from the analytical convenience embodied by its additivity property and from analogies with other

---

[8] This result assumes the welfare of the union is independent of the identity of the union members. If all members are not treated in the same way, then clearly a move toward greater equality will depend on how the move is allocated among members.

branches of economics research where extensive use has been made of utilitarian objectives. To illustrate the convenience of the utilitarian objective function, consider the following argument.

Assume all union members are identical, hours of work are exogenous, and differences in nonwage income among employed union members may be ignored (so consumption corresponds to labor earnings). Distinguish between those union members employed (E) on the union-negotiated contract at a wage of W and those employed $(\overline{E})$ at some alternative wage $\overline{W}$ exogenous to the union. In some interpretations, $\overline{W}$ represents unemployment benefits and $\overline{E}$ is the number unemployed. Under these conditions, the utilitarian objective function (3.4) may be written

$$\Gamma(W, E; h, \overline{h}, \overline{W}, M) = u(y)E + u(\overline{y})(M - E), \tag{3.6}$$

where $y = Wh$, $\overline{y} = \overline{W}h$, $M = E + \overline{E}$ and $y > \overline{y}$. In other words, y denotes earnings, the product of wage rates and hours worked. Because union membership and alternative earnings have been assumed exogenous, the previous equation is equivalent to

$$\widetilde{\Gamma}(W, E; h, \overline{h}, \overline{W}, M) = [u(y) - u(\overline{y})](E/M) \tag{3.7}$$

a formulation often described as the expected utility of an individual union member. It is as if employment at the union-negotiated wage is uncertain, all union members stand the same chance of being employed at y, and all have the information needed to construct the employment probability, E/M.

The usefulness of equations (3.6) and (3.7) derives from their additivity property: the union's marginal utility of contract wages is unaffected by changes in alternative opportunities, $\overline{y}$. The utilitarian and expected utility formulations of union objectives with a homogeneous membership, equations (3.6) and (3.7) respectively, are usually described as equivalent representations of union preferences over the choice variables, earnings and employment. This is correct under the stated assumptions of fixed membership and given alternative earnings. Note, however, that changes in these exogenous variables have different qualitative effects in the two equations: according to equation (3.6) $\partial\Gamma/\partial\overline{y} > 0$ and $\partial\Gamma/\partial M > 0$ while, according to equation (3.7), $\partial\widetilde{\Gamma}/\partial\overline{y} < 0$ and $\partial\widetilde{\Gamma}/\partial M < 0$. This means that care needs to be exercised in extending equations (3.6) and (3.7) to situations in which $\overline{y}$ or M is no longer exogenous.

The assumptions behind equations (3.6) and (3.7) of fixed membership and fixed alternative earnings are difficult to maintain. Consider first the assumption of fixed alternative earnings. No doubt part of the appeal of the expected utility formulation of union objectives arises from an analogy with decision-making at the level of a single individual, but whereas in that case it may well be appropriate to specify income in the less preferred state ($\bar{y}$) as exogenous to the individual this is surely not the situation faced by a group of individuals such as a trade union. This is because a group can pool and redistribute its incomes, thereby affecting income received by union members not employed on the union contract.[9] In other words, the expected utility objective function (3.7) results in identical (by assumption) members receiving different *ex post* outcomes even though the union has the power to affect the level of utility in the two states.

If all members pool their incomes, the task for the union is to allocate total income, $yE + \bar{y}(M - E)$, such that each individual employed on the union contract receives y_e and each of the unemployed (or those employed at the less preferred job) receives y_o. If the union allocates income to maximize the weighted average of the utilities of the employed and unemployed (that is, $u(y_e)(E/M) + u(y_o)(M - E)/M$), then not only must marginal utilities be equalized (that is, $u'(y_e) = u'(y_o)$), but also incomes are equalized ($y_e = y_o$) because all union members have been assumed to have the same, state-independent, preferences. Under these circumstances, the union does the best for its members by maximizing the size of pooled income, $yE + \bar{y}(M - E)$. When M and $\bar{y}$ are exogenous, this objective function is equivalent to equation (3.2) or, equivalently, under the assumption of given hours of work,

$$\Gamma(y, E; \bar{y}) = (y - \bar{y})E. \tag{3.8}$$

This monetary objective is sometimes interpreted as the union's counterpart to the firm's maximization of profits and I shall call it the rents from unionization. In short, when the union engages in income redistribution in this way, the assumptions behind the expected utility formulation of union objectives (3.7) imply the union will maximize rents as given in equation (3.8).

One shortcoming with the income redistribution scheme described in the previous paragraph is that it takes no account of the disutility of work: the employed union member has to work for the same income granted the unemployed union member. It is more plausible to assume that income redistribution from the employed to the unemployed continues up to the

---

[9] Income redistribution is not the only way in which nonunion wages may be endogenized. For instance, insofar as a higher union wage reduces employment in the union sector, the disemployed workers may bid down wages in the nonunion sector. Lazear (1983) incorporates such a process in his model in which the union is characterized as fully recognizing the impact of its wage policies on nonunion wages. More controversially, in Lazear's model, the union's welfare extends to nonunion as well as to union workers so the union is deterred from pushing up its wage by the negative impact of such a policy on nonunion wages.

point at which $u(y_e) = u(y_o) + k$ where k is the utility of not having to work for an income.[10] If the union again maximizes the weighted average of the utilities of the employed and unemployed members, then this is no longer equivalent to maximizing the rents from unionization, equation (3.8), because the union is not valuing a marginal dollar (or pound) received by an employed union member at the same rate as a marginal dollar paid to an unemployed member. In this instance, the union maximizes $u(y_e)$ where y_e is defined by the redistribution identity $yE + \bar{y}(M - E) = y_e E + y_o(M - E)$ and where y_e and y_o satisfy the condition $u(y_e) = u(y_o) + k$.

There is no doubt that income redistribution within the union was once a prominent feature of many unions in Britain and the United States and unemployment compensation was paid by many unions to their out-of-work members. These schemes were largely superseded by the development of state unemployment compensation although, given the presumed superior ability of the state in effecting these benefits, it is remarkable the extent to which many US unions still augment state unemployment payments with benefits negotiated as part of the collective bargaining agreement. According to the data in table 3.1, about 26 percent of unionized workers represented by major US collective bargaining contracts in 1980 are covered by clauses entitling them to supplemental unemployment benefits. Some 39 percent are covered by clauses relating to severance pay and 17 percent to some sort of minimum income guarantees.[11]

Another form of intra-union income redistribution, it may be argued, consists of seniority provisions in layoff procedures according to which those with less tenure transfer income to those with more tenure. In this instance, seniority rules simply reallocate one's income over one's working life and the union's objective function needs to be defined in terms of each worker's lifetime utility. However, once a characteristic such as seniority is introduced, all members are no longer identical so problems arise in aggregating the preferences of members whose years of tenure differ and with membership and employment changing over time the long-run objectives of the union become more difficult to define.

Redistribution within the union need not take place only through explicit payments from the employed to the unemployed union members, but also by worksharing so that all members participate in fewer working hours and in lower weekly incomes. In the United States approximately

---

[10] McDonald and Solow (1981) consider this case and describe a union of this sort as a "commune."

[11] In an analysis of 400 US collective bargaining contracts, the Bureau of National Affairs (1986) reported some sort of income maintenance provisions in 52 percent of them.

64   Trade Union Objectives

Table 3.1   Percentage of workers covered by income security provisions among those represented by major collective bargaining agreements, United States, January 1980

	Supplemental unemployment benefit plans	Severance pay	Wage-employment guarantees
All manufacturing	51.4	53.6	36.6
Food, kindred products	3.0	67.4	19.8
Tobacco	21.6	100.0	0
Textile mill products	0	0	26.0
Apparel	41.7	3.6	1.4
Lumber, wood products	17.5	7.0	0
Furniture, fixtures	13.4	9.1	0
Paper, allied products	0	53.4	0
Printing and publishing	42.1	42.4	0
Chemicals	0	73.2	1.9
Petroleum refining	0	64.5	0
Rubber and plastics	82.6	75.2	0
Leather products	0	70.3	0
Stone, clay, and glass	6.1	74.0	0
Primary metals	91.0	81.5	67.5
Fabricated metals	35.7	43.1	30.3
Non-electrical machinery	57.7	27.3	2.3
Electrical machinery	21.3	55.9	0
Transportation equipment	74.3	52.7	0
Instruments	0	30.4	0
Miscellaneous manufacturing	0	50.0	0
Nonmanufacturing	4.4	27.0	19.7
Mining, crude petroleum, natural gas	6.6	7.3	6.0
Transportation	0	6.4	78.3
Communications	1.7	89.3	0
Utilities, electric, gas	6.6	34.3	7.3
Wholesale trade	4.4	20.7	49.8
Retail trade	16.7	34.3	31.5
Hotels and restaurants	0	3.4	14.4
Services	0.6	41.6	22.9
Construction	4.4	1.0	6.1
Miscellaneous nonmanufacturing	0	0	57.1
All industries	26.0	39.2	16.8

These data relate to collective bargaining agreements covering 1,000 workers or more on January 1, 1980. They are drawn from tables 7.7 and 7.8 of US Department of Labor, Bureau of Labor Statistics (1981). Supplemental unemployment benefit plans are weekly payments designed to augment the income of a laid-off worker. Severance payments represent lump-sum compensation to workers permanently laid-off though some are made to temporary layoffs or to workers who resign for reasons of health or age. Wage-employment guarantees ensure workers of a minimum number of hours of work at a certain rate of pay. The minimum hours of work may range from a week to a year. Eligibility for these income security benefits usually depends on length of service and other factors.

36 percent of unionized workers in the early 1970s were covered by contracts that provided for some sort of worksharing.[12] They were common in the apparel industry (where they have existed for many years) and in the rubber, steel, and leather industries.[13] For example, in 1984 steelworkers and management at Jones and Laughlin Steel negotiated a plan whereby the 200 jobs at the Aliquippa, Pennsylvania, plant were to be shared by the 200 workers then employed and the 225 workers then on layoff. The intention was that each of the 425 employees would work 60 percent of the time and be on layoff 40 percent of the time. While on layoff, they would be eligible for supplemental unemployment benefits. However, these worksharing clauses appear to be invoked infrequently (Henle, 1976). One reason for this is that, in most US states (unlike much of Western Europe), the unemployment insurance system does not allow benefits to be paid to someone working only 4 out of 5 days per week and in this sense the system tilts incentives toward layoffs and against worksharing.

The conclusion from this discussion of the redistribution activities of trade unions is that some redistribution does occur in some unions. However, it is doubtful whether it is implemented to such an extent that members in the less preferred state are fully compensated (in income or in utility) for their unfortunate draw in the employment lottery. In any event, when such redistribution takes place, doubt is cast upon a formulation such as equation (3.7) that treats income in the less preferred state as exogenous to the union.

Under these circumstances, the expected utility objective function (3.7) should surely be regarded as a research hypothesis whose empirical relevance should be tested against observed behavior. This is, after all, the way in which the expected utility hypothesis has been treated in research on individual decision-making under risk where it has been found from numerous tests that, in the words of one specialist, "at the individual level expected utility maximization is more the exception than the rule. . . . [I]t

[12] In the United Auto Workers' 1984 settlement with General Motors, the union secured a requirement that the firm pay 50 cents per hour for all overtime hours in excess of 5 percent of straight-time hours into a special fund designed to finance the retraining of laid-off employees. Worksharing was also promoted by the addition of three paid holidays, bringing the total to 44 over the 3-year contract.

[13] The data describe collective bargaining contracts that cover 1,000 workers or more (US Department of Labor, 1972). Some seniority clauses may be construed as worksharing devices. Thus, in its 1973 contract, the United Auto Workers negotiated clauses permitting a worker with 35 years of experience to retire regardless of his age. In their 1963 agreement with the major steel firms, the United Steelworkers secured 13-week vacations (with pay) at 5-year intervals for senior workers. In the contracts analyzed by the Bureau of National Affairs (1986), 18 percent contained clauses providing for worksharing as an alternative or prelude to layoffs.

is doubtful that the expected utility theory should or could serve as a general model" (Schoemaker, 1982, p. 552).[14] It has been the predictive failures of expected utility that have prompted the development of non-expected utility models of preferences, such as prospect theory and regret theory, which involve more elaborate expressions both for the event probabilities and for the value functions. This evidence relates to an individual's decision-making, not to a trade union's. In fact, I know of no empirical application of the expected utility hypothesis to the study of unionism that has chosen to test whether equation (3.7) conforms to observed behavior.

The expected utility and utilitarian objective functions represent useful reference or benchmark specifications that help an understanding of certain analytical models and, indeed, along with the rent maximand, they will be used in this way in the following chapters. However, their empirical relevance has yet to be determined so their widespread use is a commentary on economists' penchant for convenient and popular, if uncorroborated, functional expressions.

The development of the utilitarian and expected utility formulations of union objectives, equations (3.6) and (3.7), in this section assumed a union consisting of a fixed number of identical members. The following three sections are concerned with differences of interest within the union: first, differences of interest between employed and unemployed workers; second, differences among employed members; and, third, differences between the interests of the rank-and-file and of the union leadership which includes a discussion of why unions care about their size.

3.3   Employed and Unemployed Members

A currently fashionable view (though one of long-standing) holds that the objectives of trade unions embrace the welfare of those currently employed, the so-called "insiders," and little or no weight is given to the unemployed who are "outsiders" to the wage determination process. This characterization of union objectives has been used to argue that, after a reduction in the union's constituency following a negative shock to employment, the union will raise its wage demands to levels that make it unprofitable for the firm subsequently to hire the unemployed.[15] Expressed differently, the union's indifference curves between wages and

---

[14] Also see Kahneman and Tversky (1979), Loomes and Sugden (1982), and Machina (1983).
[15] Versions of this argument are found in Blanchard and Summers (1986), Gottfries and Horn (1987), Lindbeck and Snower (1986), and Solow (1985).

employment are flatter or even horizontal with respect to any employment greater than current employment levels.[16] It is a union such as this that lies behind Henry Simons's well-known prescription for union behavior: as membership shrinks naturally over time through voluntary mobility and retirement so the wage should be raised to justify the employment of all, though no more than, the membership.[17] The argument appears in almost the same guise to describe the behavior of the unions in the US durable goods manufacturing sector in the 1970s and 1980s.[18]

The notion that unions disregard the welfare of the unemployed runs counter to a long tradition of working class solidarity in trade unionism where the economic status of the unemployed frequently figures in the expressed concerns of both the union leadership and the rank-and-file. These concerns may reflect genuine altruism, but also in an uncertain world in which tomorrow's unemployed may be today's employed a union policy of assistance to the unemployed can represent far-sighted

---

[16] For instance, suppose union preferences were utilitarian. If E union members were employed and $M - E$ unemployed, the union objective function may be written

$$\Gamma = \sum_{i=1}^{E} au_i + \sum_{i=E+1}^{M} bu_i$$

where $0 \leq b < a$. If union members were identical in all respects other than their employment status, the union objective function would equal equation (3.6) except that the second term on the right-hand side, $u(\bar{y})(M - E)$, would be discounted by $0 \leq (b/a) < 1$. Union indifference curves between wages and employment will exhibit a discontinuity at the existing level of employment. A fuller exposition is contained in Carruth and Oswald (1987).

[17] "Frankly, I can see no reason why strongly organized workers, in an industry where huge investment is already sunk in highly durable assets, should ever permit a return on investment sufficient to attract new capital or even to induce full maintenance of existing capital. If I were running a union and were managing it faithfully in the interest of the majority of its members, I should consistently demand wage rates which offered to existing firms no real net earnings but only the chance of getting back part of their sunk investment at the cost of the replacement outlays necessary to provide employment for most of my constituents during their own lifetimes as workers. In other words, I should plan gradually to exterminate the industry by excessive labor costs, taking care only to prevent employment from contracting more rapidly than my original constituents disappeared by death and voluntary retirement. If I were operating, as labor leader, without the valuable hostages of large sunk investment, I should be obliged to behave more moderately. But I should still seek, controlling prices via labor costs, to restrict production as rapidly as consistent with decline of my membership by death and retirement and, while permitting some return to investors, should try always to induce only as much employment and production as my original constituents could take care of without new members" (Simons, 1944, p. 8).

[18] For instance, Lawrence and Lawrence (1985) argue that, in declining industries such as motor cars and steel, far-sighted unions have recognized the demise of their industries and, while they are on their last legs, the unions extract all the quasi-rents from the installed capital equipment by pushing higher on wages.

self-interest. Of course, economists are weaned at an early professional age from the fallacy that words necessarily match behavior though, with income transfers to the unemployed and other services provided to the unemployed, there is behavior to match the rhetoric. Certainly, many of the "wage concessions" made by US unions in the early 1970s and early 1980s were prompted not by the threat of layoffs, but to enable a number of former workers currently on layoff to return to their jobs.

The fact is that unions differ in their attitudes to the unemployed, some unions approaching the insider–outsider view and others not. The diversity in income security provisions in US collective bargaining agreements is indicated by the data in table 3.1: some industries have extensive and elaborate provisions while others have few. Direct assistance to the unemployed in the form of cash payments and help in finding jobs is more common in craft unions and in unions in activities where intermittent unemployment is usual.[19] Also, the unemployed are themselves not a homogeneous group: the union is more likely to take account of the welfare of an unemployed individual who had once been an active unionist, who is likely to become one in the future, or who has friends or relatives among the employed union members.

3.4   Differences among Employed Members

The distinction between the interests of the employed and the interests of the unemployed represents just one of many possible sources of heterogeneity among union members. Indeed, the long history of factional disputes within many unions and the difficulties in effecting mergers between unions, notwithstanding their support by the AFL in the United States and by the TUC in Britain, illustrate the importance of such heterogeneity. With even the simplest of models of union behavior, it is straightforward to demonstrate the strains placed upon a trade union when there are distinct differences among union members.

Thus, postulate a union consisting of two types of workers, type 1 and type 2, that bargain together to maximize some positive monotonic

[19] "In an industry with a high rate of business mortality the union, if it is strong, is likely to show a keen interest in economic security for the permanently-displaced employee. The dress industry is illustrative. A relatively low capital investment requirement permits easy entrance into, and intense competition often causes prompt exit of firms out of, the industry. The ILGWU as early as the 1920's showed an interest in the payment of employees whose jobs were eliminated abruptly by a cessation of operation. . . . [T]he continued high rate of business demise, either because of receivership or because of migration to low-cost areas, has led the union to insist on a severance program" (Slichter, Healy and Livernash, 1960, p. 470). See also Barker, Lewis and McCann (1984).

function, φ, of their joint rents $\varphi [(y_1 - \bar{y}_1)E_1 + (y_2 - \bar{y}_2)E_2]$ where, as before, y_i denotes earnings (i.e., $y_i = W_i h_i$) and hours are treated as given. The union's opportunities to achieve its objectives are constrained such that increases in earnings can be achieved only at the cost of less employment. These trade-offs may be expressed as $E_1 = \psi_1 (W_1, W_2)$ and $E_2 = \psi_2 (W_1, W_2)$ where $\partial \psi_i / \partial W_i < 0$ for $i = 1, 2$ and $\partial \psi_i / \partial W_j \gtreqless 0$ for $i \neq j$. Then the constrained maximization of rents results in the following relative earnings gaps for the two types of workers

$$\frac{\Delta y_1}{\Delta y_2} = \frac{\psi_{21} s^{-1} - \psi_{22}}{\psi_{12} s - \psi_{11}} \tag{3.9}$$

where $\Delta y_i = (y_i - \bar{y}_i)/y_i$, $\psi_{ij} = (\partial \psi_i / \partial W_j)(W_j / E_i)$ for $i, j = 1, 2$, and $s = W_1 h_1 E_1 / W_2 h_2 E_2$.[20] It is quite evident that there is nothing about equation (3.9) to suggest that $\Delta y_1 = \Delta y_2$, that is, that the earnings gap for one group should be the same as that for the other. In fact, depending on the magnitude of the employment–wage trade-offs, one group may enjoy relatively trivial gains compared with the other. Now when there is full reallocation of income within the union, differential wage gaps should be of no concern, yet as we have already noted, though some internal redistribution takes place, transaction costs appear to render it incomplete. Therefore, with conflicts of interest within the union, there may well be reasons for one of the two groups to want to bargain separately.

In the preceding paragraph's example, differences among union members arose from differences in alternative opportunities $(\bar{y}_1, \bar{y}_2)$ and differences in the employment–wage trade-offs. Even neglecting differences of this sort, the derivation of a well-behaved union objective function by aggregating over the utility functions of individual members is a much more formidable task once heterogeneous preferences are permitted. In these circumstances, because the policies followed by most American and British unions reflect in some indirect fashion their voting members' interests, it is natural for researchers to draw on the social choice literature for assistance in specifying union objectives.

This has usually taken the form of alluding to median voter arguments and, indeed, Farber's (1977) seminal work expressed the objectives of the union in terms of the expected utility of the median voter which, in turn, was represented by the expected utility formulation in equation (3.7). Median voter arguments have been invoked in other models, too, such as those of Grossman (1983) and Booth (1984). Unfortunately, as is well known, such arguments do not represent a strong foundation on which

---

[20] Analysis along these lines appears in Rosen (1970).

to build an aggregate welfare function: even if each individual's prefer-ences are single peaked with respect to each relevant dimension, whenever utility functions contain more than one argument (say, hours of work in addition to earnings), then majority voting may not generate (in fact, probably will not generate) the sort of transitive relations for the union's preferences that we usually require of each individual's preferences.[21]

The type of heterogeneity most frequently alluded to in the literature on union objectives is that pertaining to seniority, a worker's duration of employment with a firm. It figures prominently, for instance, in Grossman's (1983) narrative which may be exposited most simply by thinking of it as if it had a recursive structure. First, each individual decides whether to be a union member on the basis of the wage expected to prevail in the next period; if the individual does join, he is locked into that sector for the duration of the period. Second, with membership given, the union selects the wage by maximizing the expected utility of the median member, the wage being determined prior to the realization of the demand for labor. Third, the state of the demand for workers is revealed and the firm unilaterally selects employment such that less senior employees have a lower probability of being employed. Of course, in an equilibrium where all expectations are fulfilled and no individual has cause to alter his behavior, the wage is such that all members are employed (and all employees are members).

Note an important restriction on the formulation of Grossman's model: although the employment probability depends on seniority, the wage does not. This is clearly a constraint on the nature of the contract; if the union has monopoly power in dictating the wage, it should exercise it in the form of setting a wage *schedule* that relates the wage to seniority. Then the employment probability and wages will be treated symmetrically in the union's objective function, each a function of seniority. And, of course, in practice usually wages *are* linked to seniority explicitly through earn-ings and fringe benefit increases that depend on length of service[22] and implicitly through the seniority rules governing promotion, work assign-ment, vacations, and other aspects of the employment contract. Hence both the logic of the argument and the practice of collective bargaining

---

[21] See Plott (1967), Kramer (1973), and Blair and Crawford (1984).

[22] In the sample of contracts analyzed by the Bureau of National Affairs (1986), "Wage progression systems specifying rate ranges rather than single rates appear in 42 percent of contracts, 45 percent in manufacturing and 37 percent in nonmanufacturing. Progression from minimum to higher rates in a range may be based on length of service, merit, or a combination of the two. Automatic increases based on length of service alone are specified in 71 percent of contracts containing rate ranges and progression scales. Seventeen per-cent of the clauses base progression on length of service, but only if performance merits advancement" (p. 118).

would suggest that the modelling procedure of allowing seniority to affect employment probabilities but not wages is unwarranted.[23]

A similar argument can be used to address the allegation that, because reductions in employment are typically by inverse seniority, the average union member is shielded from all but the most dramatic reductions in demand and, consequently, the union's indifference curves (equated to the average member's) are horizontal with respect to employment at any level of employment beyond that corresponding to the median (Oswald, 1985, 1987). Oswald's reasoning is as follows:

[T]hink of a case in which the union is considering whether to agree to their firm's offer, say, to raise the wage in exchange for a ten percent reduction in the work force. Under majority voting and "last in, first out", a group of self-interested unionized employees have an obvious incentive to accept such an offer. The reason is that union indifference curves are horizontal here because most workers in the firm know themselves to be perfectly insulated from even moderate falls in employment. (Oswald, 1985, p. 180)[24]

This argument implies that employees with varying levels of seniority will respond differently to the situation in which management call for "wage concessions" from workers so that substantial layoffs can be

[23] Frank (1985) and Weiss (1985) present models specifying wages as a function of seniority. However, because the union's objective function is equated with the original senior workers' interests, their models have the implausible implication that only original members of the union enjoy rents from union activity. Or, more casually, their models imply that, some 40–50 years after the great surge in unionization in the United States, union-nonunion wage differentials should be zero. They appear not to be.

[24] Carruth, Oswald and Findlay (1986) make use of annual time-series observations on the British coal and steel industries to determine whether employment and wages in these industries are independent of the level of unemployment benefits and of the unemployment rate. They argue that, if the unions are indifferent to employment, then the level of unemployment benefits and the unemployment rate will not figure in union objectives and, therefore, these two variables will not appear in the wage and employment reduced form equations. In fact, these variables tend to be significantly (negatively) correlated with wages and employment which induces the authors to reject the "flat indifference curve model," as they call it. But, even if they are correct in their characterization of this model as one implying the absence of unemployment benefits and unemployment from union objective functions, these variables may well appear in the reduced form wage and employment equations if they affect the outcome of union–management bargaining. For instance, the threat (or no trade) points in such a bargain may very well be related to the level of unemployment benefits and the unemployment rate. Therefore, though the authors "prefer to work with general reduced form equations" (p. 5) instead of structural specifications, I would argue that such reduced form procedures cannot distinguish among competing hypotheses: it is not that structural specification is superior; it is the only option to test the relevance of such ideas.

avoided. In particular, it implies that, when confronted with the choice between layoffs and wage cuts, the likelihood of an employee preferring a policy of no wage reductions would increase with his seniority. In fact, the opposite appears to be the case: "Older workers with extensive seniority, perhaps only a few years from retirement and with only limited alternative job opportunities, were more willing to sacrifice income for job security than younger employees with greater family responsibilities and greater opportunities for equivalent jobs," (Henle, 1973, p. 961). In other words, even in situations in which the median worker's job is not immediately at risk, there is uncertainty about whether the firm's economic difficulties will be overcome and whether layoffs will ultimately engulf very senior workers with unattractive alternative employment opportunities. Some workers possessing more seniority than the median union member before major employment reductions will have less seniority than the median voter after these layoffs so, unless they are confident the firm's economic difficulties will not persist, it might be prescient for them to accept wage concessions initially lest they find themselves without jobs in a year or two.[25]

Furthermore, the argument ignores the fact that, even if the employment status of most workers is insulated from moderate falls in demand, the effective returns from their work will not be. Where the seniority unit is wide, layoffs of the least senior workers often result in a reshuffling of employment across different departments within the firm (and even in some cases across plants) such that some senior workers are transferred to another department and displace those with less seniority. In this way, a reduction in total employment is accompanied by some retained workers being employed at a lower ranked job paying lower wages. To be sure, there is a great variation in the extent to which the senior workers may bump the junior, but in some form or other it is present in most US collective bargaining contracts.[26] The implication is that the median union member has good reason to be concerned with moderate reductions in the firm's employment because such layoffs may well result in a

---

[25] In an analysis of the voting behavior of 102 UAW bargaining units regarding the proposed General Motors contract concessions in 1982, Kaufman and Martinez-Vazquez (1988) found that "the vote for acceptance of the concessions was higher in bargaining units where employment had remained steady or had increased during the previous twelve months" (p. 194). They reasoned that wage concessions should be supported in plants where no workers are threatened with loss of jobs because, if the wage concessions are not accepted and large layoffs result, the composition of union employment and of the electorate will change such that the new median voter will be more willing to accept even larger wage concessions in the future.

[26] In the sample of contracts analyzed by the Bureau of National Affairs (1986), 60 percent specified bumping provisions.

reduction in his pay. Note that, in such cases, the negotiated pay schedules have not changed nor has the relationship between job titles and wages; workers have simply been reallocated across departments so that some now earn lower wages.

In short, the manner in which differences in seniority among workers have been taken into account in several models of union preferences is unsatisfactory. Attention has concentrated on how seniority affects employment to the relative neglect of how seniority interacts with wages.

Compared with the attention lavished on seniority, there has been little effort directed to explaining another feature of unionism, namely, the apparent preference among many unions for preserving absolute differences in wages among workers over the maintenance of relative wage differences. The phenomenon is illustrated by the data in tables 3.2 and 3.3. The former describes the wages of the main occupations in US underground bituminous coal mining as negotiated by the United Mine

Table 3.2 Full-time daily pay of bituminous coal miners negotiated by United Mine Workers of America, 1933–80 (in dollars)

Occupational group	1933	1943	1945	1957	1970	1973	1980
Inside workers							
A	5.80	10.93	12.43	24.68	36.68	47.25	84.52
B	4.76	8.69	10.19	22.44	34.44	43.25	78.34
C	4.60	8.50	10.00	22.25	34.25	42.75	76.56
D	4.36	8.21	9.71	21.96	33.96	42.25	75.98
Surface workers							
E	3.84	7.91	8.98	21.23	33.23	41.25	72.40
F	3.60	7.61	8.68	20.93	32.93	41.00	71.82
Wage ratios							
A/D	1.33	1.33	1.28	1.12	1.08	1.19	1.11
A/F	1.61	1.44	1.43	1.18	1.11	1.15	1.18
Wage differences							
A − D	1.44	2.72	2.72	2.72	2.72	5.00	8.54
A − F	2.20	3.32	3.75	3.75	3.75	6.25	12.70

Occupation group A consists of mobile loading machine operators and cutters and shearing machine operators and helpers. Occupation group B consists of motormen, rock-drillers, and rubber-tired shuttle car operators. Occupation group C consists of drivers, brakemen, spraggers, trackmen, wiremen, bonders, timbermen, bottom cagers, coal drillers, and snappers. Occupation group D consists of pumpers, trackmen helpers, wiremen helpers, timbermen helpers, and other inside labor. Occupational groups A through D work inside the mines while E and F are outside workers. Occupational group E consists of bit sharpeners, car droppers, trimmers, car repairmen, and dumpers. Occupation group F consists of sand dryers, car cleaners, and other able-bodied labor. These data are drawn from tables 4, 5, 6, and 7 of Bureau of Labor Statistics Bulletin 2062, *Wage Chronology: Bituminous Coal Mine Operators and United Mine Workers of America 1933–1981*, US Department of Labor, November 1980.

Table 3.3 Basic hourly wage rates for unionized shipbuilding and ship repair workers on the Pacific Coast, 1941–76 (in dollars)

Occupational Group	1941	1945	Jan. 1951	Aug. 1951	1960	1967	1976
A: Heavy forge blacksmiths	1.42	1.68	2.09	2.31	3.24	3.98	7.19
B: Operating engineers	1.25	1.51	1.92	2.13	3.06	3.80	7.01
C: Acetylene burners	1.12	1.38	1.79	1.98	2.91	3.65	6.86
D: Painters	1.12	1.38	1.79	1.98	2.91	3.65	6.86
E: General helpers	0.87	1.13	1.52	1.68	2.61	3.35	6.56
Wage ratios							
A/C	1.27	1.22	1.17	1.17	1.11	1.09	1.05
A/E	1.63	1.49	1.38	1.38	1.24	1.19	1.10
Wage differences							
A − C	0.30	0.30	0.30	0.33	0.33	0.33	0.33
A − E	0.55	0.55	0.57	0.63	0.63	0.63	0.63

The wage rates for 1941, 1945, and 1951 are those for new ship construction. In the August 1951 agreements, wage differentials between work on new ships and on ship repair work were eliminated. The data for operating engineers relate to those working on equipment 20 tons and over. The information is taken from table 2 of Bureau of Labor Statistics Bulletin 1982, *Wage Chronology: Pacific Coast Shipbuilders and Various Unions, 1941–77*, US Department of Labor, 1978.

Workers. The wage premium paid to the most highly paid underground workers relative to the lowest paid underground workers (that is, occupation groups A and D respectively) fell from 33 percent in 1933 to 8 percent in 1970; in fact, the absolute wage difference was precisely constant at $2.72 per day between 1943 and 1970. In other words, for a period of over 25 years, the dollar differentials in pay among all the occupations were exactly constant. Table 3.3 relates to workers in the shipyards of California, Oregon, and Washington.[27] Here the most highly paid group, the heavy forge blacksmiths, have seen their relative wage advantage over the least highly paid, general helpers, fall from 63 percent in 1941 to 10 percent in 1976. During this 35 year period, the absolute difference in their wages barely changed, being 55 cents per hour in 1941 and 63 cents per hour in 1976. Indeed, it was completely unchanged from 1951 to 1976. Similar instances have been noted many times before in

[27] For the purposes of collective bargaining, the unions form a confederation, the Pacific Coast Metal Trades District Council, which negotiates with a corresponding confederation of (almost all the major) employers, the Pacific Coast Shipbuilders Association.

Britain as well as the United States.[28]

Now it is by no means a universal practice of unionism to maintain absolute wage differentials[29] and, in any event, a general and continual increase in prices and wages ultimately disturbs the practice. However, the inclination for absolute wage differences is not only widespread, but also manifests itself in other forms: certain incomes policies in Britain in the 1970s that were designed to meet with trade union approval specified permissible maxima denominated as flat wage increases, not proportional wage increases;[30] and cost-of-living escalator clauses in union contracts are usually expressed in terms of absolute wage changes per absolute changes in the index of consumer prices.[31] There is an empirical regularity here that calls for explanation.

The most obvious line of analysis determines how a policy of maintaining absolute wage differentials affects the different constituencies within the union. Putting aside any employment or hours repercussions, lower paid workers would prefer a common absolute over a common relative wage increase that achieves the same total wage increase. If lower paid workers are relatively more numerous, they can steer union wage policy toward wage increases specified in fixed dollar amounts.[32] This argument may be correct though it is worth noting that it would be a more convincing explanation if the skill composition of the union were actually

[28] For instance, in Knowles and Robertson's classic study of earnings differentials in the British engineering industry, the weekly wage rates of skilled workers (fitters on time rates) maintained a fixed 16 shillings differential over unskilled wage rates between 1926 and 1948 while the wage ratio fell from 1.40 to 1.19. See table III of Knowles and Robertson (1951). The effects of equal cash increases on the skilled–unskilled wage differential in Britain between 1950 and 1975 are presented in Elliott (1980).

[29] Thus, for many years in the British steel industry, while mechanics sought to maintain an *absolute* wage advantage over laborers, smelters looked for a constant *relative* pay differential.

[30] See Ashenfelter and Layard (1983) for a description and analysis of them.

[31] Card (1983) rationalizes this as an approximation to a formula expressed in constant relative terms, but I find this unconvincing in view of the widespread tendency of unions to operate in terms of absolute wage differences over long periods of time when the approximation would be manifestly unsatisfactory.

[32] In other words, if occupation i receives an absolute wage increase of k in period t, its new wage is $W_{it}^a = k + W_{it-1}$ while if it receives a proportional wage increase of p its new wage is $W_{it}^* = (1 + p) W_{it-1}$. If the cost of the absolute and proportionate wage changes is to be the same over all occupations, i.e., if

$$\sum_i \theta_i W_{it}^a = \sum_i \theta_i W_{it}^*$$

where θ_i is the fraction of all union members in group i, then $k = p\overline{W}_{t-1}$ where $\overline{W}_{t-1}$ is the arithmetic mean of all wages in period $t - 1$. Occupation i will prefer W_{it}^a if $W_{it}^a > W_{it}^*$ or (substituting $p\overline{W}_{t-1}$ for k) if $W_{it-1} < \overline{W}_{t-1}$, that is, if their wage is below the arithmetic mean. Whenever the wage distribution is positively skewed, more than half of

changing in favor of the lower paid workers. If it is changing in this way, then the increasing strength of the lower paid in the union may well be reflected in a modification of relative wages expressed and facilitated by absolute wage increases.[33] But if the composition of the union is not changing, then this argument tacitly implies that the prior wage structure does not quite reveal the preferences of the union members. If it did, there would be no reason for it to be disturbed subsequently by the same absolute wage changes for all workers. I do not know of an analysis identifying the effects of changes in the internal composition of the union on movements in the wage structure, but it would be a useful contribution to knowledge.[34]

Though the preference for absolute wage changes is surely not independent of pressures from various constituencies within the union, I wonder whether this can be the whole story. Does it indicate that the benefits from money as a unit of account are so considerable that the denomination of wage differentials in terms of dollars and cents retains its usefulness to individuals even in conditions of a gradual, persistent, change in the value of money and is undermined only if society is traumatized by a long or frenzied inflation? Or perhaps, contrary to what has been presumed, trade unions are really passive agents in the determination of the wage

---

all workers are employed at less than $\overline{W}_{t-1}$ so that any union leader heeding the interests of the median member (voter) would be inclined to choose an absolute wage increase formula. As Turner (1957) writes, "trade unions prefer to demand equal wage advances for all their members. . . . [T]his preference has been strongest in certain industries (like building and woodworking) where the organization of workers was once confined to exclusive craft unions and where apprenticeship is still a necessary qualification for entry to skilled jobs. While unskilled labor remained unorganized, these craft unions were able to maintain their members' relative differentials. When the mass unions appeared, however, the craft unions were generally driven to combine with them in bargaining with employers. The choice of flat-rate wage demands by these combinations seems to have been largely dictated by the numerical preponderance of the less skilled workers" (Turner, 1957, p. 132).

[33] This distinction between the skill composition of the union's members and changes in that composition is indirectly alluded to in Turner's account of British unionism: "The preference for flat-rate advances has been almost exclusive among certain one-time craft unions that later opened their ranks to unapprenticed workers. These unions have been competing with general labor unions for membership among the unskilled. . . . But certain unions have usually presented percentage wage demands. . . . [S]uch unions have not interested themselves in expanding into other employments. . . . Some unions have generally preferred the 'percentage' form of wage demand because they wish mainly to recruit higher-paid employees. . . ." (Turner, 1957, p. 133).

[34] Of course, the union's choice need not be restricted to a common flat-rate increase or a common proportional wage increase, but could involve some mixture of these. Indeed, von Weizsacker (1978) suggests that a policy of minimizing discontent within the union (defined as the sum over all members of the difference between the potential maximum wage increase and the actual increase) would involve such a mixture.

structure and that adjusting wages by a common, flat-rate, increase is a device to narrow skill differentials which would have occurred in the absence of unionism. (This is Reder's (1955) argument.) Though this seems inconsistent with the fact that management have sometimes taken on strikes expressly directed to warding off union demands for flat-rate wage increases across the board, we would be in a better position to set aside this argument if there were a more convincing and empirically validated explanation to put in its stead.

3.5 The Union Rank-and-File and Leadership

To this point, the utilitarian objective function (3.6) and the expected utility objective function (3.7) have been treated as equivalent characterizations of union objectives. This is because we have assumed a fixed membership. In fact, it is an unusual union that plays no role in affecting its size. Such a situation might appear to occur in those industrial unions where all employees are required to be union members, union membership lapses immediately upon leaving the firm's employment (so $E = M$), and, ostensibly at least, management determines employment unilaterally. But even with such industrial unions the level of employment and, therefore, membership is determined indirectly by the union's wage policy and the dues levied. Under these circumstances, union membership is more an attribute of the job than of the individual. In any period, the objectives of the union are formed over the stock of employees inherited from the immediately preceding period, in which case M in equations (3.6) and (3.7) is represented by the level of employment in the preceding period, and some or all of those then employed are employed in the current period.

This is exactly how Kidd and Oswald (1987) proceed by specifying membership in period t as equal to employment in period $t - 1$, $M_t = E_{t-1}$ or $M_t - M_{t-1} = E_{t-1} - M_{t-1}$ or, taking limits, $dM/dt = E_t - M_t$.[35] Now suppose the union maximizes an intertemporally additive objective function, appropriately discounted. Then the modifications required of a static model depend on the precise form of the objective function: if the union maximizes a utilitarian function according to which increases in membership augment utility, then a longer planning horizon induces the union to raise its membership by setting higher employment levels than would occur in a single period model; if the union maximizes expected utility where increases in membership diminish utility, then intertemporal

[35] An analogous specification is found in Blanchard and Summers (1986), Gottfries and Horn (1987), and Lindbeck and Snower (1986).

maximization inclines the union to reduce its membership by lowering employment compared with the single period problem. Given the equation of motion, these implications follow pretty quickly once the effect of membership on the value of the union's objective function is specified.[36]

More generally, however, the essential point is that the union's goals are formulated over a longer horizon than is recognized by the single period specifications described above. The empirical importance of this longer horizon in understanding the behavior of industrial unions has not yet been addressed.

In many craft unions, an individual's union membership endures when his contract with a particular employer is ended and, in fact, starting with his apprenticeship and concluding with his pension, the craft worker may well sustain his union membership throughout his life. In this case, the union regulates membership by affecting the number of apprentices and the geographical distribution of employment through rules ensuring work for union members who move to different cities.[37] In these instances, a high value appears to be placed on securing employment for all members. As in the previous paragraphs, intertemporal elements are again introduced into the union's objectives, something not recognized in equations (3.2) and (3.3).[38]

[36] Lockwood and Manning (1987) have three criticisms of Kidd and Oswald (1987). First, they complain that, while the union has an intertemporal vision, Kidd and Oswald's model endows the firm with a single period horizon. The complaint is valid though is easily amended within the terms of the model. Second, they find Kidd and Oswald's equation of motion too simple and work instead with the more general formulation $dM/dt = aE_t - bM_t$ where the coefficients (assumed fixed) are related to the firm's separations rate and the rate at which new employees join the union or former employees quit the union. (Why should the firm's separations rate be independent of wages?) Third, they note that Kidd and Oswald restrict themselves to the case in which last period's membership places an effective constraint on this period's employment. Lockwood and Manning relax this constraint and, with their differential equation describing the evolution of union membership, examine a bargaining model in which wages are negotiated jointly while employment is determined unilaterally by the firm. When employment exceeds membership and the union maximizes the membership's rents (i.e., equation (3.8) with M replacing E), the resulting employment and wage equations are not easy to characterize and, in particular, qualitative results depend on the specific values and permutations of the parameters.

[37] American craft unions devised the "traveling card" to deal with the movement of their members to different cities. According to Ulman (1955), the problem of the traveling member hastened the development of the national federated union.

[38] In these craft unions, a distinction is drawn between apprentices, A, and journeymen, M. Let ξ be the proportion of apprentices "graduating" to journeyman status at each moment and q the rate at which journeymen retire. Hence, at each moment, the stock of journeymen is augmented by ξA and depleted by qM: $dM/dt = \xi_t A_t - q_t M_t$. Because ξ^{-1} is the period apprentices spend in training before becoming journeymen and because each apprentice receives a fraction of the wages paid to the journeymen, the value of ξ affects a union member's lifetime earnings and is a decision variable for the union. These are some of the ingredients of a complicated dynamic programming problem for the union.

However, the treatment of union membership in equations (3.6) and (3.7) may be inadequate not merely because it neglects intertemporal elements, but more importantly because it overlooks the most plausible reason for inclusion of the size of the union in a trade union's objective function: in many unions, a large membership is desired by the union leadership because a larger constituency usually furnishes the leadership with greater influence and/or wealth.[39] While a rank-and-file union member may be concerned with his employment prospects, his wages, and his hours of work, the union leader is also concerned with his tenure as an elected official at the head of what may be an influential organization.[40] Organizing drives to expand membership may be motivated not by narrow concerns of reducing effective competition from the nonunion sector, but they may represent a longer-run vision of building a more influential and politically significant organization.

In addition to these differences in interests, there will usually be opportunities for a union leader to pursue his interests at the expense of the rank-and-file's so the union membership have the familiar agency problems of monitoring the activities of their representatives. In their most blatant form, these problems are labelled as corruption within unions which may take the form of immoderate pecuniary gains or of the furtherance of political goals.[41] The rank-and-file require not only constitutional procedures ensuring the faithful representation of their preferences, but also the information to evaluate their leaders' performance. The problem here is one of comparing outcomes with what would have occurred had the current leadership been replaced by another. Naturally assessments of this sort are extremely difficult so the rank-and-file are apt to resort to simple comparisons between their situation and that of other workers. In particular, welfare evaluations are often made in terms of wage comparisons: the rank-and-file tend to judge their leadership's performance as unfavorable if they calculate their wages to have fallen below some customary differential with respect to another group of workers. Through this route, essentially one arising from incom-

---

[39] The notion that the leadership's interests account for the presence of the membership of the union in the union's objective function appears, in essence, in Ross (1948) and Rees (1962). It has been reiterated recently by Pemberton (1988) whose union objective function reflects the preferences of both the rank-and-file and the leadership where the goals of the latter are equated with the size of the membership. However, he ignores the distinction between employment and membership by assuming there are no unemployed union members.

[40] Of course, as in other organizations, it is not a matter of a simple dichotomy between the rank-and-file and the leadership, but rather there exists a hierarchical structure whereby authority is delegated and thus dispersed among many officials.

[41] James Hoffa took his returns in the form of money (James and James, 1965) while the leaders of Britain's Electrical Trades Union in the 1950s had a political agenda.

plete information concerning their leadership's performance, the union's welfare appears to depend on *relative* wages instead of or in addition to wages relative to consumer prices.

This provides a justification for the inclusion of alternative wages, $\overline{W}$, in the union's objective function, equation (3.3), but it should be noted that the justification is quite different from that underlying the presence of alternative wages or earnings in the utilitarian objective function, equation (3.6). In the latter, $\overline{y}$ (or $\overline{W}$) represents the alternative income available to a union member who loses his job at his preferred employment. By contrast, according to the argument in this section, $\overline{W}$ is not the wage the union member could elect to receive by switching jobs; rather it is the case that $\overline{W}$ serves as a yardstick with which to evaluate whether the union leadership is attending to the interests of the rank-and-file. Lacking the information to undertake a careful and thorough assessment of the leadership's performance, the rank-and-file adopt readily available (though imperfect) rules of thumb and the most common of these is the comparison between their wage and the wage paid to another group of workers. Hence the leadership need to be sensitive to any increase in the comparison wage relative to the wage paid to their own rank-and-file because such an increase will engender dissatisfaction among their members.

The relevant comparison wage (or wages) varies considerably across different groups of employees. Often it is represented by the wages of another group within the plant, but on other occasions it may be given by the wages of another employer. This variation implies that, in any empirical work, the specification of alternative wages in union objective functions requires careful attention to institutional detail. Though economists are inclined to employ some broad measure of comparison wages, such as the average hourly earnings of all manufacturing production workers, it is hardly ever consistent with the industrial relations setting and must rest heavily on the empirical regularity that the wage structure usually changes sluggishly so that operational distinctions among different wage rates are difficult to discern.

The notion that the rank-and-file and the leadership have distinct interests is underscored by their different attitudes to lump-sum bonuses in US collective bargaining contracts. These bonuses are payments whose amount is set down in advance in the collective bargaining agreement. They are not contingent on the firm's or the workers' performance, they take the form either of a uniform dollar amount for all workers or of a percentage of earnings, and they are usually paid shortly after a new contract is signed. Before 1983 there were very few contracts with provisions for lump-sum bonuses, but by 1989 perhaps two-fifths of private unionized workers were covered by them.[42] Lump-sum payments do not affect a worker's base wage which implies first that they do not incorporate the compounding that would result from annual percentage base wage increases and second that they leave undisturbed the base on which overtime and certain benefits (including pensions) are determined. For these reasons, union leaders have generally opposed them. By contrast, the rank-and-file are more favorably disposed toward them perhaps because they are paid early in the contract. Because lump-sum bonuses are paid only to current employees and not to future employees (unlike the monetary equivalent of a wage rate increase), the leadership's opposition to them may be viewed as their looking after the interests of future employees. Whatever the appropriate interpretation, the divergent attitudes constitute a topical example of the distinct interests of the rank-and-file and the leadership.

3.6   Empirical Research on Union Objectives

Evaluating what is known from analytical studies of trade union objectives is not straightforward. The reason is that these objectives are themselves not directly observed. What is observed is the outcome of a bargaining process where the union's goals are confronted with management's goals. Therefore, inferences about the preferences of the union are critically dependent upon auxiliary hypotheses about how these preferences are revealed through the bargaining process. In fact, of course, this is no different from, say, the literature on the behavior of the consumer where the preferences of the household need to be joined with assumptions about the form of the budget constraint before empirical evidence can be brought to bear on the nature of the household's utility function. The difference is that researchers typically display much more confidence about the nature of households' budget constraints than about bargaining processes. Budget constraints are often obscured by nonlinear taxes, transaction costs, price discounts, and other factors so I am unsure whether this difference in confidence is warranted, but nevertheless the point is that our knowledge of the preferences of trade unions is necessarily dependent on hypotheses about elements of union-management bargaining.

In empirical research on consumer behavior, the results of various

---

[42] Erickson and Ichino (1989) cite the Bureau of Labor Statistics as reporting that, in the first half of 1989, 42 percent of all private sector workers under major collective bargaining contracts were covered by lump-sum provisions.

studies may usefully be compared by listing the implied values of various income or price elasticities of demand. This convenient summary is possible because, with the assumed common linear budget constraints, the variation in the values estimated for the elasticities originates entirely from the variation in the form of the utility functions. By contrast, in the literature on union objectives, not merely have different bargaining processes been posited to derive the estimates, but even when the same form of the bargaining process has been assumed its precise characteristics differ.

For instance, consider the common assumption that the union selects a wage rate to maximize its objective function and management responds by determining employment unilaterally: even among studies that share this assumption about the determination of wages and employment, the effect of an increase in any exogenous variable on wages or employment will depend on the particular parameters of the labor demand function as well as on the form of the union's objective function. The point is illustrated in my study (Pencavel, 1984a) of six locals of the International Typographical Union. Assuming the model of wage and employment determination just described (i.e., the union selects the wage and management follows by choosing employment) and assuming the same *form* of the union objective function and the same *form* of the employment–wage tradeoff, I fitted wage and employment equations to each of six ITU locals for the years from 1946 to 1965. Estimates were derived of the parameters for each union's objective function and for each employment–wage tradeoff. I then simulated the wage and employment equations in two ways: the first assumed all unions shared the identical wage–employment tradeoffs, but possessed the various objective function parameters actually computed for them; and the second assumed all unions had identical objective functions, but faced the employment–wage tradeoffs estimated for them. This exercise suggested that differences in the employment–wage tradeoff were much more important than differences in union objectives in accounting for wage and employment variations across union locals. In other words, assuming the same preferences for these union locals offended the data less than assuming the same employment–wage constraints. Of course, one might expect greater uniformity in preferences across locals of the same trade union representing a narrow group of workers, but the relevant point here is simply that empirical estimates of union objective functions are not usefully compared by examining the implications of models embodying different expressions for the constraints through which union preferences are revealed.

The alternative is to draw some inferences directly from the objective functions themselves. This is not straightforward because researchers have used different expressions to characterize union objectives so the estimates of a common functional form cannot be compared. Moreover, unions of radically different sizes have been analyzed, some whose members number in the hundreds of thousands and others with almost a handful of members. This means, of course, that any useful comparison of these objective functions should make use of a metric that is independent of the particular units of measuring wages and employment. The obvious candidate is Allen's elasticity of substitution which is relatively easy to compute in view of the fact that most studies claim to have focused on two variables only, wages and employment, and (explicitly, at least) have neglected hours of work.

Therefore, table 3.4 presents under $\hat{\sigma}$ the calculated values of the elasticity of substitution between wages and employment in various microeconomic studies of trade union objective functions. According to the functional forms used in these studies, the elasticity of substitution is not a fixed parameter so it should be understood that the values of $\hat{\sigma}$ in table 3.4 (which are evaluated at approximate sample mean values of variables) are sensitive to the point of evaluation. By way of comparison, I have computed for each study the elasticity of substitution implied by the rent maximand. This is simply $1 - (0.5)(\overline{W}/W)$ which lies between one-half and unity.[43] The estimates of σ range between 0.18 and 2.10. Moreover, although standard errors are not provided, it should be noted that at least for typographers,[44] the values of σ are not estimated at all precisely and usually a wide range of values are consistent with the results. For instance, for typographers, hypotheses that σ equals zero or unity often cannot be rejected by conventional criteria.

With the exception of Farber's (1977) and MaCurdy and Pencavel's (1986) studies, $\hat{\sigma}$ is less than unity and, in this sense, accords with the implications of rent maximization. Such values of σ suggest quite restricted opportunities for substituting wages for employment in the union objective function. This is consistent with Cartter's conjecture:

[43] As the measure of $\overline{W}$, I have taken the specification of alternative or comparison income used in each study. In Carruth and Oswald (1985), $\overline{W}$ is the weekly unemployment benefit. In Farber (1977) and MaCurdy and Pencavel (1986), $\overline{W}$ is average hourly earnings of production workers in durable goods manufacturing industry. In Pencavel (1984a, b), $\overline{W}$ is average hourly earnings of nonsupervisory workers in retail trade. In Card (1986), $\overline{W}$ is production workers' average hourly earnings in manufacturing.

[44] Card (1986), Carruth and Oswald (1985), and Farber (1977) do not calculate the value of the elasticity of substitution and there is insufficient information in their work for me to determine the standard errors of this parameter. To illustrate the imprecision with which σ is estimated for typographers, my augmented addilog estimates of 0.71 and 0.19 come with standard errors of 0.33 and 0.06, respectively.

Table 3.4   Estimates of the elasticity of substitution between wages and employment in union objectives

Research	Union	Average employment	Form of objective function	$\hat{\sigma}$	σ for rents
Card (1986)	US airline mechanics	31,509	Expected utility with constant relative risk aversion	0.46	0.70
Card (1986)	US airline mechanics	31,509	Slightly modified rent maximand	0.78	0.70
Carruth and Oswald (1983)	British coal miners	430,240	Expected utility with constant relative risk aversion	0.77	0.92
Farber (1977)	US coal miners	232,545	Expected utility with constant relative risk aversion	1.34	0.73
MaCurdy and Pencavel (1986)	13 printers' locals	37	Stone–Geary	2.10	0.60
MaCurdy and Pencavel (1986)	13 printers' locals	37	Quadratic	1.96	0.60
Pencavel (1984b)	5 small printers' locals	78	Augmented addilog	0.71	0.58
Pencavel (1984b)	5 large printers' locals	418	Augmented addilog	0.19	0.76
Pencavel (1984a)	Cincinnati's printers	172	Stone–Geary	0.76	0.76
Pencavel (1984a)	Columbia's printers	105	Stone–Geary	0.27	0.72
Pencavel (1984a)	Dubuque's printers	68	Stone–Geary	0.43	0.70
Pencavel (1984a)	Memphis's printers	323	Stone–Geary	0.26	0.76
Pencavel (1984a)	Fond du Lac's printers	41	Stone–Geary	0.18	0.72
Pencavel (1984a)	Columbus's printers	602	Stone–Geary	0.22	0.77

The values of σ for MaCurdy and Pencavel (1986) are derived from estimates specifying the production technology to be Cobb–Douglas. For a constrained translog production function, the estimates are 1.69 for a Stone–Geary objective function and 2.12 for a quadratic objective function for the union. These estimates for MaCurdy and Pencavel represent the average of the σs calculated for each observation in the sample.

It would seem most likely, once a union is already enjoying a particular wage–employment combination, that it would take a considerable increase in wages to compensate for a reduction in employment, and it would take a considerable increase in employment to compensate for a wage reduction. This is reasoned to be true because of the internal political pressures the union would be subject to if it openly agreed to either of these reductions (Cartter, 1959, pp. 89–90).

However, summary measures of empirical findings, such as the estimates of the elasticity of substitution between wages and employment in table 3.4, do not do full justice to what has been learned from this work. Moreover, table 3.4 blurs some important differences among the studies in their definitions of the wage and employment variables and, therefore, in the implicit role occupied by hours of work. In fact, it is not difficult to provide more information because most empirical work on union objective functions has been conducted on just two types of unions, coalminers and printers. Let us consider these in turn.

Coalminers

In both the United States and Britain, the coalminers boast of a long history of vigorous unionism where conflict within the union has been almost as established as disputes with management. Also, for much of the postwar period, the American and British unions have had to accommodate themselves to the fact that the demand for union coal has been declining. In the United States, not only has there been competition from other sources of energy, but the nonunion sector has grown substantially in importance: the United Mine Workers of America has not been able to organize the surface mines in the western USA to anything like the same extent as the underground mines of the east and midwest.[45] Contributing to the decline of the union sector have been the large wage gains won by the UMW – some 32 to 40 percent in the 1960s according to Lewis's (1970) estimates – and the handsome pension, health, and welfare benefits that have been negotiated. For the purpose of bargaining with the UMW, the employers join together to form the Bituminous Coal Operators' Association. This tends to be dominated by a few large corporations.[46]

[45] In the late 1970s, the UMW represented about 35.5 percent of total employment of the surface mines in the west (Perry, 1984, p. 65).

[46] The votes of the BCOA members are proportional to their relative output so "the largest producers control the industry's positions and strategies in collective bargaining"

By contrast, throughout the postwar period the National Union of Mineworkers in Britain has had to deal with the managers of a nationalized industry on whom political pressures have been more immediate and obvious.[47] Though coal production in Britain rose to the mid-1950s before falling almost uninterruptedly since then, employment in the industry declined throughout the postwar period.[48] The relative earnings of mineworkers has fluctuated markedly over the period: whereas in 1948 the average hourly earnings of adult males in the coal industry were about 40 percent greater than the average for all wage-earners in British industry, this figure had fallen to 2 percent by 1970; with a rejuvenated militancy, this figure rose in the 1970s so that it regained the 40 percent differential by the end of the decade.[49]

Both Farber (1977) for the United Mine Workers of America and Carruth and Oswald (1985) for the British National Union of Mineworkers characterized the union's objective function in the utilitarian or, equivalently (given the assumed exogeneity of membership and of alternative wages), the expected utility framework. Also, both posited similar (constant relative risk aversion) utility functions for the typical member.[50] For Farber,

---

(Perry, 1984, p. 114). In 1975, "15 percent of the companies produced more than 88 percent of total tonnage, and 2.8 percent of the companies accounted for nearly 60 percent of all the coal produced" (Miernyk, 1980, p. 9).

[47] The role of the federal government in the labor relations of the US coal industry has been by no means negligible. See Perry (1984, chapter 9).

[48] Total saleable mined coal rose from 198 million tons in 1948 to approximately 210 million tons in the mid-1950s and thence down to 88 million tons in the financial year 1985–86. There were 724,000 wage earners on the colliery books in 1948, 704,000 in 1957, and 155,000 in 1985–86. These data are taken from issues of the United Kingdom's *Annual Abstract of Statistics*.

[49] See Handy (1981), pp. 172–3 and 284.

[50] Like Farber and Carruth and Oswald, Svejnar (1986) posits an expected utility maximand for the union with a utility function displaying constant relative risk aversion. He assumes a Cobb–Douglas production function and a contract in which earnings, y, and employment, E, are jointly and efficiently negotiated. He specifies the following equation where TLC stands for the total labor cost, $1 - \delta$ the coefficient of relative risk aversion, and γ' the relative bargaining strength of the union $(0 < \gamma' < 1)$:

$$(TLC/E) - y = \left[(1 - \gamma')/\gamma'\right]^{\delta - 1}\left[1 - (\bar{y}/y)^{\delta}\right]y$$
$$= \delta^{-1}\left[1 - (\bar{y}/y)^{\delta}\right]y.$$

The stochastic form of this equation slightly rearranged is fitted to time-series data for each of 12 major unionized companies. (In effect, γ' is estimated from a second equation.) His estimates of δ span a huge range, the lowest being -1.81 and the largest being nine billion (another being six billion). But not too much should be made of these estimates as in almost every case, interesting special cases such as δ equal to zero or equal to unity are consistent with the data. In other words, there is really very little useful information about union preferences in this study.

$$\Gamma(W, hE; \overline{W}) = (1 - \alpha)^{-1}\left[\, W^{(1-\alpha)} - \overline{W}^{(1-\alpha)}\,\right](hE)$$

where W is an estimate of the average hourly earnings of unionized miners plus some proportion of retirement and health benefits and $\overline{W}$ is average hourly earnings in US durable goods manufacturing. For Carruth and Oswald,

$$\Gamma(Wh, E; B, \overline{Wh}) = \{\alpha_0 + (1 - \alpha_1)^{-1}\left[(Wh)^{(1-\alpha_1)} - B^{(1-\alpha_1)}\right]$$
$$+ \alpha_2(\overline{Wh})\}E$$

where Wh represents weekly earnings (including allowances in kind) of all coal industry workers, B average weekly unemployment benefits, and $\overline{Wh}$ average weekly earnings of manual workers in UK manufacturing industry. Farber and Carruth and Oswald characterized the union as setting the wage to maximize its objective function subject to management choosing employment. The authors estimated the first-order conditions describing this problem together with the employment–wage relationship that represents the union's constraint.[51] This constraint is, more precisely, a manhours–wage rate function for Farber and an employment–earnings function for Carruth and Oswald; hours of work occupy contrary roles in the two studies. Farber used 27 annual observations from 1947 to 1973 while Carruth and Oswald used 31 annual observations from 1950 to 1980.

Farber estimated α to be 2.98 while Carruth and Oswald estimated α_0 to be 9.1, α_1 0.78, and α_2 −0.2. The authors claim that all these coefficients are significantly different from zero which, they say, implies the union objective function diverges systematically from the maximization of rents (which would require α and α_1 to be zero).[52] The authors remark on the greater weight attached to employment in union objectives than would be implied by the maximization of rents.[53] Nevertheless,

[51] Farber's model is slightly more complicated than appears from the description in the text. Because the UMW levies a tax on coal output to finance its pension and health benefits, there are two first-order conditions for the maximization of the objective function, one condition for wages and the other for the tax rate. He estimates two loglinear equations representing the demand for underground and for surface coal and an equation describing the fraction of coal output mined by the UMW. Carruth and Oswald's employment–wage constraint is linear in variables and parameters.

[52] Both Farber and Carruth and Oswald refer to the special case in which $\alpha = \alpha_1 = 0$ as wage bill maximization. In Farber's case, $\alpha = 0$ implies $\Gamma = (W - \overline{W})(hE)$ which is equivalent to what I call rents in equation (3.8) (not the wage bill maximand) if $h = \bar{h}$. In Carruth and Oswald's case, if $\alpha_1 = 0$, then $\Gamma = \{\alpha_0 + \left[(Wh) - B\right] + \alpha_2(\overline{Wh})\}E$ which is an unconventional definition of the wage bill.

[53] "[T]he union members are quite concerned about the employment effects of the union wage-ton tax policy. . . . [M]embers of the UMW put significantly greater stress on employment relative to wages than would be implied by [rent] maximization" (Farber, 1977, pp. 92–3). "[T]he NUM does appear to place a greater weight on employment relative to wages than would be predicted by [rent] maximization" (Carruth and Oswald, 1985, p. 102).

quite different estimates of relative risk aversion (2.98 for the UMW and 0.78 for the NUM) were thus derived. It should be noted that these two studies take the utilitarian (or expected utility) maximand as a maintained hypothesis. There is no attempt in either study to test whether the parameter restrictions implied by this maximand accurately describe union objectives.

Printers

The internal structure of the International Typographical Union and its bargaining conventions with employers form a striking contrast with the US mineworkers' union. While since 1950 the US coalminers have negotiated agreements for the entire unionized sector, the chapters of the ITU negotiate contracts with local printing establishments and, most notably, newspaper firms. Authority within the union resides in the ITU local. The printers represent probably the most democratic union in the United States. For many years, two political parties competed for office and the electoral process effected a frequent turnover of officers. There are few perquisites associated with being a union official who enjoys little discretionary authority, the rank-and-file being consulted at many stages of contract negotiation and ratification.[54] At least until the past 20 years when the development of computerized typesetting has threatened the very existence of the union, the ITU exercised extensive control over operations in printing establishments. Not merely were all printers required to be union members even before being hired, but all issues of production technology were negotiated with the union. As a craft union very conscious of its long and prestigious history, it appears to place a heavy emphasis on securing employment for all its members. Various worksharing procedures were codified and it was standard to hold on to "unneeded" workers until they could be induced to take an early retirement or work could be found for them in other cities.

[54] "Its members have an income and status which minimizes the disparity between the perspectives and styles of life of workers and union leaders. . . . Side by side with the high average wages earned by journeymen printers is the tendency of the union's political system to operate to keep the income differential between workers and union officers small. Official salaries can be raised only by referendum of the whole membership of the local or international, and the membership persistently refuse to give their officers large or frequent raises. . . . [Union leaders] have very little financial stake in union office, and are that much less inclined to entrench themselves in office to the detriment of the democratic process. . . . [W]orking printers themselves have very much the sense of meeting their union officers as status equals, with nothing like the deference paid by most semiskilled workers to their white-collared middle-class union officers. Moreover, the union officer's work is not always very attractive to the skilled typographer with pride in his craft" (Lipset, Trow and Coleman, 1956, pp. 214–15).

The purpose of Dertouzos and Pencavel's (1981) original analysis[55] of the ITU was to discriminate between popular alternative hypotheses about union objectives. To this end, we posited the following Stone–Geary objective function for the union:

$$\Gamma(W, M) = (W - \gamma)^{\theta}(M - \delta)^{1 - \theta} \qquad (3.10)$$

where W denotes the negotiated hourly wage rate and M local union membership (except for one local, Cincinnati, where employment data were available). Because of the emphasis placed by the closed shop ITU in securing employment of all members, we wrote as if M actually represented employment, but nevertheless it is worth keeping the employment–membership distinction in mind and noting that in most cases the data related to membership.

Equation (3.10) could be rationalized in terms of an approximation to the Bernoulli–Nash social welfare function (cf. equation (3.5)), but in fact it was put forward both because it nests other objective functions as special cases and because it leads to convenient reduced form equations. The special case of the wage bill maximand is obtained by the restrictions $\theta = 1/2$ and $\gamma = \delta = 0$. The special case of rents requires $\theta = 1/2$, $\delta = 0$, and γ equal to the alternative wage. Or γ may be related to a comparison wage rate that is relevant to the formation of the ITU's objectives. With γ measured by some alternative or comparison wage, the formulation of equation (3.10) corresponds to the tendency mentioned in section 3.4 for many unions to think in terms of absolute differentials in wages rather than of relative differentials. The notion that the union cared about wages only and not about employment implies $\theta = 1$. Hence popular specifications of union objectives may be tested as parameter restrictions on a more general functional form.

We assumed the ITU locals selected the wage to maximize equation (3.10) subject to a linear wage–employment constraint and fitted the resulting reduced form wage and employment equations to annual data from 1946 to 1965 for eight locals. The estimates of θ, the weight of "supernumerary" wages relative to "supernumerary" employment, ranged from 0.15 to 0.87 suggesting considerable diversity in union objectives. In all but one case, $\hat{\theta}$ differed significantly from both zero and unity. The "reference" parameters, γ and δ, were estimated to be higher in large cities where alternative wages and employment opportunities were greater. The special cases of wage bill and rent maximization were rejected by the data.

My subsequent study (Pencavel, 1984b) of the ITU used almost the same data and had the same goal, to test certain common specifications

[55] This analysis was based on Dertouzos's (1979) PhD dissertation.

of union objectives. For this purpose, I posited an addilog function defined over hourly wage rates and membership (which, again, was presumed synonymous with employment):

$$\Gamma(W, M; \overline{W}) = \mu(1+\rho)^{-1}(W - \beta\overline{W})^{1+\rho} + (1-\mu)(1+\eta)^{-1}M^{1+\eta}$$

(3.11)

where $\overline{W}$ is given by average hourly earnings of nonsupervisory workers in retail trade. This function nests the Stone–Geary ($\rho = \eta \rightarrow -1$) and, a fortiori, rents ($\mu = 0.5$) and the wage bill ($\beta = 0$). Again, the ITU was assumed to select the wage to maximize equation (3.11) subject to a wage–employment constraint. Assuming a particular expression for the slope of this constraint, the first-order condition for this maximization problem was estimated with data for ten ITU locals. This estimation procedure requires, therefore, fitting just one equation. The results indicated that, for the five largest locals, a rent maximand came closer to an appropriate description of the data,[56] but this was not the case for the smaller union locals. For all observations corresponding to all estimates, the quasi-concavity condition for the union objective function was always satisfied.

My work with MaCurdy (MaCurdy and Pencavel, 1986) made use of an entirely different sample of ITU locals. When we came to estimating the union objective function, we posited a different resolution of the bargaining problem, namely, that management and the union jointly determine wages and employment and negotiate efficient contracts.[57] Using annual observations on 13 ITU locals from 1945 to 1973, we estimated the first-order condition for efficient contracts and specified several different union objective functions including the Stone–Geary and quadratic preferences. The specification permitted less diversity in union preferences among the ITU locals than was allowed in the previous research.

In general, the results were consistent with the notion of a well-behaved (quasi-concave) union objective function defined over wages and membership (employment). However, the parameter restrictions implied by rent maximization were clearly rejected by conventional statistical criteria. From the implied marginal rates of substitution between wages and employment, we inferred that, compared with a rent maximization objective, the union placed considerable weight on employment in pursuing their goals.

---

[56] Closer in the sense that, taken one at a time, the hypotheses $\hat{\mu} = 0.5$, $\hat{\rho} = -1$, $\hat{\eta} = -1$, and $\hat{\beta} = 1$ could not be rejected at conventional levels of significance.

[57] This is discussed in section 4.2 in chapter 4.

Conclusions

This research on the coalminers' and printers' unions has convincingly demonstrated that the problems of specifying and estimating union objective functions are not intractable as was once thought. It is not merely the case that parameters have been estimated that appear sensible and plausible; if that were all, then little would have been accomplished. More than this, meaningful (i.e., quasi-concave) objective functions have usually been estimated[58] and values of other parameters, such as slopes of wage–employment constraints, have conformed to prior beliefs. When inferences can be drawn from the estimates about differences in wages and employment, these accord with other information we have about the workings of these labor markets.[59]

As in other areas of research, there is always the possibility that these results reflect more on the ingenuity or tenacity of the researchers in organizing and permuting the data than on the intellectual worth of the enterprise. But, as a practitioner in some of these studies, I simply report that artful or contrived work was neither needed nor used in the research on the printers. I suspect this is also the case for the research on the coalminers. This does not mean, of course, that the form of union objectives has been determined with some assurance. On the contrary, the estimated standard errors attaching to the various parameters quite clearly signal a good deal of imprecision.

Taken at face value, the point estimates of the coalminers' and printers' objective functions suggest substantial diversity in preferences: the British and American coalminers' unions do not place the same weight on wages relative to employment; and the various ITU locals appear to have distinctly different wage–employment indifference curves. At the same time, almost every study has been able to reject popular, simple, assumptions about the nature of union objectives. Not only do the assumptions of rent and wage bill maximization usually conflict with the data, but so does the proposition that unions care about wages only and not about employment. On the contrary, most studies find a greater weight attached to employment, greater, that is, compared with what rent maximization would imply.[60]

---

[58] The qualification "usually" here indicates that quasi-concavity is not always found. For instance, estimates of the Stone–Geary function have sometimes yielded values of the reference parameters, γ and δ, that exceed observed wages and employment, respectively, in which case the function is simply not defined. Of course, this particular problem with the Stone–Geary has often been encountered in the literature on consumer behavior.

[59] For instance, the positive association between firm size and printers' wages in the newspaper industry is given structural interpretation as is the tendency for wages to be higher in larger cities. See Pencavel (1984a).

[60] To repeat what was stressed at the beginning of section 3.6, estimates of the union

The major shortcomings of these studies stem from the rather casual correspondence between variables as they appear in the conceptual framework and those actually used in the empirical research.[61] These slips mean there remains considerable ambiguity about the primary issue motivating the research on union objective functions, the tradeoff between wage rates and employment. Some studies have measured union objectives in terms of earnings (the product of wage rates and hours of work) and employment and others in terms of wage rates and manhours. There has been no attempt in these microeconomic studies to determine the validity of the implicit assumptions concerning the role of work hours in union objectives. Similarly, though the research on the printers' unions has characterized their objectives in terms of wages and employment, in fact in the empirical work union membership has been used in place of employment. In this particular research, membership does seem to bear a positive weight in union objectives, but it would have been better to have drawn more clearly the distinction between employment and membership and, where possible, to allow for separate effects of these variables.[62]

Another class of issues with respect to the research on union objectives concerns the role of auxiliary hypotheses about the solution to the bargaining problem. In each study described above, the manner in which wages, hours, and employment are determined in unionized markets was taken as a maintained hypothesis. No researcher seems to have investigated the robustness of the estimates of union objectives with respect to departures in assumptions concerning the solution to the bargaining problem. Conceptually this is a well-defined issue for research and one whose results could be of great value. If our knowledge of union objective functions is sensitive to what is assumed about the solution to the bargaining problem, then this substantially compounds the empirical tasks facing us. Because our prior beliefs about bargaining procedures and conventions are not held with assurance, estimates of union objective functions would have to be made under several different assumptions about the methods by which wages, hours, and employment are determined.

---

objective function are conditional upon assumptions about the solution to the bargaining problem. Arguing along these lines, Farber (1986, p. 1068) has wondered whether the weight attached to employment in these estimated union objectives stands more appropriately for management's bargaining resistance.

[61] Also, the empirical work largely ignores uncertainty by assuming ex ante beliefs are realized. For an attempt to incorporate uncertainty into empirical research on union objectives, see Chen (1987).

[62] The difficulty here is obtaining reliable data for most typographers locals on employment in newspaper firms.

3.7 Summary

In this chapter, I have argued the case for the specification of union objectives in terms of an equation such as (3.3):

$$\Gamma = g(y, h, E, \overline{W}, M).$$

This is understood to represent the preferences of the union leadership who incorporate in some fashion the interests of their members. This explains why g increases with respect to the rank-and-file's earnings and to total employment and why g decreases with respect to the hours worked by each employee. The leadership's desire to preside over a large and potentially influential organization accounts for g increasing with union membership while a comparison wage, $\overline{W}$, serves as a gauge for the rank-and-file to appraise the union leadership's performance; g decreases with respect to $\overline{W}$. As shown from the discussion of the coalminers and the printers, analytical work has provided a little support for these arguments even though the evidence is not straightforward to read.

In the introduction to this chapter, I emphasized the narrow conception of union objectives considered here: not only does equation (3.3) concentrate on ends, not processes, but questions relating to the structure of the union organization are put aside. But even so restricted, equation (3.3) omits dimensions of the employment relationship that unions have at times been especially concerned with and that in certain circumstances may assume considerable importance. I am thinking, in particular, of issues associated with the organization of work and the choice of production methods, issues that unions have affected through rules relating to the minimum number of workers per machine, the pace of work, the class of employees eligible to work at a particular task, the types and numbers of machines, and others.

These rules are usually interpreted as being of no value to the union in and of themselves, but as indirect attempts to regulate employment[63] and in this vein, in chapter 5, I shall consider constraints on the capital–labor ratio designed to affect the level of employment. However, there are occasions on which the union is interested in these rules not as devices for controlling employment, but because they affect the level of work effort, the degree to which employees enjoy independence from supervision, and other aspects of the quality of the workers' lives at their place of work. Thus, for instance, various rules governing crew sizes and the types of machines place restrictions on the capital–labor ratio in order to control work effort per hour, a dimension of the labor input that has yet to be

[63] See, for instance, McDonald and Solow (1981).

fully integrated into economic analysis. I shall be following standard practice and neglecting work effort as well as other features affecting the quality of the workers' environment even though a number of union rules and policies are likely to be best understood as directed to these ends.

4 Efficient Contracts

4.1 Introduction

The previous chapter discussed the objectives of trade unions as far as they concerned wages, hours of work, and employment. This chapter takes these objectives as given and inquires into the determination of these variables in a bargaining relationship with the firm's management. In the following section, I discuss the characteristics of efficient contract models. I then consider what modifications of these characteristics are required when negotiations involve several unions or firms and when the parties are uncertain of the values of future exogenous variables. The literature purporting to test for the presence of efficient contracts is examined and evaluated. I turn to models within the class of efficient contracts proposing specific outcomes and discuss certain bargaining theories. Their empirical implications are assessed and the experimental evidence on bargaining reviewed. I close this chapter with some conclusions.

At the outset I need to say a few words on management's objectives. In most cases, the *representatives* of the union are bargaining with the *representatives* of the firm's owners – workers do not bargain directly with the owners, a feature that has inspired the development of bargaining models of nonunionized as well as unionized firms (see, for instance, Aoki, 1984). So one class of the firm's employees (management) are bargaining with another class of the firm's employees (the union leadership). And all the reasons why the objectives of the union leaders may not exactly mirror the objectives of the union rank-and-file hold also for the relationship between management's objectives and those of the owners. Recognition of this may well suggest specifying management's interests in terms of an objective function in which the owners' profits constitute just one argument. I am not going to follow this course here for two reasons.

First, many of the results below will hold when profits represent one element of a more general set of management objectives. It is difficult to generalize because specific results depend upon the particular arguments of management's objective function. In those cases where management is concerned with its own perquisites and where it is indifferent to the number of employees and to their pay and hours of work except insofar as these factors affect profits, then little is gained by the generality afforded by objective functions in which profits constitute one of a number of arguments.

Second, profit maximization by the firm conventionally provides the reference point for analyzing non-standard assumptions and models about labor market behavior. It is important, therefore, to establish that certain results about the determination of wages, hours of work, and employment are not the consequence of departures from profit maximization. For these reasons, I shall assume that management takes as its goal the maximization of net revenue or profits. The precise definition of profits remains to be given.

I find it convenient to distinguish two classes of bargaining models. There are those where the values of all the variables are determined jointly and concomitantly. I call these Efficient Contracts and they are the subject of this chapter. Then there are those models where the variables are ordered in some fashion and the value of one or more of these variables is determined before the value(s) of the other variable(s). Such contracts in which the variables are ordered and then determined in sequence, I call Recursive Contracts. They are the subject of the following chapter where reasons for such an ordering are discussed.

I use the term "efficient contracts" reluctantly. I have found that, in this literature, the adjective "efficient" is sometimes an impediment to understanding. Not only does it beg the question of what particular resources are being economized, but also it requires only a little imagination to rationalize seemingly anomalous or discrepant behavior as efficient. So a Recursive Contract in which the determination of wages is made prior to employment may be fully efficient in a world where information about future production requirements is incomplete and where the transaction costs of specifying a full set of contingencies are prohibitive. If then a broad set of circumstances and arrangements is consistent with efficiency, the usefulness of the term to distinguish different types of contracts is compromised.[1] Given economists' predilection for notions of efficiency,

---

[1] This is recognized in the game theoretic literature on non-cooperative bargaining where a number of different concepts of efficiency are employed. For example, Holmstrom

the word becomes an epithet to declaim against another. This is not a useful way to conduct scientific inquiry and I do not mean to use the concept of efficiency in this eristic way. However, I do use the concept as, in this literature, it seems to have become associated with a particular class of models.

The bargaining setting below presupposes a number of features, some of which should be explicitly noted. First, it is assumed in this chapter that both sides consent to the items constituting the bargaining agenda. Of course, this assumption is not satisfied in all labor–management bargaining: for example, management often insists on retaining unilateral control over the level of employment and hours of work and a number of disputes have centered on these prerogatives. In this instance a compromise may be reached such that management's authority over employment and hours is not explicitly or formally denied, but unwritten understandings are reached about normal or typical levels. In any event, in this chapter the two parties are assumed to bargain over the values of the negotiated variables, not over what constitutes the set of the negotiated variables.

Second, any agreement the two parties arrive at is assumed to be enforceable. In some cases the enforcement mechanism is provided by recourse (or threat of recourse) to an arbitrator or to courts of law. In other cases the incentive to honor the agreement is supplied by the costs associated with the loss of reputation in future bargaining negotiations. Naturally there are situations in which these enforcement mechanisms operate ineffectively and, indeed, they operate at all only insofar as each party is able to identify the other party's actions that are prohibited by the contract. Moral hazard problems are a well-known feature of collective bargaining contracts. Moreover this enforceability assumption requires that the parties to the agreement police their own constituents to ensure contractual performance.

Third, the irregularity of collective bargaining negotiations is ignored. That is, the opportunity costs of time spent in negotiation and enforcement activity as well as the out-of-pocket expenses associated with contract negotiation mean that collective bargaining agreements are rarely renegotiated within a year and are often of two or three years in duration. Though some contracts contain contingent clauses, they are clearly incomplete in this regard, a consequence perhaps of problems associated with bounded rationality, the limited capacity of individuals to imagine all possible future contingencies and to process the information necessary

---

and Myerson (1983) distinguish among the characteristics of solutions under different assumptions about the information available to the bargainers by defining ex post classical efficiency, ex ante incentive efficiency, and interim incentive efficiency.

to allow for these contingencies in the negotiated contracts. The implication of these transaction costs is that, during the lifetime of a collective bargaining contract, the values of some or all of the negotiated variables may not move smoothly or may not move at all as the values of the exogenous variables change. These costs of transacting are neglected in what follows.

Fourth, except when discussing some of the experimental literature on bargaining, the analysis in this chapter neglects any important informational asymmetries that impede the negotiation and enforcement of contracts. Information is not assumed necessarily to be complete nor need it be public. I simply ignore "hidden information" that materially affects the nature of the negotiated settlements. The specification of such informational asymmetries has become popular in recent years although the implications of these models are distressingly sensitive to small changes in their assumptions. A discussion of certain asymmetrical information models is contained in chapter 5.

4.2   Efficient Contract Models

For the moment, simply write profits π as a function of per worker earnings (Wh), hours per worker (h), the employment of labor (E), and the services of any nonlabor input (K):

$$\pi = \pi(Wh, h, E, K; Z) \tag{4.1}$$

where Z stands for variables that affect profits but are beyond the firm's control. At present, one trade union representing all the firm's non-management employees is assumed to be bargaining with the management of one firm. Following the discussion in the previous chapter, the trade union's objectives are represented by

$$\Gamma = g(Wh, h, E; \overline{W}, M) \tag{4.2}$$

where $\overline{W}$ is some comparison or alternative wage rate and M is union membership.

Under these circumstances, many economists (though not, I believe, most industrial relations specialists) are inclined to the view that union-management bargaining will not leave unexploited any opportunities to raise one party's welfare that do not reduce the other party's welfare. In other words, efficient contracts will be negotiated, efficient, that is, from the point of view of this trade union and management, not necessarily from the point of view of society's resource allocation. This means the values of the bargained variables are determined jointly and lie on the parties' contract "curve" (surface) which is derived by maximizing one party's welfare, say, the union's, subject to a given value for the other party's welfare, say, π_0. Attaching the multiplier $\lambda < 0$ to π_0, the first-order conditions describing this contract curve are as follows:

$$g_i = \lambda \pi_i \qquad i = 1, 2, 3, 4 \tag{4.3}$$

where $g_1 \equiv \partial g / \partial (Wh)$, $g_2 \equiv \partial g / \partial h$, $g_3 \equiv \partial g / \partial E$, $g_4 \equiv \partial g / \partial K$, $\pi_1 \equiv \partial \pi / \partial (Wh)$, $\pi_2 \equiv \partial \pi / \partial h$, $\pi_3 \equiv \partial \pi / \partial E$, and $\pi_4 \equiv \partial \pi / \partial K$. In each case, the variable is set at a level such that the marginal "utility" of that variable to the union is proportional (λ) to the effect of a small increase in its value on management's profits.[2] Obviously, for any variable absent in one party's objective function (as would be the case if the union were indifferent to K), its value is determined entirely in accordance with the interests of the other party.

If a closed form solution of the first-order conditions is feasible, then the decision variables may be specified as functions of the exogenous variables:

$$y = \psi_1(Z, \overline{W}, M, \pi_0)$$

$$h = \psi_2(Z, \overline{W}, M, \pi_0)$$

$$E = \psi_3(Z, \overline{W}, M, \pi_0)$$

$$K = \psi_4(Z, \overline{W}, M, \pi_0)$$

$$\lambda = \psi_5(Z, \overline{W}, M, \pi_0)$$

where $y = Wh$.

Of course, one variable assumed to be given above, namely, π_0, is not predetermined in most bargaining situations so there will normally be a different "efficient" value for each decision variable as π_0 is altered. Hence, except for special cases, there is a whole gamut of efficient values of y, h, E, and K, each combination corresponding to a different point on the contract curve. In short, requiring contracts to be efficient is not normally sufficient to generate a unique combination of values of the decision variables.

An illustration of the first-order conditions (4.3) with specific forms for the union's and firm's objective functions is instructive. With respect to the firm's profits, assume the absence of costs of adjustment and fixed costs of employment:

---

[2] If management maximized an objective function $U = U(\pi, J)$ where U is increasing in π and where J represents some other argument, then equation (4.3) becomes $g_i = \lambda$ $(U_\pi \pi_i + U_J J_i)$ where $U_\pi = \partial U / \partial \pi$, $U_J = \partial U / \partial J$, and J_i is the derivative of J with respect to the ith variable. When J is independent of this variable, $g_i = \tilde{\lambda} \pi_i$ where $\tilde{\lambda} = \lambda U_\pi$.

$$\pi(Wh, h, E, K; Z) = R(h, E, K; Z) - WhE - rK \qquad (4.4)$$

where R is gross revenue and r is the (fixed) user cost of each unit of physical capital services. Here Z stands for exogenous variables that alter the firm's gross revenues. If the union's objective function takes the general form $\Gamma = g(Wh, h, E)$, then the first-order condition for earnings relative to employment may be written

$$\frac{g_3}{g_1} = \frac{y - R_3}{E} \qquad (4.5)$$

where $y = Wh$ and $R_3 = \partial R/\partial E$.[3] Clearly, as emphasized by Leontief (1946), provided both $g_3 > 0$ and $g_1 > 0$, at any point on the earnings-employment contract curve, earnings exceed the marginal revenue product of employment. It is convenient for our arguments later if the previous equation is rearranged as follows:

$$R_3 = y - (g_3 g_1^{-1})E \qquad (4.6)$$

This is one form of the condition for the marginal revenue product of employment under efficient contracts. Because this equation has a prominent place in our discussion below, for expository convenience, I dub this the efficient contracts employment condition. Alternatively, making use of the first-order condition for working hours,

$$R_3 = y + (g_3 g_2^{-1})R_2 \qquad (4.7)$$

where $R_2 = \partial R/\partial h$. In other words, according to the efficient contracts employment condition, the profit-maximizing firm is using more labor at any earnings level than it would do if it exercised unilateral control over employment.[4] This "excess" labor may be manifested in the form of

---

[3] If management maximized an objective function $U = U(\pi, J)$ with π given by equation (4.4), then equation (4.5) would take the following form:

$$\frac{g_3}{g_1} = \frac{u_\pi(y - R_3) - U_J J_E}{U_\pi E - U_J J_y}$$

where $J_E = \partial J/\partial E$ and $J_y = \partial J/\partial y$. Equation (4.5) holds when $J_E = J_y = 0$.

[4] If management maximized an objective function $U = U(\pi, J)$, then equation (4.6) would become

$$R_3 = y - g_3 g_1^{-1}E - U_\pi^{-1} U_J(J_E - g_3 g_1^{-1} J_y)$$

with the definitions of U_π, U_J, J_E, and J_y given in the preceding footnotes. It is impossible to determine whether R_3 here is greater or less than R_3 in equation (4.6) until some restrictions are imposed on J_E and J_y. It remains likely, however, that the firm will be using labor in excess of the "marginal revenue product equals earnings" condition.

minimum crew rules, featherbedding, make-work practices, and other manifestations of over-manning requirements.[5] Insofar as the negotiated earnings exceeds the transfer price of labor, then mechanisms such as long apprenticeship programs, high entrance fees and dues, and nepotism will tend to be adopted to ration employment among those offering themselves for work. Therefore, these efficient contracts will tend to be characterized both by devices to restrict entry into union employment and by rules that serve to absorb the excessive number of workers employed (excessive, that is, given the relationship of the marginal revenue product of labor to the wages).

The slope of the earnings–employment contract curve (holding hours constant) is given by the expression

$$\frac{\partial y}{\partial E} = \frac{(R_3 - y)g_{13} + g_1 R_{33} + g_3 + E g_{33}}{g_1 - (R_3 - y)g_{11} - E g_{13}} \tag{4.8}$$

where $R_{33} = \partial^2 R/\partial E^2$, $g_{13} = \partial^2 g/\partial y \partial E$, $g_{11} = \partial^2 g/\partial y^2$, and $g_{33} = \partial^2 g/\partial E^2$. It is easy to establish that this expression (4.8) may be positive, negative, or infinite. More structure needs to be placed on the union's objective function if qualitative results are to be derived. Thus, consider the following simple form:

$$\Gamma(y, h, E; \bar{y}) = (y - \varphi(h) - \bar{y})^\mu E \tag{4.9}$$

where $\mu > 0$, $\varphi' > 0$, $\varphi'' > 0$, and $\bar{y} = \overline{Wh}$. This is almost the same as the Stone–Geary utility function, equation (3.10), and, for expository convenience, I shall designate it below as the Stone–Geary.[6] Here $\varphi(h)$ may be interpreted as the disutility of work and $\bar{y}$ as earnings in the next best activity or perhaps earnings in nonunion employment. The sum, $\varphi(h) + \bar{y}$, will be termed the opportunity cost of an employee's work in this unionized job. In this case, again assuming interior solutions for all the variables, the first-order conditions (4.3) (including the equation for the multiplier λ) are as follows:

$$y: \quad \mu(y - \varphi - \bar{y})^{\mu-1} = -\lambda \tag{4.10}$$

$$h: \quad -\mu(y - \varphi - \bar{y})^{\mu-1}\varphi'(h)E = \lambda(\partial R/\partial h)$$

$$E: \quad (y - \varphi - \bar{y})^\mu = \lambda[(\partial R/\partial E) - y]$$

$$K: \quad r = \partial R/\partial K$$

---

[5] Note that my use of the term "featherbedding" corresponds not to a situation where the marginal revenue product of employment is zero, but simply to a situation where the marginal revenue product of employment falls short of earnings.

[6] To be precise, assume $E = M - \delta$, $\varphi(h) + \bar{y} = \gamma$, and $y = W$. Then equation (4.9) yields (3.10) exactly with $\mu = \theta/(1 - \theta)$.

$$\lambda: \quad R(h, E, K; Z) - WhE - rK = \pi_0.$$

Combining the equations for y and E,

$$\partial R/\partial E = y - \frac{1}{\mu} \left(y - \varphi(h) - \bar{y} \right)$$

which is the form of the efficient contracts employment condition, equation (4.6), corresponding to the Stone–Geary objective function (4.9). In the special case of $\mu = 1$, $\partial R/\partial E$ equals $\varphi(h) + \bar{y}$. As $\mu \to \infty$, employment becomes of no concern to the union (its indifference curves are horizontal with respect to employment) and $\partial R/\partial E = y$. In general, the marginal revenue product of labor equals a weighted sum of y and $\varphi(h) + \bar{y}$ with weights $1 - (1/\mu)$ and $1/\mu$, respectively.

The slope of the contract curve between y and E (holding h given) is

$$\frac{\partial y}{\partial E} = \left(\frac{\mu}{\mu - 1} \right) \frac{\partial^2 R}{\partial E^2}.$$

Assuming $\partial^2 R/\partial E^2 < 0$,[7] this contract curve will be positively sloped if $\mu < 1$, it will be negatively sloped if $\mu > 1$, and it will be vertical if $\mu = 1$. See figure 4.1. Suppose E_n represents employment in the event of this firm not being unionized. Then upon unionization employment would rise if efficient contracts were negotiated along $\mu < 1$, employment would fall along $\mu > 1$, and employment would be unchanged along the contract curve corresponding to $\mu = 1$.

The case of a vertical contract curve ($\mu = 1$) yields such convenient results that its appeal has proved irresistible.[8] When $\mu = 1$, it is straightforward to check from equation (4.10) that $\lambda = -1$ so the Lagrangean equation to be maximized is $\Gamma - (\pi_0 - \pi)$ or $\Gamma + \pi$ except for the constant π_0. In other words the two parties have a common interest in maximizing

$$R - yE - rK + (y - \varphi(h) - \bar{y})E = R - rK - (\varphi(h) + \bar{y})E.$$
$$(4.11)$$

Suppose $\gamma = \varphi(h) + \bar{y}$ as in equation (3.10). Then in their employment, hours, and physical capital decisions, the union and management together

---

[7] If p denotes the price of output and X the amount of output produced and sold, then

$$\frac{\partial^2 R}{\partial E^2} = \left(p + X \frac{\partial p}{\partial X} \right) \frac{\partial^2 X}{\partial E^2} + 2 \frac{\partial p}{\partial X} \left(\frac{\partial X}{\partial E} \right)^2 + X \left(\frac{\partial^2 p}{\partial X^2} \right) \left(\frac{\partial X}{\partial E} \right)^2.$$

The first two terms on the right-hand side are negative, but the third term is ambiguous in sign. In what follows, I shall assume $\partial^2 R/\partial E^2 < 0$.

[8] For instance, a vertical contract curve is presumed in Hall and Lilien (1979) and the same assumption forms the basis of de Menil's (1971) seminal work.

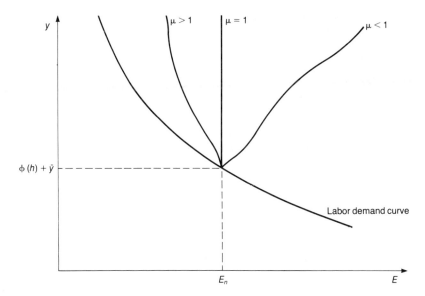

Figure 4.1   Conventional employment demand curve and earnings-employment
contract curve corresponding to objective functions equations (4.4) and (4.9).

replicate the choices that would be made by a profit-maximizing mono-
polist whose price per unit of employment was γ. In other words, as
Fellner (1947) emphasized, the unionized firm's allocation of resources is
not affected by the presence of the union.[9] The potential difference
provided by the union is the division of the firm-specific net revenues,
equation (4.11), between shareholders and workers: the higher is y, the
greater the share of these rents allocated to workers and, indeed, each
dollar increase in y raises the union's utility by the same amount as
management's profits are reduced:

$$\frac{\partial \Gamma}{\partial y} = - \frac{\partial \pi}{\partial y} = E. \tag{4.12}$$

This implication of union–management settlements on a vertical contract curve is easily confused with an accounting identity. That is,
consider the effects on profits and on union rents of an increase in y
computed by holding employment fixed. Define the firm's net revenue
(NR) as $NR = R - yE - rK$ and define the net wage bill (NWB) as
$NWB = (y - \bar{y})E$. Then the effect of an increase in y on NR holding E

---

[9] In the long run, any reduction in rates of return to capital will discourage the supply
of capital to the firm.

constant is the same (except for sign) as the effect of an increase in y on NWB holding E constant:

$$\frac{\partial(NWB)}{\partial y} = -\frac{\partial(NR)}{\partial y} = E_0 \qquad (4.13)$$

where E_0 denotes the fixed value of employment. Whereas equation (4.12) holds because there is a behavioral incentive not to alter employment, equation (4.13) follows as a matter of computation and is without any behavioral significance. It is important not to confuse (4.12) with (4.13).

4.3   Efficient Contracts and the Collective Bargaining Structure

The argument in the preceding section has assumed a bargaining setting in which a single union negotiates with a single firm. A departure from this assumption is an important one to consider in view of the importance of multi-union and multi-employer contracts in the United States and Britain.[10] Where a single firm bargains with several unions, each representing a distinct group of workers, the basic reasoning above requires little modification: now an objective function needs to be defined for each union and equation (4.3) holds as a description of the first-order conditions for the earnings, hours, and employment of each of several classes of workers.[11]

This assumes, however, that each union's objectives are not affected by the levels of employment, hours, and pay of the workers represented by other unions. Suppose, on the contrary, that union j's objective function depends upon the earnings paid to workers represented by union k: $\Gamma^{(j)} = g^{(j)}(y_j, h_j, E_j; y_k)$. Then, where a firm bargains separately with one group of its workers, the first-order condition for earnings paid to workers k in an efficient contract will take the form

[10] Among major collective bargaining agreements in the United States in January 1980, almost 60 percent were contracts made with a single employer and these represented about 57 percent of all unionized workers covered by such agreements. Fifty percent of these single employer contracts related to a single plant. (See US Department of Labor, 1981, table 1.8.) By contrast, in Britain most collectively bargained pay increases in a 1984 survey were the product of national or regional agreements covering several plants (see Millward and Stevens, 1986, chapter 9.)

[11] Of course, the satisfaction of these first-order conditions should not be construed as implying that labor's bargaining strength is independent of whether unions bargain together or separately. See, for instance, Davidson (1988) and Horn and Wolinsky (1988) for arguments on how bargaining structures may affect the solution.

$$\frac{\partial g^{(k)}}{\partial y_k} = \lambda \frac{\partial \pi}{\partial y_k} + \lambda^{(j)} \frac{\partial g^{(j)}}{\partial y_k}$$

where $\lambda^{(j)}$ is the Lagrange multiplier attached to union j's welfare. In other words, interdependencies among different unions' objectives imply less straightforward characterizations for contract efficiency. Of course, if these interdependencies are important, then incentives exist for the unions to internalize them and to redistribute rents among different classes of workers within an amalgamated union. The impediments to this process consist of the transaction costs discussed in the previous chapter. In addition, there are the attitudes of management to take into account: some will try to frustrate union amalgamations while others will see it in their interests to encourage them.

When a single union bargains with a number of different firms, the first-order conditions are again just like equation (4.3) except that the right-hand side elements are firm-specific. This statement presupposes that the multi-employer collective agreement allows for differences in wages among firms. Some do, but others do not (at least, not explicitly). For example, in the agreements between the United Mine Workers and the Bituminous Coal Operators Association (BCOA), a single wage rate is negotiated and all the companies in the Association are supposed to pay it. (Indeed, these wages are paid also by some firms not belonging to the Association.) In this case, the first-order condition for earnings takes the form of

$$\frac{\partial g}{\partial y} = \sum_{j=1}^{m} \lambda^{(j)} \frac{\partial \pi^{(j)}}{\partial y}$$

where $\lambda^{(j)} < 0$ is the Lagrange multiplier attached to the jth firm's profits and there are m firms in all. As was the case with equation (4.6), there is an inequality between the marginal revenue product of employment in any firm and earnings. In particular, the efficient contracts employment condition (equation (4.6)) holds except that firm-specific subscripts are needed on all the non-earnings variables. Of course, a settlement where earnings are constrained to be the same in each firm is consistent with contract efficiency only if the union places some value on wage equality.

4.4 Contingent Efficient Contracts

Now consider the nature of efficient labor contracts under conditions where all exogenous events occurring during the life of the contract are not fully known. These considerations of uncertainty were raised by

Azariadis (1975), Baily (1974), and others and have spawned an extensive literature on what is commonly labelled as "implicit contracts." The notion that certain labor market contracts are implicit conveys the suggestion that these models are applicable to nonunion no less than unionized markets and, moreover, as the agreements are supposed to be tacit, it is simply irrelevant for critics to point out that contingent contracts are absent in many labor markets. In essence, this approach to labor market contracts is a straightforward marriage between, on the one hand, the theory of optimal risk sharing as developed by Borch (1962), Arrow (1971), and others and, on the other hand, the earlier union–management bilaterial monopoly models of Leontief (1946), Fellner (1947), and others.

Suppose the firm's product demand schedule may vary across different states indexed by s where $s = 1, \ldots, \bar{s}$. There are no important information asymmetries meaning that the union and management concur in their evaluation of the probability distribution of these states so that the probability of state s is given by $q_s > 0$ and

$$\sum_{i=1}^{\bar{s}} q_i = 1.$$

The collective bargaining agreement now specifies wages, hours, and employment as contingent on the occurrence of event s. Consider a natural extension of the parties' objective functions above (equations (4.4) and (4.2)) whereby management maximizes the expected value of profits

$$\mathcal{E}\pi = \sum_{s=1}^{\bar{s}} q_s [R_s(h_s, E_s, K_s) - W_s h_s E_s - r_s K_s]$$

and the union's objective is to maximize the expected value of its Γ function

$$\mathcal{E}\Gamma = \sum_{s=1}^{\bar{s}} q_s g_s(W_s h_s, h_s, E_s; \overline{W}_s, M)$$

where $g_s(\cdot)$ is the union's state-specific welfare function. Observe that in the union's objective function M has been assumed independent of s. This corresponds to the usual (implausible) assumption in the implicit contract literature whereby a given pool of workers is attached to a firm and the workers in this pool do not migrate to other sectors of the economy nor does the firm recruit workers beyond M in any state.

If the union and management negotiate efficient contracts, equation (4.3) holds in any given state s. With respect to the determination of earnings in different states, say in s and t, the first-order condition requires $(\partial g_s / \partial y_s) E_s^{-1} = (\partial g_t / \partial y_t) E_t^{-1}$ and the earnings features of the state-contingent contract will depend upon relative employment in the two states and upon the form of the union's objective function in the two states.[12] In fact, a widespread if not universal assumption in the implicit contracts literature is that each worker's (risk averse) objectives are given by an expected utility formulation such as

$$g_s(y_s, h_s, E_s; \bar{y}_s, \bar{h}_s, M) = \left[u(y_s) - \varphi(h_s) \right] \frac{E_s}{M}$$

$$+ \left[u(\bar{y}_s) - \varphi(\bar{h}_s) \right] \left(1 - \frac{E_s}{M} \right)$$

where $\bar{y}_s$ and $\bar{h}_s$ represent earnings and work hours in some alternative activity. In this case, $\partial g_s / \partial y_s = u'(y_s)(E_s/M)$ for all s and the first-order condition for earnings becomes $u'(y_s) = u'(y_t)$ implying $y_s = y_t = y$ because $u'(y)$ is a monotone function of y. In other words, the expected utility hypothesis generates the result that real earnings are invariant to the state s and the option to express earnings as a function of s is not taken up. As is well known, this result arises from the gains to trade in a situation in which one party (in this case the worker) is risk averse while the other is risk neutral: the worker obtains implicit insurance against fluctuations in his earnings.

The other parts of the union–management contract deal with work hours and employment. Even with the assumption that each worker maximizes expected utility, the particular results depend upon how hours and employees enter into the production (or revenue) function and upon the manner in which hours affect preferences.[13] In Azariadis's (1975) original formulation, the hours of work dimension was essentially sidestepped by assuming each employee works either full time or not at all. Under these circumstances, the results for employment depend upon what $\bar{y}$ represents in the preceding equation – whether, for instance, $\bar{y}$ is unemployment compensation distributed by the government and not charged against the firm. When the firm pays its own unemployment compensation, the contract guarantees not only the same wages independently of s, but also it ensures "full employment" (meaning here $E_s = M$) for all s.

On the other hand, when the unemployment compensation is not fully charged against the firm, the efficient contract exploits the fact that some workers can draw on an independent source of income (independent, that is, of the firm's and the worker's resources) and so, in some realizations of s, the firm will employ less than the total number of workers available

---

[12] For instance, for the Stone–Geary objective function (4.9) above, the first-order condition for earnings requires $y_s - \varphi(h_s) - \bar{y}_s = y_t - \varphi(h_t) - \bar{y}_t$.

[13] A clear statement of this appears in Rosen (1985).

($E_s < M$). In this instance, for there to be less than full employment, the marginal revenue product of labor evaluated at $E_s = M$ must be less than the worker's unemployment compensation $\bar{y}$ (see, for instance, Akerlof and Miyazaki, 1980). This is exactly the condition under which a worker would choose to receive the unemployment compensation in a spot auction market in which the firm's offered wage always equalled its marginal revenue product of labor. In this sense the implicit contracting framework is generating less than full employment in precisely the same circumstances as a conventional spot market.

The motivation behind the original work on implicit contracts was to offer an explanation for greater employment variability and smaller real wage variability over the business cycle than is implied by naive characterizations of the way in which auction labor markets operate. In fact, as pointed out in the preceding paragraph, the symmetric information versions of implicit contract models do not succeed in providing a more meaningful explanation for employment variability. Whether each worker's wage compensation tacitly contains an insurance component (as the theory proposes) is difficult to assess. While many US collective bargaining agreements specify conditions under which wages may be changed during the lifetime of the contract, the link between contractual wages and consumer prices is not merely nonlinear but discontinuous and explanations of the incidence and form of these indexation provisions make little or no recourse to the sorts of considerations emphasized in implicit contract models. In short, this literature has yet to persuade us that its central ideas are empirically relevant.

4.5 Tests of Contract Efficiency

What opportunities might be available for a researcher to test whether union–management contracts are efficient? Later in this chapter I shall consider research where efficient contract models are augmented with hypotheses about the particular point at which the parties settle on the contract curve, but here I want to see whether the conditions for efficiency alone imply inclusion or exclusion restrictions that might form the basis for fruitful empirical research.

Brown and Ashenfelter (1986) have addressed this question and have used the efficient contracts employment condition, equation (4.6), as the basis of their empirical work. Recall this condition:

$$R_3 = y - \left(g_3 g_1^{-1}\right) E.$$

Brown and Ashenfelter write, "it is clear that, in any efficient bilateral contract, the alternative wage rate must determine, at least in part, the marginal revenue product of employment" (p. S43). In other words, in terms of the efficient contracts employment condition, they point out that the marginal revenue product of employment, R_3 ($= \partial R/\partial E$), will be correlated with alternative earnings insofar as g_3/g_1 depends on $\bar{y}$.

Using essentially the pooled cross-section time-series data collected by Dertouzos (1979) for his original study of the International Typographical Union, Brown and Ashenfelter proceed to approximate the efficient contracts employment condition, equation (4.6), by the following regression equation:

$$\ln E_{it} = b_0 + b_1 X_{it} + b_2 \ln y_{it} + b_3 \ln \bar{y}_{it} + u_{it} \tag{4.14}$$

where u_{it} is an unobserved stochastic term and X_{it} represents a vector of nonwage variables such as the lagged values of the dependent variable, time trends, fixed city effects, and indicators of the output produced by typographers. Employment, E, is measured in some cases by membership and in other cases by total manhours so that, as was the case for the studies described in section 3.6, the distinctions among employment, work hours, and union membership are obscured. The earnings variable, y, in equation (4.14) is measured by the hourly contract minimum wage and the alternative earnings variable, $\bar{y}$, by a number of different indicators including the average hourly earnings of manufacturing production workers. When $\ln y$ was treated as endogenous,[14] the estimates of b_2 and b_3 fluctuated in sign across equation specifications and, more often than not, their values were less than their estimated standard errors. Other than rejecting the hypothesis of a vertical contract curve, the authors conclude on a quite agnostic note.

Their research raises two questions: (1) does the absence of alternative earnings, $\bar{y}$, from the efficient contracts employment condition necessarily imply that contracts are inefficient, as they maintain?; and (2) is the presence of alternative earnings in their estimating equation (4.14) consistent with a first-order condition from inefficient bargaining models? I shall answer "no" to the first question which implies that contracts may be efficient even if the marginal revenue product of employment is uncorrelated with $\bar{y}$ and I shall answer "yes" to the second question which implies that a partial correlation between E and $\bar{y}$ is compatible with a first-order condition corresponding to an employer being on his wage-taking labor demand curve.

First consider the argument that efficiency requires that $\bar{y}$ ". . . determine, at least in part, the marginal revenue product of employment." The validity of this argument rests on the presumption that g_3/g_1 is a

---

[14] Their instrumental variables for $\ln y$ were lagged values of y and current and lagged values of the consumer price index.

function of $\bar{y}$. In fact, there are quite plausible cases in which this is not the case. As an illustration, if $\Gamma = \varphi_1(E)\varphi_2(h)(y/\bar{y})^\eta$ where φ_1 is a monotonically increasing function of employment and φ_2 a monotonically decreasing function of hours of work, then g_3/g_1 is independent of $\bar{y}$ and so the marginal revenue product of employment in equation (4.6) is not associated with alternative earnings.[15] The efficient contracts employment condition does not necessarily imply that employment or the marginal revenue product of employment will be correlated with alternative earnings.

Second, let us show that the estimating equation (4.14) is fully consistent with the first-order condition corresponding to certain inefficient bargaining models. For the purpose of this argument, suppose the union sets the wage to maximize $\Gamma = g(y, h, E; \bar{y})$ subject to management determining employment unilaterally according to the trade-off $E = f(y, X)$. The first-order condition describing this optimum is $-g_1/g_3 = f'$. To illustrate with particular functional forms suppose

$$\Gamma = (\text{constant})y^{(1+b_2)}\bar{y}^{b_3}e^u + b_4 E$$

where hours of work are included in the constant and

$$f(y, X) = \exp(a_0 - a_1 y e^{-b_1 X}).$$

In this case, the first-order condition $-g_1/g_3 = f'$ yields the estimating equation (4.14) exactly. Further, compounding the difficulty of identification, if $\partial\Gamma/\partial\bar{y} < 0$, then b_3 will have the negative sign that Brown and Ashenfelter maintain is its expected sign if contracts are efficient. In other words, a partial correlation between E and $\bar{y}$ is consistent both with the first-order condition for an efficient contract and with the first-order condition for certain inefficient contracts.

---

[15] More generally, suppose all variables are constant except employment and reference earnings, $\bar{y}$, and express the relationship between employment and the marginal revenue product of employment by $E = \psi(R_3)$ where $\psi' < 0$. Then differentiation of equation (4.6) yields

$$\frac{\partial R_3}{\partial\bar{y}} = \frac{Eg_1^{-2}(g_{14}g_3 - g_{34}g_1)}{1 + Eg_1^{-2}\psi'(g_1g_{33} + g_1g_3E^{-1} - g_3g_{13})}$$

where the 1 subscript relates to derivatives taken with respect to y, the 3 subscript to E, and the 4 subscript to $\bar{y}$. (Virtually the same expression appears in Nickell and Wadhwani (1987).) The numerator of this equation is difficult to sign because, even if $g_{34} \leq 0$ (i.e., the union's marginal utility of employment does not increase when $\bar{y}$ is higher), g_{14} may well be negative (i.e., the marginal utility of earnings falls when $\bar{y}$ increases). In general, the sign of $\partial R_3/\partial\bar{y}$ is ambiguous so it is not clear why instances in which their measures of $\bar{y}$ affect R_3 positively are described by Brown and Ashenfelter as "contrary to the hypothesized direction of this effect" in efficient contracts.

Other researchers have also examined the partial correlation between employment and alternative earnings and have used equation (4.14) as a device for evaluating the empirical relevance of efficient union-management contracts. For instance, pooled cross-section time-series data have been used to fit an equation such as (4.14) to the British coal mining industry (Bean and Turnbull, 1987), to aircraft mechanics for seven US airlines (Card, 1986), and to British manufacturing firms (Nickell and Wadhwani, 1987). These authors seem to be aware of the fact that virtually any results from fitting (4.14) are consistent with contract efficiency so their rather equivocal conclusions on this are hardly surprising.[16] These authors seem less alert to the fact that, as the previous paragraph argued, equations such as (4.14) (that is, equations where employment is related both to y and $\bar{y}$) are perfectly consistent with the first-order condition corresponding to models in which employment is set unilaterally by profit-maximizing management. Hence the somewhat negative judgements expressed by Bean and Turnbull, by Card, and by Nickell and Wadhwani about those models are unpersuasive.[17]

Abowd (1989) has taken a quite different route to test whether union-management contracts are efficient. Indeed, his research hypothesis is not merely that contracts are efficient, but also that they lie on a vertical contract curve. This means the union's objective function corresponds to the rent maximand and has an unambiguous monetary dimension. As noted by equation (4.12), this implies that a negotiated increase in earnings raises the union's utility by the same amount as it decreases management's profits. This remarkable result does not hold for positively sloped or negatively sloped contract curves of the sort corresponding to $\mu > 1$ and $\mu < 1$ in figure 4.1 although equation (4.12) holds as an approximation as the contract curve becomes steeper. Nor is it likely to be implied by certain bargaining models whose solutions lie off the contract curve though again there are circumstances under which the settlement will approach a dollar-for-dollar tradeoff.[18]

---

[16] For instance, Bean and Turnbull write, "the results . . . are at least consistent with the predictions of the efficient bargain model. Validating the latter is likely to be a very tricky business since the model does not appear to place any obvious testable restrictions on the data generation process."

[17] Card's conclusion is both well expressed and representative: "Both the labor demand model and the simplest efficient contracting model, which equates the marginal product of workers to their alternative wage rate, are rejected in favor of a more general model that includes contract and alternative wages in the employment equation. The parameter estimates for this model, however, are extremely imprecise and the implied reduced form employment equation fits poorly relative to an unrestricted auto regression" (Card, 1986, p. 1067).

[18] For instance, as George Johnson has pointed out, suppose $\mu = 1$ and the union maximizes $\Gamma = (y - \varphi(h) - \bar{y})E$. But suppose the union moves first by setting the

Of course, this implication holds only when the firm's total surplus, $\pi + \Gamma$, is fixed: when total rents, $\pi + \Gamma$, increase or decrease, management's profits and the union's utility will tend to move in the same direction, not in the opposite direction. Hence the empirical implementation of equation (4.12) needs to distinguish carefully between factors causing the joint surplus to change and factors causing the division of this surplus to change. The way Abowd effects this distinction is by drawing upon the efficient capital markets literature to argue that, at each moment, the value of the shareholders' traded equity incorporates all the information available about factors (current and future) affecting that wealth. The announcement of a collective bargaining agreement is presumed not to affect the firm's total value, but it is potentially new information relevant to the division of that value between the shareholders and the union. So when a new collective bargaining agreement is negotiated, the deviation of the shareholders' wealth from what was expected (say) three months earlier on the basis of available information will correspond exactly (though with opposite sign) to the deviation of the union's wealth from what was expected three months earlier on the basis of available information at that point.

Expressed differently, at settlement date s involving the jth firm–union pair, let $\Delta\pi_{sj}$ be the difference between the level of the shareholders' wealth and that level expected three months earlier and let $\Delta\Gamma_{sj}$ be the difference between the actual level of the relevant union's wealth and the level expected three months earlier. Then, if the collective bargaining settlement provides no new information about the total rents, $\pi + \Gamma$, but only information pertinent to its division between the shareholders and the union, then in a regression equation of the following form fitted to many firm–union pairs,

$$\Delta\pi_{sj} = \alpha + \beta\Delta\Gamma_{sj} + \epsilon_{sj}, \tag{4.15}$$

α should equal zero and β has an expected value of minus unity. (Here ϵ_{sj} is a mean zero randomly distributed disturbance term.) It is this equation that Abowd fits to data on 2,228 non-government non-construction contracts negotiated in the United States between 1976 and 1982.

He presents a number of different estimates of α and β depending upon the precise way in which the variables were constructed. The generalized least-squares estimates of α range from -17.4 (with an estimated

---

wage and, with the wage thus determined, management selects employment unilaterally. This inefficient bargaining outcome implies that, evaluated at the optimum, $\partial\pi/\partial y = -E$ (Hotelling's lemma) and $\partial\Gamma/\partial y = E(1 - e \cdot \Delta y)$ where $e = -(\partial E/\partial y)/(y/E)$ and $\Delta y = (y - \varphi(h) - \bar{y})/y$. The value of $\partial\pi/\partial y$ differs from $-\partial\Gamma/\partial y$ insofar as e or Δy diverges from zero.

standard error of 6.8) to 3.8 (with a standard error of 6.7). In most cases the null hypothesis that $\hat{\alpha}$ equals zero cannot be rejected. The estimates of β have a wider range. Where the values of the variables are constructed on the basis of a horizon of the same length as the collective bargaining contracts, the estimates of β range from -0.63 with a standard error of 0.19 to -0.93 with a standard error of 0.32. The central tendency of $\hat{\beta}$ is -0.77 with a standard error of about 0.27. So the hypothesis that $\hat{\beta} = -0.50$ is no less consistent with the data as $\hat{\beta} = -1.0$. $\hat{\beta}$ is consistently greater than minus unity though never significantly so by conventional criteria.[19]

When the effects of positive changes in $\Delta\Gamma_{sj}$ are distinguished from the effects of negative changes in $\Delta\Gamma_{sj}$, the estimated coefficients attaching to these separate variables are inclined not to be the same. In particular, increases in $\Delta\Gamma_{sj}$ tend to be associated with larger declines in $\Delta\pi_{sj}$ than the accompanying decreases in $\Delta\Gamma_{sj}$ and increases in $\Delta\pi_{sj}$. Abowd claims this is an "anomaly" generated by outliers involving the steelworkers' agreements in May 1980.

Abowd's study is a very conscientious piece of work and provides the most important evidence to date in support of the notion of labor-management settlements being negotiated on a vertical contract curve. The study's shortcomings are not so much errors in its execution, but more a consequence of what seem to be unavoidable difficulties in implementing equation (4.12). That is, the method depends crucially on the researcher being able to identify and hold constant shifts in the contract curve. In Abowd's work, this is effected by assuming that the constructed measures of shareholders' wealth and of union wealth expected three months before the collective bargaining agreement incorporate all relevant information concerning variables shifting the contract curve. But this is a heroic assumption. In modern empirical work, it is usual to allow for the fact that the researcher has less information than the actors whose behavior is being modelled. If, for instance, shareholders and unions have information about firm-specific product market conditions and this information is unavailable to the researcher,[20] then firm-specific shifts in the contract curve will not be held constant and the consequent non-random errors in measuring $\Delta\pi_{sj}$ and $\Delta\Gamma_{sj}$ will affect the estimates of α and β.

Also it should be noted that, in computing expected union rents over the life of the contract, Abowd fixes employment (or, more precisely, the

[19] It might be argued (though Abowd does not) that a coefficient estimate of β greater than minus unity is to be expected in the presence of taxes.

[20] This is an apt example: in Abowd's calculations of expected union wealth, no firm-specific information about product market conditions is used.

number of workers covered by the collective bargaining contract) at its level at the date of the agreement.[21] Actual employment over the life of the contract will probably diverge from this fixed level. There is the real possibility here that what Abowd has constructed in $\Delta\Gamma_{sj}$ is the effect *holding employment constant* of an increase in earnings on the net wage bill $(NWB) : \partial(NWB)/\partial y = E_0$. Suppose the left-hand side of equation (4.15) corresponds to the effect of an increase in earnings on the firm's net revenues (NR) holding employment constant. Then the estimating equation (4.15) may well be mapping not the behavioral relationship (4.12), but the accounting identity (4.13). I don't know how this identification problem can be resolved, but it seriously handicaps using this method to test for a vertical contact curve.

4.6   Specific Solutions of Efficient Contract Models

The previous sections discussed the characteristics of efficient contracts. As was emphasized, normally there are many different combinations of earnings, hours, and employment that satisfy the requirements of contract efficiency. It is not surprising, therefore, that the empirical work discussed in the preceding section should have made so little headway in determining whether collective bargaining contracts are efficient: little structure is imposed on the data by simply requiring contracts to be efficient. A natural response is to impose more structure on the problem by formulating relationships that have the effect of selecting one combination of variables among the many satisfying the conditions of efficiency. This issue is central in the literature on bargaining.

In essence, this literature is concerned with alternative rules that, for given values of a set of exogenous variables Y, associate with each value of π allocated to management a particular outcome Γ for the union:

$$\Gamma = \Omega(\pi; Y) \tag{4.16}$$

where $\partial\Gamma/\partial\pi \equiv \Omega' > 0$. One interpretation of this equation is that it describes the relative bargaining power of the two parties and the goal of the researcher is to determine the form of Ω corresponding to different rules of behavior for a pair of rational bargainers. A second interpretation of equation (4.16) has a heavy normative component according to which

---

[21] Abowd reports that about 40 percent of his observations lacked data on employment so, using information on the industry with which the contract was identified, he assigned an employment figure to these observations. In a personal communication (September 12, 1988), he says that when equation (4.15) was fitted to the sample whose employment was not imputed in this way, his estimates of α and β were barely affected.

the function Ω embodies the criteria that a fair or dispassionate arbitrator (making interpersonal utility comparisons) would follow in resolving the dispute between the parties.[22] Indeed, in the literature on the operation of arbitration systems for public workers, arbitrators are often (tacitly) endowed with a mechanism such as equation (4.16) to guide them in making awards.

For the profit maximand (4.4) above, the combinations of earnings, hours, employment, and capital that satisfy equation (4.16) for given values of Y are given by the equation

$$(g_1 + \Omega'E)dy + (g_2 - \Omega'R_2)dh + \left[g_3 - \Omega'(R_3 - y)\right]dE$$

$$+ \left[g_4 - \Omega'(R_4 - r)\right]dK = 0 \qquad (4.17)$$

where $R_2 \equiv \partial R/\partial h$, $R_3 \equiv \partial R/\partial E$, and $R_4 \equiv \partial R/\partial K$. Thus, for instance, the trade-off between earnings and employment (holding hours and capital constant) implied by the previous equation is

$$\frac{\partial y}{\partial E} = \frac{\Omega'(R_3 - y) - g_3}{\Omega'E + g_1}.$$

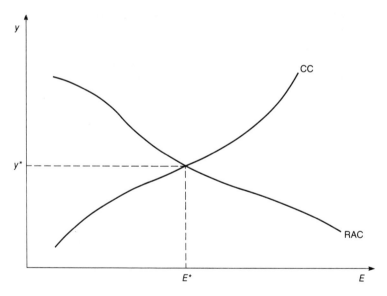

Figure 4.2   A rent allocation curve (RAC) and contract curve (CC) between earnings and employment.

[22] The positive interpretation is stressed by, for instance, Harsanyi (1977) and the normative interpretation by Raiffa (1953) who defines equation (4.16) as an arbitration scheme.

This describes a negatively sloped relationship between y and E illustrated by the rent allocation curve (RAC) in figure 4.2. An upward sloping contract curve (CC) has also been drawn in figure 4.2 and the combination of earnings and employment satisfying both the condition for contract efficiency and the rule for the allocation of rents is $y*E*$. A combination of earnings and employment along RAC, but off of CC, satisfies the rent allocation rule but is inefficient.

In the special case where the union's objective function is the Stone-Geary, equation (4.9), the slope of the earnings–employment tradeoff along the rent allocation curve is

$$\frac{\partial y}{\partial E} = \frac{\Omega'(R_3 - y) - (y - \varphi(h) - \bar{y})^{\mu}}{E[\Omega' + \mu(y - \varphi(h) - \bar{y})^{\mu - 1}]}$$

and, at the point where this rent allocation curve intersects the contract curve, the slope of the RAC is

$$\frac{\partial y}{\partial E} = -(\mu E)^{-1}(y - \varphi(h) - \bar{y}).$$

The literature on bargaining is designed to place more structure on the form of the rent allocation curve. There are two branches of this literature. The earlier approach was pioneered by Nash (1950) who modelled the bargaining process as a cooperative game. He specified a set of postulates or axioms about the nature of the game, and he identified properties the solution should possess and derived from these a particular function characterizing the solution of the bargaining problem. In the context of our labor-management bargaining model, Nash's proposed solution consists of those values of earnings, hours, employment, and capital that maximize the function Ψ:

$$\Psi(y, h, E, K; Z, \overline{W}, M) = (\Gamma - \overline{\Gamma})^{\alpha}(\pi - \bar{\pi})^{1-\alpha} \qquad (4.18)$$

where $\alpha = 1/2$ and $\overline{\Gamma}$ and $\bar{\pi}$ are the values of the union's and firm's payoffs in the event of no agreement being reached. This implies that, at the solution point, Ω' in equation (4.17) is a constant equal to the negative of the slope of the payoff frontier.[23] Because Ψ is a function of Γ and π, maximization of Ψ implies the parties will maximize their respective payoffs. Hence the maximand Ψ embodies the postulate of contract efficiency.

Using the same axiomatic approach to the bargaining problem, postulates different from Nash's have been examined and other solutions

---

[23] The payoff frontier is the locus of points where one party's payoff is maximized given a value for the other party's payoff.

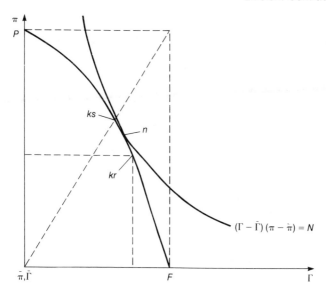

Figure 4.3   Alternative solution concepts.

proposed. The relationship between these solutions and Nash's is suggested by figure 4.3 where the payoff frontier is denoted by PF and the origin corresponds to the no-trade points $\bar{\pi}$, $\bar{\Gamma}$. Nash's solution is satisfied at point n where the curve $(\Gamma - \bar{\Gamma})(\pi - \bar{\pi}) = N$ is tangent to PF. Kalai and Smorodinsky (1975) suggested a division based on the relative maximum attainable net payoffs of the two parties. The same solution was proposed by Raiffa (1953) in one of his "arbitration schemes." It is satisfied at point ks in figure 4.3. Kalai (1977) and Raiffa (1953) have also proposed an egalitarian solution with the property that, among the points on the payoff frontier, its coordinates are equal. It is denoted by point kr in figure 4.3.[24] All three solutions graphed in figure 4.3 will coincide when the payoff frontier is symmetrical.

The other branch of the bargaining literature examines the process by which a sequence of offers and counteroffers converges over time to an agreement (or perhaps does not converge and no agreement obtains). Each party is endowed with a strategy that specifies particular rules of bargaining behavior. Thus in Zeuthen's (1930) early model, at any round in negotiations, the party with the smaller tolerance of risking conflict will revise its past offer and move toward a compromise. According to Harsanyi's (1956) interpretation, Zeuthen's bargaining process yields an

[24] Quite evidently, Kalai and Smorodinsky's solution and Kalai's and Raiffa's solution do not satisfy the axiom of independence of irrelevant alternatives.

outcome identical to Nash's. The work of Bishop (1964), Foldes (1964), Cross (1965), Stahl (1972), and others introduces the costs imposed on each party as time passes without agreement having been reached. The interesting feature of these models is that, when certain simplifying assumptions are made, they imply a solution to the bargaining problem that corresponds to the maximum value of the function Ψ in equation (4.18) except that α may take any value between zero and unity (and need not be one-half as in Nash's solution).

For instance, in Rubinstein's (1982) influential version, the parties make alternating offers concerning the division of a pie, X, that shrinks in size over time as they delay reaching an agreement. Party 1's portion of the pie is x and party 2's portion is $1 - x$. Assume that, after t negotiating periods, the value of party 1's portion of the pie is $x\delta_1^t$ and that of party 2 is $(1 - x)\delta_2^t$ where δ_1 and δ_2 are fixed discount rates with $0 < \delta_1, \delta_2 < 1$. In the finite horizon version of the model, let T denote the maximum number of periods over which negotiations take place. Assuming it is player 1's turn to make an offer, then in period T this constitutes an ultimatum so he proposes a division whereby he receives (virtually) all of the payoff X. Consequently, in period $T - 1$, player 1 (whose turn it is to respond to player 2's offer) will refuse any offer of less than $\delta_1 X$, but accept any offer of more so that player 2 receives the share $X - \delta_1 X$. Working backwards, in period $T - 2$, party 2 must be offered $\delta_2 (X - \delta_1 X)$ and party 1 receives $X - \delta_2 (X - \delta_1 X)$. In period $T - 3$, party 2 offers $X - \delta_1 (X - \delta_2 (X - \delta_1 X))$ and party 1 gets $\delta_1 (X - \delta_2 (X - \delta_1 X))$. And so on. As the number of periods over which negotiations take place gets larger, the (unique subgame perfect) equilibrium division involves party 1 receiving the portion $x^* = (1 - \delta_2) / (1 - \delta_1 \delta_2)$ with party 2 receiving the portion $1 - x^*$.

The equilibrium division appears to depend on which party happens to make the first offer as, indeed, it does in this discrete version of the bargaining process. In the continuous time version where party 1's utility is $xe^{-r_1 t}$ and party 2's is $(1 - x)e^{-r_2 t}$, if a length of one period of negotiation is Δ, then $\delta_i = e^{-r_i \Delta}$ and

$$\lim_{\Delta \to 0} x^*(\Delta) = \frac{r_2}{r_1 + r_2},$$

implying that the partition depends on relative time preferences only. This result is derivable from equation (4.18) if $\alpha = r_2 / (r_1 + r_2)$. In other words, differences in time preference make one party less willing to tolerate delay in reaching an agreement. The more impatient party will have a smaller exponent attached to his surplus payoffs in equation (4.18).

Another rationalization of an asymmetric solution to the bargaining problem relies on differences between the union and management in estimates of the probability of an agreement never being reached (see Binmore, Rubinstein and Wolinsky, 1986). As Harsanyi and Selten (1972) have shown, equation (4.18) will even accommodate bargaining problems in certain situations of mutual incomplete information such as when the total rents to be apportioned are not known with certainty, but the two parties agree on the probability distributions of these rents.

I am not arguing that the theoretical bargaining literature provides a persuasive, *a priori*, case for the asymmetric Nash solution. On the contrary, the strict assumptions needed to derive definitive results signal the special circumstances in which the models operate. For instance, the models often assume the parties are bargaining over a single variable and each possesses no private information about its valuations. On the other hand, the extent to which the asymmetric Nash solution crops up is noteworthy and, among the particular efficient solutions proposed, it is clearly the leading candidate for characterizing outcomes.

Applying the asymmetrical Nash solution, therefore, for the definition of π in equation (4.4) above, namely,

$$\pi(Wh, h, E, K; Z) = R(h, E, K; Z) - WhE - rK,$$

and for the Stone–Geary definition of Γ in equation (4.9), that is,

$$\Gamma(y, h, E; \bar{y}) = (y - \varphi(h) - \bar{y})^\mu E$$

where $\mu > 0$ and $\bar{y} = \overline{Wh}$, and assuming $\overline{\Gamma} = \bar{\pi} = 0$, the first-order conditions for a maximum of Ψ in equation (4.18) are as follows:

$$y: \left(\frac{\alpha}{1-\alpha}\right) = \frac{yE}{\pi} \cdot \frac{\Delta y}{\mu}$$

$$h: \left(\frac{\alpha}{1-\alpha}\right) = \frac{y R_2}{\pi \varphi'} \cdot \frac{\Delta y}{\mu}$$

$$E: \left(\frac{\alpha}{1-\alpha}\right) = \frac{yE}{\pi} \cdot \frac{(y - R_3)}{y}$$

$$K: r = R_4 \tag{4.19}$$

where $\Delta y \equiv (y - \varphi(h) - \bar{y})/y$, $R_2 \equiv \partial R/\partial h$, $R_3 \equiv \partial R/\partial E$, and $R_4 \equiv \partial R/\partial K$. The equations for y and E involve the ratio of the income received by labor, yE, to the income received by the firm's owners, π. In fact, this may help to rationalize the interpretation sometimes offered of movements in the share of wages in total incomes: periods when labor's share has increased have been construed as occasions when labor's relative bargaining power (here measured by α) has risen.[25] The first-order condition for employment, above, may be arranged to express per worker earnings, y, as proportional to the sum of the marginal revenue product of employment, R_3, and the per worker net revenue, $(R - rK)/E$:

$$y = (1 - \alpha)\left[\left(\frac{R - rK}{E}\right) + R_3\right]$$

and this holds independently of $\mu \geqq 1$.

4.7   Empirical Implications of Efficient Bargaining Models

For the profit maximand (4.4) and the Stone–Geary representation of Γ, equation (4.9), the first-order conditions describing the generalized Nash solution to the bargaining problem imply the following relationships between the bargaining variables on the one hand and the exogenous variables on the other hand:

$$\left\{ \begin{array}{l} y = y(\bar{y}, r, Z, \bar{\Gamma}, \bar{\pi}, \alpha) \\[4pt] h = h(\bar{y}, r, Z, \bar{\Gamma}, \bar{\pi}, \alpha) \\[4pt] E = E(\bar{y}, r, Z, \bar{\Gamma}, \bar{\pi}, \alpha) \\[4pt] K = K(\bar{y}, r, Z, \bar{\Gamma}, \bar{\pi}, \alpha) \; . \end{array} \right. \tag{4.20}$$

The qualitative content of this system is not straightforward to assess because it depends, *inter alia*, upon the form of the firm's revenue function $R(h, E, K; Z)$ and upon specific properties of the union's objective function (such as whether μ is greater or less than unity). Of course, restrictions on these functions may be posited, but then our interest in the comparative statics is thereby compromised by the unappealing assumptions made to derive them.

Some plausible conjectures can be submitted. For instance, increases in Z (denoting rightward shifts in the firm's product demand curve) move the contract curve to the right and this will tend to be associated with increases in employment. The corresponding changes in earnings and hours are more difficult to sign. An increase in $\bar{y}$ shifts the contract curve upwards and to the left and this will tend to raise negotiated earnings and reduce hours of work.

To illustrate the potential qualitative content of this approach, return to the profit maximand, equation (4.4), and the Stone–Geary function,

---

[25] Such an interpretation has been offered guardedly by, for instance, Phelps Brown and Hart (1952).

equation (4.9), and express equation (4.18) as $\Psi = [\,(y - \varphi\,(h) - \bar{y}\,)^{\mu}E\,]^{\alpha}$ $[\,R - yE - rK\,]^{1-\alpha}$. Suppose hours of work are predetermined at $\bar{h}$, suppose the production function is $X = AK^{a}E^{b}$ where A incorporates the effects of hours of work and $0 < b < 1$, and suppose the product demand curve is $p = X^{-c}Z^{d}$ where $0 < c < 1$ and $d > 0$. Increases in Z correspond to increases in consumers' expenditures and shift the product demand curve rightwards. Then the equations for earnings and employment are

$$\begin{cases} y = \tilde{\alpha}_{1}\left[\varphi(\bar{h}) + \bar{y}\right] \\ E = \tilde{\alpha}_{2}Z^{\tilde{\beta}_{1}}\left[\varphi(\bar{h}) + \bar{y}\right]^{\tilde{\beta}_{2}}r^{\tilde{\beta}_{3}} \end{cases} \qquad (4.21)$$

where $\tilde{\beta}_{1} = -\mathrm{d}\tilde{\beta}_{2} > 0$, $\tilde{\beta}_{2} = [\,(1 - c)\,(a + b) - 1\,]^{-1} < 0$, $\tilde{\beta}_{3} = a(1 - c)\tilde{\beta}_{2}$, and $\tilde{\alpha}_{1}$ and $\tilde{\alpha}_{2}$ involve convolutions of the other parameters. In this particular example, where the union's objectives are represented by the Stone–Geary function, earnings are independent of changes in Z and r so that, if Z were a cyclical indicator such as consumers' expenditure or if r were the price of oil, then these equations rationalize the widespread belief that employment is relatively volatile and wages relatively insensitive over the business cycle and that oil price shocks affect employment but not earnings.

If this bargaining model accurately describes the outcome of union-management negotiations, then the system of equations (4.20) should provide some guidance for understanding the empirical regularities with respect to earnings, hours, and employment described in chapter 2. In fact, usually the literature reviewed in chapter 2 has made only casual attempts to relate their findings to bargaining models of this sort. Thus it has long been surmised that unions stand to gain more from dealing with firms which enjoy certain monopolistic advantages in their product market.[26] Evidence for this proposition is mixed: on the one hand, Mellow (1983) found that union–nonunion wage differentials in US manufacturing tended to be lower in more highly concentrated industries and Stewart (1987) reported union–nonunion wage differentials for British skilled manual workers that were lower in the less competitive public sector; on the other hand, a number of economists have asserted (and a few have provided evidence to the effect) that in the United States unions have captured a share of the monopoly rents in industries whose

[26] The arguments are not always compatible with the bargaining model outlined in this chapter. For instance, one line of reasoning runs that collective bargaining earnings-employment agreements are not on the parties' contract curve but on the firm's employment demand curve and that this demand curve tends to be more inelastic for monopolistic firms whose product demand curve is likely to be more inelastic than that for competitive firms.

prices are regulated by government commissions.[27] In either event, the presence of Z in equations (4.20) rationalizes the notion that product demand conditions affect collective bargaining outcomes.

Also, it is not clear how the empirical regularities discussed in chapter 2 relate to the role of $\bar{y}$ in equations (4.20). In part this ambiguity arises because (as the discussion in chapter 3 emphasized) in some instances $\bar{y}$ may represent a comparison or reference level of earnings and in other instances $\bar{y}$ may stand for the level of earnings obtainable in some alternative activity. With respect to the former, I do not know of quantitative research relating the gains achieved by one union to the level of earnings negotiated by another union.[28] With respect to the latter, certainly there is a positive correlation across worker types between the earnings of union employees and those of nonunion employees, but whether this is the causal relationship implied by equation (4.20) is another (unaddressed) matter. As mentioned in section 4.5, recently a number of economists have investigated the association between employment and measures of $\bar{y}$ though most of these studies have entered both y and $\bar{y}$ on the right-hand side of employment equations in an attempt (misguided, according to my argument above) to determine whether collective bargaining contracts are efficient.

As far as $\bar{\Gamma}$, $\bar{\pi}$, and α in equations (4.20) are concerned, the theory outlined provides little guidance for their empirical counterparts. In one of the few attempts to apply this generalized Nash approach to the outcomes of a number of collective bargaining contracts, Svejnar (1986) expressed $\bar{\Gamma}$ as a function of alternative earnings, $\bar{y}$ (the same $\bar{y}$ that appears in the union's objective function), and specified α to be a function of variables such as the economy-wide unemployment rate, the rate of change of the consumer price index, and incomes policy variables. In fact, a good case could be made for a contrary allocation of these variables: for instance, the union's disagreement point, $\bar{\Gamma}$, may well depend on alternative job opportunities indexed by the unemployment rate; and the union's relative bargaining power, α, may be enhanced by an increase in alternative earnings, $\bar{y}$. The same sort of capricious specification characterizes Alogoskoufis and Manning's (1987) model of the aggregate British labor market: they maintain the ratio of wages to unemployment compensation affects the union's welfare (Γ) but not its bargaining power (α) while the union–nonunion wage differential affects the union's bar-

---

[27] See the arguments and evidence in Ehrenberg (1979) and Hendricks (1977). Convincing evidence on the trucking industry is reported by Hirsch (1988) and Rose (1987).

[28] There is a good deal of non-quantitative research maintaining the existence of pay comparisons among unionized workers. For example, see the discussion and the references cited in Chamberlain and Kuhn (1965, pp. 203–9), and also the analysis in chapter 6.

gaining power but not its welfare. Neither restriction seems compelling and this illustrates how the value of their bargaining model is undermined by the theory's reliance upon constructs whose observable counterparts are poorly defined.

Svejnar's (1986) research represents the most serious attempt to use this generalized Nash bargaining model to describe actual union–management settlements. His observations relate to US collective bargaining agreements for each of 12 major companies over the period from the mid-1950s to the late 1970s. Neglecting all inputs (including hours of work) other than employment and assuming a vertical earnings–employment contract curve,[29] Svejnar writes the first-order condition for earnings as follows:

$$(y - \bar{y})_t = \alpha \left(\frac{R - \bar{y}E - C}{E} \right)_t + \epsilon_t$$

where C denotes all nonlabor costs and ϵ is a stochastic disturbance.[30] He measures $\bar{y}$ by an index of industry-wide earnings either for the US as a whole or for the region in which each firm is located. As he notes, $\bar{y}$ is a mixture of union and nonunion wages. The ordinary least-squares[31] estimates of α range from a low of 0.06 (with an estimated standard error of 0.016) to a high of 0.72 (with a standard error of 0.031). Nash's symmetry postulate $\alpha = 0.5$ cannot be rejected for four of the 12 firms. This test of Nash's special case is perhaps the most useful aspect of

---

[29] In fact, he starts with a specification that allows for a nonvertical contract curve by writing each union's (net) welfare as

$$\Gamma - \bar{\Gamma} = \delta^{-1} \left(y^\delta - \bar{y}^\delta \right) (E/M)$$

from which a first order condition for earnings can be derived. Rearranging this and adding a stochastic error term (ϵ') yields the following equation where C denotes all nonlabor costs (which are treated as fixed):

$$E^{-1} = y(R - C)^{-1} + (1 - \alpha)\alpha^{-1}\delta^{-1}\left[y - y(\bar{y}/y)^\delta \right](R - C)^{-1} + \epsilon'.$$

This equation is fitted jointly with a stochastic form of the first-order condition for employment, this second equation helping to identify α. As mentioned in chapter 3, the point estimates of δ are very diverse and often startlingly high (one being six billion and another nine billion). Moreover, in virtually every case, most interesting hypotheses about δ (such as $\hat{\delta} = 1$ or $\hat{\delta} = 0$) cannot be rejected. In short, there is simply not much useful information in Svejnar's paper regarding the form of the union objective function so I concentrate in the text on his estimates of α conditional upon a vertical contract curve.

[30] This equation may be derived from the conditions (4.19) above for the Stone–Geary objective function on the assumption that $\mu = 1$, $\varphi(h) = 0$, and $C = rK$.

[31] Because disturbance terms never appear in Svejnar's paper, it is not easy to determine the appropriateness of his estimating techniques. As for the use of ordinary least-squares for Svejnar's equation, it could be regarded as audacious to maintain that, for instance, the firm's gross revenues are distributed independently of ϵ_t.

Svejnar's article because it is difficult to evaluate the performance of the general bargaining model as a description of wage and employment behavior in these firms.

4.8 Experimental Evidence on Bargaining

The evidence discussed above makes use of field data, that is, observations generated by the actual workings of the economy. For several decades now, there has been another source of evidence on bargaining, namely, that garnered from laboratory experiments. In these, individuals are presented with monetary payoffs and placed in a bargaining setting with the parameters of the environment carefully controlled. Corresponding to the two classes of bargaining models outlined in section 4.6, the axiomatic approach initiated by Nash and the sequential, alternating offers, approach characterized by Rubinstein's model, there are two classes of experimental work.

The experimental framework designed by Roth and Malouf (1979) and adopted by a number of other researchers[32] is designed to test Nash's solution. In this framework, two individuals bargain over the allocation of lottery tickets, each ticket enabling the holder to win a monetary prize. The value of the prize is sometimes the same to each party and sometimes it is different. The more lottery tickets held, the greater the probability of winning the prize and, provided each individual's preferences can be represented by an expected utility formulation, then the utility functions of each player are known exactly (up to a linear transformation).[33] The expected utility postulate constitutes one of the maintained hypotheses of this branch of the experimental literature and, in chapter 3, I have already expressed serious misgivings about it as a characterization of trade union objectives.

Nash's solution predicts, of course, that each party should receive one-half of the lottery tickets (the equal probability agreement) and that this is invariant to the monetary value of the prizes. In fact, equal probability agreements tend to be the outcome when each party is fully informed of his and his opponent's prizes and when the two parties have equal prizes. However, when the parties have different prizes, the full information games tend to generate two outcomes (or "focal points"), one being the

---

[32] The literature prior to 1979 is summarized in Roth and Malouf (1979) and the literature from 1979 is reviewed in Roth (1987).

[33] That is, because the information regarding preferences embodied in an expected utility function is meaningful only up to an arbitrary origin and scale, each player's utility can be expressed so that the utility of the prize is unity and the utility of not winning is zero.

equal probability agreement and the other being the equal expected value agreement (i.e., each bargainer obtains the same expected value so that the party faced with a higher prize accepts fewer lottery tickets). So, contrary to Nash's prediction, outcomes are affected by the monetary values of the prizes.

The results of these experiments are particularly sensitive to the amount of information available to each of the parties. When each party knows his own prizes only, equal probability agreements tend to be negotiated. But when one party knows both prizes and the other knows his prize only, the equal expected value agreement is a focal point provided it is the player with the smaller prize who knows both prizes. Also, in many cases, the parties simply fail to reach an agreement. The frequency of disagreement is greatest when the player with the smaller prize knows both prizes and the player with the highest prize knows his prize only, but the smaller prize player does not know that the other player does not know both prizes. In this game, the increased share obtained by the player with the smaller prize when agreements are negotiated almost exactly offsets the increase in the number of disagreements, a result consistent with the hypothesis that the bargainers are trading higher payoffs for a higher probability of disagreement.

The experimental research relating to the sequential, alternating offers, models of bargaining differs from that just described in that the amount of money being divided (the portions being the topic of bargaining) shrinks as negotiations continue without agreement being reached. Such a situation might correspond to union–management negotiations once a strike has occurred, the strike imposing costs on both parties.[34] It is assumed that the bargainers' utilities are identical to their monetary payoffs, an assumption that might call into question the bearing of this research to the union–management bargaining discussed in this chapter. The experiments involve tracking the outcomes of bargaining between pairs of individuals where the control parameters consist of T, the maximum number of periods over which negotiations take place, and δ_1 and δ_2, the rates at which the monetary payoffs shrink for party 1 and for party 2, respectively. As shown in section 4.6, when bargaining takes place by alternating offers in a sequence of fixed time intervals, a unique division of the payoffs can be determined for given values of δ_1, δ_2, and T so there is a clear prediction for the experiments to test.[35]

[34] Of course, nothing is implied about why a strike has occurred. Some of the literature on strikes is discussed in the next chapter.

[35] To be precise, a unique division would be implied if the units bargained over were perfectly divisible, but where they are restricted to integer quantities the equilibrium division may specify a range of values.

In fact, in most of the experiments to date, the equilibrium implied by Rubinstein's theory does not describe the outcomes well. In some instances, the theory implies quite lopsided splits, but such unequal divisions are infrequently observed.[36] In many cases, player 1's first-period offers are rejected by player 2 and, furthermore, player 2's counteroffer involves less cash for himself than player 1 had offered in his previous proposal! This latter result flatly contradicts the postulate that player 2's utility is measured by his monetary payoff. Even in the last round of bargaining, when the game enters an ultimatum phase, there seem to be a remarkable number of instances in which offers of unequal splits are rejected and both parties walk away with nothing.

In their forthright review of their and other experimental research, Ochs and Roth (1989) suggest that the parties' concepts of equity, of a fair resolution of the game, enter into bargaining problems. Offers diverging "too much" from equal splits are more likely to be rejected even if the rejecting party loses money as a result. Disagreements (with their associated costs) are tolerated if avoiding them means accepting an unfair division. Ochs and Roth conclude that the players "try to estimate the abilities of the player they are bargaining with and . . . at least some agents incorporate distributional considerations in their utility functions. Since offers (not to mention agreements) reflect a bargainer's estimate of his opponent's behavior, they do not directly reveal anything about the utility of either individual. . . . [T]he utilities cannot simply be assumed to be equal to the monetary payoffs of the players" (p. 379).

The importance in economic decision-making of perceptions of fairness has been noted in many situations other than those of pure bargaining. For instance, when prices and wages are adjusted to changed economic circumstances, Kahneman, Knetsch and Thaler (1986) find consistent

---

[36] To illustrate this, consider the following example. Suppose $T = 2$ and player 1 makes the first offer by proposing a division of $20 which player 2 may accept or reject. If player 2 rejects, it is his turn to make an offer, but in this second round the total value of the "pie" shrinks to $4 (implying $\delta_1 = \delta_2 = 0.20$). If player 2's offer is rejected, both parties receive nothing. When it is player 2's turn to make an offer he can present player 1 with an ultimatum: $3.99 for player 2 and $0.01 for player 1. So, at the first round, any offer that player 1 makes to player 2 that is an improvement on $3.99 should be accepted by player 2. Hence player 1 offers $4.00 to player 2 which should be accepted. The prediction is then that player 1 takes $16 and player 2 takes $4 of the $20 pie, an 80 percent–20 percent split. In fact, such unequal splits are rarely observed in the experimental literature: player 2 rejects such unequal offers even though he is guaranteed to lose money by so doing. One of the experiments designed by Ochs and Roth (1989) comes close to this example. When $T = 3$, $\delta_1 = 0.6$, and $\delta_2 = 0.4$, the equilibrium of the alternating offers model predicts that player 1 will receive 84 percent of the payoff and player 2 will receive 16 percent. In fact, player 1's opening offer proposed roughly 55 percent for himself on average and 45 percent for player 2. In other words, the offers came much closer to an equal division of the payoffs.

patterns of attitudes regarding those adjustments deemed justified and those deemed unacceptable. To avoid the disfavor and disrepute of behaving "unfairly," actors will depart from behavior predicted by the standard model of decision-making.[37] Kahneman, Knetsch and Thaler suggest that the standard of fair behavior is provided by the "reference transaction." This is usually the terms on which a transaction was made in the past and it assumes the status of a relevant precedent defining what is normal or acceptable.[38]

If their arguments are correct and the experimental literature on bargaining intimates they may well be,[39] an understanding of current

[37] A vivid illustration of this is provided by the severe gasoline shortage on the west coast of the USA in 1920. Olmstead and Rhode (1985) have described how the gasoline companies responded to the shortage not by raising prices, but by developing and administering a complex allocation scheme of the sort usually associated with government rationing programs. Why did firms use non-price rationing methods? The authors argue, "Internal documents show that Standard Oil of California's leaders . . . were clearly concerned with their public image and tried to maintain the appearance of being "fair". . . . To the extent that the gas famine was seen as the result of the drought (an act of nature) and the illegal railroad walkout (an act against society), it would be improper for a "bastion of capitalism" to exploit the situation. The recent wartime experiences also strengthened the sentiment for nonprice rationing as a patriotic way to deal with market adjustments" (p. 1053).

[38] "A central concept in analyzing the fairness of actions in which a firm sets the terms of future exchanges is the *reference transaction*, a relevant precedent that is characterized by a reference price or wage, and by a positive reference profit to the firm. . . . Transactors have an entitlement to the terms of the reference transaction and firms are entitled to their reference profit. . . . Market prices, posted prices, and the history of previous transactions between a firm and a transactor can serve as reference transactions. When there is a history of similar transactions between firm and transactor, the most recent price, wage, or rent will be adopted for reference unless the terms of the previous transaction were explicitly temporary. . . . The relevant reference transaction is not always unique. Disagreements about fairness are most likely to arise when alternative reference transactions can be invoked, each leading to a different assessment of the participants' outcomes. . . . [T]he reference transaction provides a basis for fairness judgments because it is normal, not necessarily because it is just. Psychological studies of adaption suggest that any stable state of affairs tends to become accepted eventually, at least in the sense that alternatives to it no longer readily come to mind. Terms of exchange that are initially seen as unfair may in time acquire the status of a reference transaction" (Kahneman, Knetsch and Thaler, 1986, pp. 729–31).

[39] In addition to the experimental results already described, the experiments of Roth and Schoumaker (1983) also bear on the potential relevance of the reference transaction. They presented players with computer programs as opponents, the computers being programmed to work towards a particular (often quite unequal) outcome of the game. The players were not aware that their opponents were computers programmed to produce a particular outcome. After a number of rounds played against the computer, the players were pitted against other human beings. In these games, the player who had been "conditioned" by the games with the computer to expect a particular (perhaps unequal) split carried these expectations over to the all-human games. Expressed differently, the splits in the games involving the computer served as a reference transaction in subsequent games.

union–management bargaining outcomes cannot be reached without reference to the history of the outcomes: what is negotiated today depends, in part, on how the negotiations were resolved the last time the contract was renewed. This would help to rationalize the common practice of relating current values of variables to their values in the past, a practice often paralogized by a vague allusion to costs of adjustment but which is rarely expressed explicitly in terms of the parameters of an adjustment cost function. If perceptions of fairness affect bargaining outcomes and if fairness is related to outcomes in the past, then shocks experienced in a given period specific to a particular bargaining pair may affect the entire historical evolution of wages, employment, and hours of work in that firm or industry.

If, on the other hand, standards of fairness are more closely tied to bargaining outcomes in other, neighboring, union–management negotiations, then this calls for the values of variables determined in one bargain to be related to those negotiated in other bargains. There already exists, in fact, research examining such interactions and it is reviewed in chapter 6. Indeed, the notion of a reference transaction will not be foreign to many industrial relations specialists who for a long time have testified to the relevance of custom and fairness in understanding certain labor market outcomes. It is also consistent with arguments in chapter 3 where I made a case for the presence in a union's objective function of wages in other comparable jobs: workers do not conceive of this other job as a genuine, alternative, employment opportunity, but they use the wage on this job as a reference with which to gauge the performance of their leaders in working for the interests of the rank-and-file. However the reference transaction is formed, the experimental work strongly suggests that economics research on collective bargaining outcomes should pay closer, explicit, attention to notions of fairness and equity.

4.9 Conclusions

This chapter has been devoted to an exposition of the central features of simple efficient collective bargaining contracts. I have argued that the requirement for contracts to be efficient imposes very little structure on observations of wages, hours, employment, and other variables so that economists' ability to assess the empirical relevance of contract efficiency in labor markets is severely circumscribed. Under these circumstances, it has perhaps been surprising that, in order to place more structure on these models, economists have invoked particular solution concepts so infrequently. The primary purpose of appealing to a particular solution concept is to reduce the multiplicity of equilibria compatible with efficiency. It is not clear whether, for this purpose, the use of such solution concepts to help organize data on wages, hours, and employment is in some sense a more drastic assumption than assumptions made when undertaking empirical work in other areas of economics. Economists have tended to handicap themselves unduly by their reluctance to examine the empirical implications of particular solution concepts and much more might be learned about efficient contracts in labor markets if economists shook off this reluctance.

The experimental literature on bargaining has been a most useful contribution to knowledge. Because the experiments endow the parties with simple, monetary, payoffs, it is natural to question their value for union–management bargaining where, at least on the union's side, objectives are typically less straightforward. However, it is the purity of the experimental environment that makes the experimental results so very interesting. The fact that, even in so simple and unaffected a setting, bargaining outcomes are sensitive both to the information available to the parties and to common notions of equity strongly suggests the relevance of these considerations in actual union–management bargaining. Of course, the Nash bargaining solution was originally designed with little consideration given to the role of incomplete information so it would seem unwise to apply it widely to many different circumstances. It needs to be used circumspectly and other solution concepts should be given due consideration.

5 Recursive Contracts

5.1 Introduction

The labor contracts discussed in the previous chapter are fully efficient. The notion of efficiency has a powerful hold on economists weaned on the principle that, if left unconstrained, individuals will exhaust the possibilities of mutual gains from trade with each other. However, the circumstances under which such efficient contracts will obtain are restrictive. There are several reasons for this.

First, the arguments in chapter 4 have presumed that wages, employment, and hours of work represent the bargaining agenda, but there is really the prior question of how the bargaining agenda are determined. In fact, one party may ascertain that its bargaining power is greater if it can successfully maintain exclusive control over a particular variable and omit an item from the scope of bargaining. For instance, management may calculate that its profits associated with an efficient contract in which employment is jointly negotiated with the union would be smaller than its profits associated with a contract in which it exercises unilateral control over employment. (In terms of figure 5.1 (p. 134) management may determine that negotiations with the union over employment will result in an efficient contract at a where profits are π_1 whereas, if it is able to negotiate y_c and prevent any joint negotiations over employment, it can realize profits of π_3 at b.) In this case, management calculates it would not realize a higher payoff from a move to the contract curve and so it would be willing to spend resources to maintain its exclusive control over employment. The potential for higher profits from an efficient contract will not be realized if the union cannot or will not persuade management that it will suffer no reduction in profits by admitting the level of employment into the bargaining agenda. More generally, the attainment of efficient contracts may be frustrated if the parties cannot reach a mutually satisfactory agreement on what it is that they will bargain about.

Second (and related to the first), each party is better informed about its own valuations than its opponent's. Thus management may well have a poor knowledge of the union's objective function and so may make an offer that appears to management to be Pareto superior to the initial contract but that is not judged by the union to be Pareto superior. Indeed, as numerous observers of the mechanics of collective bargaining have noted, the very nature of bargaining between management and labor usually involves each party engaging in threats, bluffs, and deceptions designed to misrepresent its true valuations. In other words, it is by no means clear that the negotiation process in collective bargaining provides incentives for the parties to reveal their respective valuations and thus there can be no assurance that an efficient contract will be reached.

Third, even if, at the time of their negotiation, collective bargaining contracts are efficient, they are not renegotiated each time the environment alters. This means that, unless wages, hours, and employment are specified fully as functions of the environment, efficient contracts negotiated at the time of a new collective bargaining agreement may lie off the contract curve soon after when circumstances change. In fact, a number of contracts contain provisions for altering their terms when certain circumstances change, but the set of contingencies is incomplete, a consequence in part of the well-known problems of observing and verifying whether the contingencies have actually occurred. The union and management are well aware that circumstances unforeseen at the time of contract negotiation occur during the lifetime of the contract and consequently some discretion is permitted in altering certain variables. For instance, few contracts actually specify the precise number of employees, but it is common for management to be required to follow certain procedures regarding hires, training, transfers, promotions, work scheduling, layoffs, and retirements. These rules constrain management's decisions over the level and structure of employment. Whether the resulting employment is on or off a shifting contract curve is difficult to determine.

Fourth, efficient contracts need to prevail over moral hazard problems. That is, the previous paragraph has referred to the costs of adjusting the terms of an efficient contract to changes in the environment. Even when the environment does not change, each party has an immediate incentive to disregard its contractual agreements and to engage in behavior that enhances its own welfare at the expense of the other party's. For instance, employees' hours at the workplace may correspond to those negotiated, but through malingering they may diverge from effective work hours. Correspondingly, management may reduce contractual employment by failing to hire replacements for those who separate through voluntary quits, illnesses, deaths, and retirements. Hence, each party needs to monitor the performance of the other to ensure the terms of the contract are being fulfilled. Disputes during the administration of a contract are common and some of them may well reflect attempts by one party to improve its payoffs by moving off the contract curve.

Therefore, there should be no presumption that collective bargaining contracts are fully efficient: first, the negotiation of efficient contracts may be obstructed by a failure to reach agreement over the bargaining agenda; second, it is not clear whether the bargaining process provides incentives for each party to reveal its true valuations and thereby effect agreements on the contract curve; third, negotiation costs and considerations of bounded rationality imply that contractual terms are not fully contingent on the values of the exogenous variables; and, fourth, it is costly to determine whether the parties are honoring their agreements. Under these circumstances, it would seem appropriate to treat contract efficiency as a research hypothesis rather than as a maintained hypothesis and to inquire into other types of bargaining outcomes.

The purpose of this chapter is to explore certain models of wage, employment, and hours determination that do not necessarily satisfy the conditions of full contract efficiency as defined previously. The following section describes *recursive* models according to which wages and perhaps the capital–labor ratio are first negotiated and then management determine the level of employment and other factor inputs. I then assess what the literature on dispute resolution (strikes and arbitration) has to contribute to the study of wages, employment, and hours of work. A discussion of how hours of work might fit into recursive bargaining models is the topic of section 5.5. Particular functional forms are presented in section 5.6 to provide an application of a recursive model. The case of producer cooperatives is discussed in section 5.7. In section 5.8, I outline an empirical procedure for assessing whether the determination of employment in unionized markets is best understood through the use of a conventional wage-taking labor demand function.

5.2   Recursive Bargaining Models: Employment and Wages

Most non-efficient models of collective bargaining treat the negotiated variables asymmetrically. The asymmetry arises from the observation that collective bargaining agreements tend to specify wage rates and fringe benefits precisely while the provisions relating to employment are typically indirect. There are two classes of these indirect employment provisions.

One class takes the form of procedures to be followed with respect to turnover – hires, promotions, layoffs, retirements, etc. For instance, in unionized construction and longshoring in the United States, a large portion of hiring takes place through the union or a union hiring hall. Outside these industries, closed or union shop agreements are designed to restrict the pool of new hires to existing union members or those willing to join the union.[1] With respect to layoffs, a number of contracts restrict layoffs by requiring labor input adjustments to take the form first of hours of work reductions while other contracts specify those workers (usually temporary workers or workers on subcontract) whom management may first layoff. Advance notice of layoffs is common as is severance pay. Some of these provisions are directed to the composition of employment rather than to the number of employees, but there may well be occasions on which the employment level is not independent of its structure.

Another class of collective bargaining provisions relates not to the number of workers, but to the assignment of workers to machines, processes, and activities. There are regulations on the number of workers operating a machine, on the particular activities that each type of worker may be required to undertake, on the speed of assembly-line work, on the maximum weights that each worker may be asked to lift, and so on. Each industry has its own particular set of work rules that makes it difficult to generalize about their specific form. However, their presence in collective bargaining contracts seems indisputable: in the United States among major contracts in 1980, approximately 22 percent of workers were covered by rules limiting or regulating crew size and 61 percent were covered by rules restricting work by those outside the bargaining unit.[2]

No doubt, some of these work rules are not binding on management or are not honored, but equally there will be customs and conventions regarding capital–labor ratios and work pace that are not enshrined in formal agreements yet operate as effective constraints on work behavior. There is a long line of research documenting how social pressure and tradition in nonunion as well as union plants may operate as effectively

---

[1] The *British Workplace Industry Relations* surveys (Millward and Stevens, 1986) reported that in 1980 the management of 69 percent of all establishments and in 1984, 38 percent of all establishments negotiated with their trade unions at some time about the number of people recruited. In 1984, 30 percent of manual employees and 8 percent of non-manual employees in Britain were covered by closed shop agreements.

[2] See table 7.5 of US Department of Labor (1981) Bulletin 2095. In the British Workplace Industrial Relations Survey for 1984, 55 percent of unionized plants bargained at one time over staffing or manning levels for manual workers. This figure was as high as 77 percent in the nationalized industries. (See Millward and Stevens, 1986, table 9.19.)

as formal rules to regulate the work performed by each employee and to sustain a particular level of employment.[3]

A general assessment regarding the consequences of these indirect provisions on employment – those relating to turnover and those relating to work activities or to the work pace – is difficult. In some cases they may operate to keep employment on or very close to that corresponding to the contract curve. In other cases, the effects of these provisions on the level of employment may be of little account and, taking the wage rate as given by the collective bargaining contract, management adjusts employment to its profit-maximizing level. The situation is depicted in figure 5.1 where CC denotes the contract curve and DD a conventional wage-taking employment demand curve. The coordinates to a specify the earnings-employment combination corresponding to an efficient contract while at b management has taken earnings as given at y_c and has reduced employment from E_c to E_d (thereby raising profits from those on isoprofit curve π_1 to those on π_3). At b, management is on its wage-taking profit-maximizing employment demand function where the marginal revenue product of employment equals per worker earnings:

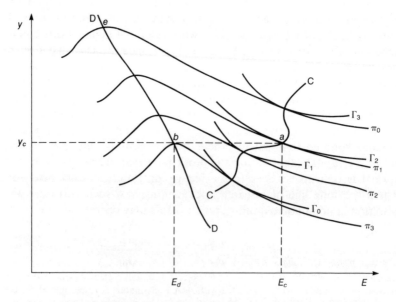

Figure 5.1   Employment on a contract curve (CC) and on an employment demand curve (DD).

[3] The classic work is Mathewson (1931) though the literature is extensive. For instance, Lupton (1963) and Roethlisberger and Dickson (1939).

$$R_3 = y \qquad (5.1)$$

where $R_3 \equiv \partial R / \partial E$.

Of course these indirect controls over employment may place the parties neither at a nor at b, but somewhere in between. Indeed, George Johnson (1990) has shown this to be precisely the case when the collective bargaining contract successfully specifies the capital–labor ratio. In his model, at the first stage, the union and management jointly determine the wage rate and the capital–labor ratio and, at the second stage, with the production "activity" thus specified, management unilaterally selects the levels of employment and of capital services. The earnings–employment combinations satisfying this type of collective bargain lie on a curve between DD and CC in figure 5.1.[4] Given the expression for the firm's profits in equation (4.4) above, Johnson's characterization of the collective bargaining contract implies that, at the second stage, the employment-capital ratio must satisfy the relation

$$\frac{E}{K} = - \frac{(r - R_4)}{(y - R_3)} \qquad (5.2)$$

where $R_3 = \partial R / \partial E$ and $R_4 = \partial R / \partial K$. For positive values of both inputs, this means that, whereas labor is employed such that the marginal revenue product of employment falls short of earnings, capital's marginal revenue product exceeds its price. Put differently, more workers and less capital are being used compared with a situation in which profit-maximizing management hires its inputs freely at given prices. With the union's objectives given by equation (4.2) above, that is, $\Gamma = g(Wh, h, E; \overline{W}, M)$ it can be shown that the marginal revenue product of employment may be expressed as follows:

$$R_3 = y - \chi(g_3 g_1^{-1}) E \qquad (5.3)$$

where, for plausible forms of the revenue function, $0 \leq \chi \leq 1$.[5] Comparison with equation (4.6) indicates that, with a fully efficient labor contract, $\chi = 1$, while when profit-maximizing management exercises unilateral control over employment, as indicated in equation (5.1), $\chi = 0$.

---

[4] Johnson's specific results are derived from particular assumptions about the forms of the production function (constant returns to scale) and the union objective function (Stone-Geary). However, these assumptions are primarily for expositional purposes only and the general conclusion about employment being off both the labor demand curve and the contract curve holds under more general conditions. Also see Clark (1989a, b).

[5] Here $\chi = 1 - \mu^* g_3^{-1} (R_{34} + EK^{-1} R_{33})$ where μ^* is the Lagrange multiplier on the constraint (5.2) and $\mu^* = - g_3 (EK^{-1} R_{33} + 2R_{34} + E^{-1} KR_{44})^{-1}$. $R_{34} = \partial^2 R / \partial E \partial K$, $R_{33} = \partial^2 R / \partial E^2$, and $R_{44} = \partial^2 R / \partial K^2$. With the sort of efficient contracts described in the previous chapter (that is, without constraints on the labor–capital ratio), $\mu^* = 0$ and $\chi = 1$.

In the case of equation (4.6), employment was jointly negotiated with earnings and hours of work while, in the narrative underlying equations (5.1) and (5.3), some structure was placed on the time *sequence* of decision-making: earnings (and, in Johnson's model, the capital–labor ratio) are determined at the first stage and then management unilaterally adjusts employment. Such a causal chain is characteristic of a *recursive* system according to which the variables negotiated at the first stage affect those determined at the second stage.[6]

5.3 Asymmetrical Information, Strikes, and Specific Human Capital

Models with recursive features are common in the recent literature on industrial disputes or strikes. In this literature, the union and management are usually modelled as negotiating over the wage rate; either employment is assumed to be fixed or it simply does not enter the analysis.[7] The central issue motivating this literature (what Kennan (1986) calls "the Hicks Paradox") is why strikes occur if their effect is to shrink the joint rents available for division between the parties. If the union and management are endowed with the same (perhaps incomplete) information about each other's objectives and opportunities, they should be able to negotiate an outcome that is no worse than what would emerge from a strike and yet that avoids these wasteful costs. Hence, it is argued, models admitting the possibility of strikes would seem to require informational asymmetries, one party being privy to information not available to the other.

The first analytical model of strikes incorporating such asymmetrical information was Ashenfelter and Johnson's (1969).[8] They argued that, in certain circumstances, the union rank-and-file are inclined to hold exaggerated expectations about the wage obtainable on a new contract. A strike has the effect of moderating the workers' aspirations.[9] Hence

[6] Of course, in the econometrics literature, a recursive system also requires uncorrelated disturbances across structural equations.

[7] An exception is Hayes (1984) who examines the incentives for strikes both in contracts restricted to wages and in contracts specifying wages and employment.

[8] It bears similarities with Hicks's (1963) theory of industrial disputes, Hicks maintaining that "the majority of actual strikes are doubtless the result of faulty negotiation" (p. 146).

[9] In fact, three parties figured in Ashenfelter and Johnson's commentary: the management, the union rank-and-file, and the union leadership. No informational asymmetries were posited between the union leadership and the management, but the union leaders were presumed not always able to convince their members of what was attainable. Therefore, their analysis holds even without the union leadership interposed between the membership and the management.

there is a negative trade-off, a "resistance curve," between wages, W, and strike length, D, that the firm may optimize against:

$$W = W(D, X_1)$$ (5.4)

where X_1 stands for exogenous influences on this resistance curve. The firm's profits may be written $\pi = \pi(W, D, X_2)$ where $\partial\pi/\partial W < 0$ and $\partial\pi/\partial D < 0$ and where X_2 represents other exogenous variables. Taking the union's resistance curve as given, the firm chooses the strike length (perhaps zero) to maximize $\pi(W(D, X_1), D, X_2)$ which implies for $D > 0$ that the marginal rate of substitution of strike length for wages in the firm's profit function be equal to the slope, $-\partial W/\partial D$, of the union's resistance curve. According to this characterization, if the workers were not so poorly informed of the firm's profit function, the wage agreement that concluded the strike could have been obtained without the cost of a strike. The model offers an explanation for the occurrence of strikes, for their duration, and for the wage on the new contract although the authors restricted their empirical analysis to an investigation of only the first of these, a time-series study of aggregate strike frequency.[10]

The profound insight of Ashenfelter and Johnson's model is that a satisfactory account of strikes requires the presence of private information and it is this idea that has characterized the more recent literature.[11] Indeed, some of this literature may be understood as trying to provide some behavioral underpinnings to the resistance curve, equation (5.4). In these models,[12] the union is portrayed as incompletely informed about the firm's profits and makes wage demands which the firm can meet if its profits are robust, but which the firm will not grant otherwise. In the latter situation, the firm prefers to accept a strike, the effect of which is to signal to the union that, indeed, the firm's profitability does not warrant its original wage demands.[13] The strike induces the union to

[10] In fact, one of the model's endogenous variables (strike frequency) was regressed on another endogenous variable (wage changes).

[11] As a comment on fashions in economics, I might note that, for about a decade after the publication of their article, the asymmetrical treatment of the union and management was regarded as a shortcoming of Ashenfelter and Johnson's model. By contrast, in the most recent decade, it has been regarded as a significant insight.

[12] See, for instance, Fudenberg, Levine and Ruud (1983) and Hayes (1984).

[13] And there is some evidence that this happens in just this way sometimes. "Unions are likely to be skeptical of management's claim that a reduction in labor costs is needed to help the plant or enterprise survive. They have heard managements in wage negotiations argue time and again that they could not afford to meet certain demands, and yet when the demands have been conceded, the enterprises have met them. Consequently, even when the inability-to-pay argument is valid and the management must have relief, the union may not realize it. For this reason,. . . management may have to prove its sincerity by taking a strike" (Slichter, Healy and Livernash, 1960, p. 825).

moderate its wage demands until a point is reached when a settlement with the firm is possible. In some versions of this private information theory of strikes, bargaining takes place over time with a fixed delay specified between succeeding offers (Hart, 1989).

An evaluation of this approach to the study of strikes necessarily involves assessing the likely importance of these problems introduced into bargaining by the union's misperceptions of the firm's profits. No doubt, in many cases, the union is incompletely informed about the firm's current and future profits, but it is certainly not ignorant of them. The workers, after all, are contributing to the production of the goods for sale and are well informed of the length of production runs, overtime, subcontracting, and other indicators of output. In the service industries, for accounting purposes, output is often measured simply in terms of the labor input in which case the workers may be almost as well informed of sales as management.

It is sometimes not difficult for the union leadership to get access to sales and inventory data and, in these models, it is in management's interest to supply these data. Indeed, some firms post such information. Many unions have research departments whose job includes following sales and profits. Furthermore, what matters for union–management negotiations is not merely current profits but future profits, and management must estimate these just as much as the union. Differences between management and the union may certainly induce a strike, but in this instance it is no longer clear that the relation between strike length and wage identifies a union resistance curve, equation (5.4), rather than some hybrid union–management concession schedule.

It should also be recognized that, in most cases, collective bargaining contracts specify automatic extensions beyond their expiration dates unless the firm or the union explicitly terminates the contract and, in fact, it appears that most instances in which a settlement occurs after the expiration of the previous contract do *not* involve a strike.[14] Presumably, as negotiations extend beyond the expiration of the old contract, information is being transmitted between the two sides. However, this is being accomplished without the signal of a strike being provided so, at least in a large number (perhaps a majority) of cases, strikes are not being used as a screening mechanism.

In any event, the obvious difficulty in applying these models is that their central features depend upon the characteristics of the union's informa-

---

[14] In the Bureau of National Affairs' (1986, p. 4) sample of contracts, 86 percent of agreements have automatic renewal provisions. In Herrington's (1988) sample of 1,191 contracts between 1955 and 1985, 60.5 percent of the contracts signed after the expiration of the previous contract did *not* involve a strike.

tion set so that to put them to use in any practical context a researcher needs to augment the model with auxiliary hypotheses about the way in which each party's beliefs are formed. For instance, Tracy (1987) postulates that the union's uncertainty about the firm's profits is indicated by the volatility of the firm's market value and he finds that in US manufacturing industries between 1973 and 1977 both the probability of a strike and its duration are positively associated with this volatility. Along similar lines, Herrington (1988) supposed that the variance in a forecast error of sales indexed the union's ex ante uncertainty and, with data for 82 firms over 30 years (1955–85), he found both the probability of a strike and its duration to be positively correlated with this variance. However, when Hirtle (1985) applied Tracy's procedure to a sample of contracts covering a longer period of time (1957-80), she reported little association between such indicators of uncertainty and strike incidence. These results bear as much on the plausibility of the auxiliary hypothesis (that the union's uncertainty about the firm's profits is measured by these indicators) as on the key implication of the asymmetrical information models.

The central concerns of this book are with wages, employment, and hours of work so of more relevance for our purposes is an assessment of this class of models' implications for wages. Recall that, according to these private information models, the firm rejects the union's wage demands and prompts a strike when its profits are relatively low, and as the strike continues so the wage demands fall. In other words, as a strike goes on, the parties move down the resistance curve, equation (5.4), so that, conditional upon X_1, a negative association should be revealed between wages and the length of strikes.[15]

McConnell (1989) has undertaken a thorough analysis of this association using information on 1,986 contracts in the United States between 1970 and 1981. These contracts describe 883 management–union bargaining pairs in 20 manufacturing and 25 non-manufacturing industries. The core of her findings is contained in ordinary least-squares estimated equations in which the logarithm of real wages projected over the life of a contract are regressed on a dummy variable indicating whether a strike occurred and on a variable measuring the length of the strike in days (this variable assuming the value of zero when no strike occurred).[16]

[15] Of course, if the X_1 s are completely and perfectly measured, all bargaining pairs will operate at the same point on equation (5.4) and no variations in wages and strike lengths will be observed to identify the resistance curve. Differences in the union's discount rate or in the way it forms its expectations about the firm's profits or in something else are needed for the identification of equation (5.4).

[16] The resistance curve is supposed to represent the union's trade-off between strike length and wages and, insofar as it describes the union's opportunity set, it is not obvious

According to McConnell's results, the estimated coefficient on the strike dummy variable is typically smaller than its standard error.

As for the strike duration variable, its coefficient is rarely estimated with precision and a negative sign is obtained only when bargaining pair fixed effects are introduced into the estimated equation. In this case, its coefficient implies that a ten day strike is associated with a decline in wages of about 0.3 percent. The conditional mean duration of strikes in her sample is 41 days so, for this average strike, the real wage was about 1.2 percent lower than that on an equivalent contract that did not experience a strike. When she allows the slope of the wage–strike length resistance curve to vary by broad industrial groups, a significant negative effect is estimated only for nondurable manufacturing industry for which a strike of ten days is associated with a 0.67 percent reduction in the real wage. McConnell may well have found a negatively sloped wage–strike length resistance curve, but it seems not to be a solid or manifest relationship and considerably more work is needed before a convincing case can be made that strikes represent a first-order consideration in explanations for variations in union wages.[17] For the record, I know of no research examining the relationship between strikes and employment or hours of work.

A different class of asymmetrical information models takes as its central issue not the existence of strikes but the determination of wages in situations in which workers embody specific human capital. In these models management are better informed about the current state of the firm's sales and therefore of the value of the workers' productivity while workers are better informed about their latest alternative employment opportunities. If each party were as well informed on these matters as the other, then the terms of their contract could be specified as dependent upon these exogenous factors, but each party has an incentive (at least in the short run) to misrepresent its position and thereby enjoy a bargaining advantage, the workers exaggerating the value of their alternative opportunities and management understating the value of their employees' work. Given the costs of negotiating a contract in these circumstances in which

---

why wages and not strike length was selected as the left-hand side variable. The regressors representing X_1 in McConnell's analysis include current and recent prices, the average wage across all industries, indicators of aggregate employment and unemployment, incomes policies dummy variables, features of the collective bargaining contract (such as its expected duration and the presence of the cost-of-living adjustment clauses) and of the bargaining unit, and a quadratic time trend.

[17] Herrington (1988) reported virtually no association between wage changes and his indicators of uncertainty as mentioned earlier. Examining a sample of 2,868 manufacturing contracts in Canada from 1964 to 1985, Card (1987) found no contemporaneous correlation between real wages on the one hand and strike length and strike incidence on the other hand.

both parties have private information, the two parties may determine it is preferable to specify a fixed wage (or to specify an easily administered formula for setting the wage) before the realization of and independent of the workers' outside opportunities and of their productivity.[18]

The wage contract negotiable under conditions of bilateral asymmetric information will depend upon management's assessment of the future productivity of its employees and upon the union's assessment of its alternative opportunities during the lifetime of the contract. Sometimes these assessments will turn out to be incorrect so that we will observe layoffs in the case in which management's expectations about the future productivity of workers proved too optimistic and we will observe quits by workers in the case in which workers' expectations about alternative job opportunities proved too conservative. In the latter case, even though some workers may have particular alternative options that dominate continued employment with this firm, there should be an adequate supply of new workers to replace any who have quit provided the union has secured a genuine wage differential over alternative employments. In this event, notwithstanding these quits, management is in the position of unilaterally selecting the level of employment appropriate to its goals.

5.4 Arbitration

The research on strikes described in the previous section represents one class of models whose purpose is to investigate how the procedures used to resolve collective bargaining disputes affect the outcomes. Another class of models has been used to analyze the operation of different dispute resolution mechanisms regulating the collective bargaining process of certain state and local government employees in the United States. These schemes have emerged as a response to the predicament created by the growth of unionism in the past 25 years or so among public sector workers, many of whom lack the statutory right to strike. The distinguishing feature of these mechanisms is their use of third parties to help resolve disagreements.

These third parties may serve as mediators, fact-finders, or arbitrators: mediators help in communicating accurate information both between the union and management and also between groups within the union constituency or within management; fact-finders usually issue reports describing the issues in dispute and the publication of their reports is often

---

[18] Michael Riordan (1984) shows that, when the union and management are risk neutral, one incentive compatible contract is, indeed, recursive such that the union (say) sets wages (or the formula for wages) and management follows by determining employment.

designed to bring public pressure to bear on the parties to resolve their disagreements; and arbitrators have the authority to impose settlements on the two parties. As the most invasive of the third party methods used to resolve public sector disputes, arbitration methods have come under special investigation. In essence, two types of interest arbitration methods[19] have been studied, conventional arbitration (CA) and final-offer arbitration (FOA). Under CA, the arbitrator may draw up the terms of the settlement that he deems appropriate. With FOA, the arbitrator is constrained to select either the union's "final" offer or management's "final" offer.[20]

For a number of years, industrial relations specialists wondered whether the outcome of the union–management contest would be affected by the particular arbitration procedure used. After all, it was speculated, an arbitration system that restricts the arbitrator's choice to two points (either the union's position or management's position) will rarely yield the same outcome as an arbitration system that does not so constrain his choice.[21] In particular, under CA, arbitrators were sometimes said to split-the-difference between the union's and management's positions yet tacitly arbitrators were assumed to alter their behavior when operating under FOA: instead of choosing between the union's and management's positions randomly (the FOA equivalent of splitting-the-difference under CA), the arbitrators were supposed to invoke their own criteria of an appropriate award and thereby FOA would discourage the two parties from presenting wildly divergent offers.

These views have been seriously challenged by Farber in a series of papers presenting what might now be called the standard model of union–management bargaining in situations where a third party arbitrator will impose a settlement on parties in the event of their not reaching a negotiated settlement.[22] The basic issue to be addressed is: what is the arbitration system's counterpart to the strike costs that provide the incentives for the parties to negotiate a settlement themselves? In answering this question, Farber and Katz (1979) characterize the union and management as bargaining over a single variable, the wage rate, in a simple zero-sum (pie-splitting) game. The model sits squarely in the class

[19] Interest arbitration is the use of third parties to determine the terms of a collective bargaining contract. Grievance arbitration is the use of third parties to resolve disagreements over the operation of a collective bargaining agreement.

[20] Though FOA was in use in the British coal and steel industries before the Great War and also in certain industries in Weimar Germany, the issues surrounding the operation of this system lay dormant until raised by Carl Stevens (1966) in an important article.

[21] This presumption will not hold if the union and management behave differently under the two systems so that their last offers under one system diverge from their offers under the other. Indeed, Farber and Katz (1979) argued this is just what should be expected.

[22] See Farber and Katz (1979), and Farber (1980, 1981).

of recursive models with employment and hours of work determined at a different time from wages. The union's utility from a negotiated wage W_n is $\Gamma(W_n)$ with $\Gamma'(W_n) > 0$ and the management's utility from the negotiated wage W_n is $\pi(W_n)$ with $\pi'(W_n) < 0$. Their expected utilities from a settlement devised by an arbitrator is $\mathcal{E}\Gamma(W_a^u)$ and $\mathcal{E}\pi(W_a^m)$ where W_a^u is the union's estimate of the arbitrated wage and W_a^m is management's estimate of the arbitrated wage. W_a^u and W_a^m are the union's and management's threat points. The union will prefer a negotiated settlement if $\Gamma(W_n) - \mathcal{E}\Gamma(W_a^u) > 0$ and the management will prefer a negotiated settlement if $\pi(W_n) - \mathcal{E}\pi(W_a^m) > 0$. Clearly, these two conditions can hold if each party adheres to pessimistic expectations about the arbitrated settlement, the union believing W_a^u to be relatively low and management believing W_a^m to be relatively high. Pessimistic (and conflicting) expectations about the arbitrator's expected award will certainly provide an incentive for a negotiated settlement.

However, suppose the union and management form not only mutually consistent expectations $W_a^u = W_a^m = W_a$, but also believe the expected value of the arbitrator's settlement will equal the negotiated settlement W_n. In other words, suppose the union and management are faced with a fair bet. The union will still prefer the negotiated settlement if $\Gamma(W_n) - \mathcal{E}\Gamma(W_n) > 0$ and correspondingly management will prefer the negotiated settlement if $\pi(W_n) - \mathcal{E}\pi(W_n) > 0$. Equivalently, if the parties are averse to the risk accompanying arbitration, they stand ready to compromise their wage offers in negotiations to avoid going to arbitration. That is, the union will be willing to subtract W_u^* from the certain negotiated settlement W_n to make it indifferent between a negotiated and an arbitrated settlement where W_u^* is defined as $\Gamma(W_n - W_u^*) - \mathcal{E}\Gamma(W_n) = 0$ while management will be willing to add W_m^* to W_n to make it indifferent between a negotiated and an arbitrated settlement where W_m^* is defined as $\pi(W_n + W_m^*) - \pi(W_n) = 0$. In each case, W_u^* and W_m^* are the cost of risk, a second-order approximation to which is proportional to the variance in wages, $\sigma_u^2(W)$ and $\sigma_m^2(W)$:

$$W_u^* = R^u(W)\,\frac{\sigma_u^2(W)}{2} \quad \text{and} \quad W_m^* = R^m(W)\,\frac{\sigma_m^2(W)}{2}$$

where $R^u(W)$ and $R^m(W)$ are the union's and management's Arrow–Pratt measures of absolute risk aversion.[23] Hence if either W_u^* or W_m^* is

[23] That is, $R^u(W) = -\Gamma''(W)/\Gamma'(W)$ and $R^m(W) = -\pi''(W)/\pi'(W)$. The second-order approximation is derived and discussed in Pratt (1964). Assuming R^u and R^m are constant and assuming $W_a^u = W_a^m$, Farber and Bazerman (1989) compute W_u^* and W_m^* using experimentally generated data and construct the contract zones for CA and FOA.

positive (or if both are positive), the parties will avoid going to arbitration and will negotiate a settlement themselves. As the expressions for W_u^* and W_m^* make clear, this negotiated "contract zone," as Farber and Katz call it, increases with the parties' risk aversion and with their expectations of the variance of the arbitrator's awards, $\sigma_u^2(W)$ and $\sigma_m^2(W)$. If an accumulation of experience with arbitration reduces $\sigma_u^2(W)$ and $\sigma_m^2(W)$, we should observe fewer negotiated settlements over time. In short, it is uncertainty about the settlement the arbitrator would impose that drives the risk-averse parties toward a negotiated settlement. The parties may protect themselves against a possible unfavorable arbitration award by compromising in their negotiations with one another.[24]

As for the behavior of the arbitrator, Farber (1981) characterizes him as forming an estimate of the "appropriate" decision based in part on the intrinsic features of the situation and in part on the parties' offers where the weight on the latter declines as the parties' offers get farther apart. Under CA, this will induce the parties to influence the arbitrator by choosing positions roughly equidistant (if the two parties have approximately the same attitudes toward risk) from their estimate of the arbitrator's appropriate award; the arbitrator's average award will give the appearance of splitting the difference between the two parties' positions, but only because the two parties have aligned themselves around the arbitrator's appropriate award. Under FOA, if the arbitrator selects that offer closer to his estimate of the appropriate award and if the two parties select their final offer with this in mind, the more risk-averse party will adopt a more moderate position implying it will "win" FOA awards more frequently, but will do so with more modest awards than if it were less risk-averse. Whether FOA provides more incentives than CA for a negotiated settlement cannot be determined a priori, but depends upon the form of the probability distributions of the arbitrator's appropriate award. The operation of FOA erases both the middle part and the tails of the prior distribution of the arbitrator's appropriate wage so that the net effect on risk compared with the undeleted distribution under CA is difficult to assess. In general, Farber's arbitration model guards us against expecting the form of the arbitration procedure to affect the outcome of the union–management contest in a straightforward way.

In fact, naive comparisons of the wage increases resulting from the operation of different dispute resolution procedures do not indicate any clear pattern. For instance, since 1977, collective bargaining agreements between police unions and local governments in different New Jersey

---

[24] The argument here is designed to explain the incentives for the parties to settle without recourse to arbitration. Of course, these incentives are sometimes superseded by other factors (including mistakes and misperceptions) causing the parties to go to arbitration.

municipalities have been subject to binding arbitration if the two parties cannot reach an agreement by themselves. In an early analysis of the operation of the New Jersey statute, Bloom (1979) found no significant difference between increases in salaries negotiated by the parties themselves and those salary increases that were the product of binding arbitration.[25] In a later study comparing the operation of FOA and CA, Ashenfelter and Bloom (1984) reported no statistically significant difference between the average wage increases awarded under the two arbitration systems in 1978, 1979, and 1980.[26] Moreover, the decisions made under FOA appear to be very close to (not significantly different from) those that would be inferred from analyzing the CA decisions. An interpretation in the spirit of Farber's arbitration model is that the union "won" approximately two-thirds of the FOA cases because the union's final wage demand came closer to the arbitrator's notion of the appropriate wage increase where what is appropriate is inferred from the awards made under CA.[27] Expressed differently, the arbitrator seemed to be applying pretty much the same criteria under the two arbitration systems. In return for its more conservative wage demands, the union appears to have enjoyed a smaller variance in the awards (that is, a smaller risk of unfavorable outcomes).

Suggestive as these empirical regularities are, they do not satisfy the conditions of an experiment whereby a set of union–management contests are randomly assigned to resolution by different procedural rules. The reason is that in the typical case the parties are choosing whether to go to arbitration and also sometimes choosing the form of the arbitration system. Because the various union–management contests are not being

---

[25] Also he reported no differences in salary increases between those settlements that made use of fact-finders and those that did not. The results regarding the use of mediators were variable: between 1976 and 1978, those settlements involving mediators were significantly above other settlements while the reverse was true between 1977 and 1979; between 1977 and 1978, there was no significant difference between those settlements using mediators and those not. This pattern is consistent with mediators being involved in relatively low settlements in 1976 and 1979 and in relatively high settlements in 1977 and 1978.

[26] The percent mean (and standard deviation in parentheses) wage increases under FOA were 6.63 (1.19) in 1978, 7.57 (1.48) in 1979, and 8.10 (1.41) in 1980 while the corresponding increases under CA were 6.55 (2.23), 8.59 (2.32), and 8.26 (2.14).

[27] A similar interpretation would apply to the fact that, under Iowa's FOA system, two-thirds of the decisions between 1976 and 1983 were "won" by the employer. In Iowa, before FOA is invoked, a fact-finder may propose terms to settle the dispute. In those instances in which an FOA decision was preceded by a fact-finder's proposal, Ashenfelter (1985) shows that the employer's last offer was closer on average to the fact-finder's recommendation than the union's last demand. In other words, whereas in New Jersey the union came closer to the arbitrator's view of the appropriate wage increase and accordingly the union "won" relatively more decisions, in Iowa the employer played the more conservative role.

randomly allocated to different dispute resolution schemes, the natural question that arises is whether the factors determining the choice of resolution mechanism are also affecting the characteristics of the outcomes. Given the well-known problems in satisfactorily answering this type of question with field data, there seems a good case for examining experimentally generated data which by design can produce the random assignment of contests to arbitration mechanisms. This is essentially Farber and Bazerman's (1986) goal in asking a number of arbitrators to rule on 25 different contrived union–management contests. Without being supplied with any decision-making criteria, the arbitrators were asked both to make CA awards and to select an award following FOA rules. Five-hundred-eighty-four arbitrators were sent these simulated contests and 64 responded with wage decisions.[28] These decisions suggested that the arbitrators behaved in very much the same way under the two arbitration systems. In arriving at their awards, arbitrators took account both of the intrinsic features of the contest (and especially the value of recent wage increases in "comparable arbitrated settlements") and of the last offers made by the parties where the relative importance of the parties' final offers declined as the gap between them increased.[29] There remained, however, a good deal of variability in arbitrators' decisions so there seems ample reason for the parties to regard the arbitration process as one immersed in uncertainty.

Much of the more recent literature on arbitration has been directed to the question of whether the arbitrator's decisions are influenced more by the two parties' wage offers or by the particular circumstances of the case at issue. Typically, to describe the arbitrator's awards, an equation along the following lines is specified:

$$W_a = \alpha_0 + \alpha_1 W_u + \alpha_2 W_m + \alpha_3 X + e \qquad (5.5)$$

where W_a is the arbitrator's wage award, W_u and W_m are the union's and the management's final wage offers, X represents the intrinsic circumstances of the case (such as the rate of price inflation, other arbitrated

---

[28] Before jumping to the conclusion that 11 percent is a pitifully low response rate (Olson, 1988), it should be remembered that wage arbitration represents a very small fraction of all arbitration cases so that many of the members of the National Academy of Arbitrators who did not reply to Farber and Bazerman's experiment lacked the expertise to do so.

[29] This particular conclusion differs from Bloom's (1986) findings in a comparable experiment regarding the operation of CA. He concluded arbitrators placed little weight on the intrinsic features of the cases and were inclined to split the difference between the parties' final offers. However, in his experiment (unlike Farber and Bazerman's) the intrinsic features of the cases were correlated with the parties' offers so the inferences about the effects of each are a little more ambiguous.

wage decisions, and so on), and e stands for factors omitted from the equation. Usually the Ws are expressed in terms of percentage wage increases and often, instead of entering W_u and W_m separately, their arithmetic mean is specified. When the analysis uses data from FOA, the dependent variable is dichotomous, identifying whether the union won or lost. It is a common finding in this literature that the estimates of α_1 and α_2 are "large" and of unquestionable statistical significance while those of α_3 often lead to acceptance of the null hypothesis that variations in X are uncorrelated with W_a. This has led to the inference that arbitrators are strongly influenced by the wage offers and place relatively little weight on the intrinsic circumstances of the cases.

This is an unwarranted inference, as some researchers recognize, simply because the parties' final wage offers, W_u and W_m, are themselves dependent upon X, the intrinsic circumstances of the cases. In other words, consider the following characterization of the sequence of the arbitrator's decision-making. First, suppose that on the basis of the particular circumstances, the arbitrator forms an initial estimate of the appropriate wage award. Denote this initial estimate by W_I:

$$W_I = \lambda X + e_1 \tag{5.6}$$

where X stands for the set of circumstances known to the arbitrator and to the researcher while e_1 represents the relevant variables known to the arbitrator but not known to the researcher. λ is a set of weights formed from the arbitrator's previous experience. The arbitrator also makes an informed guess of what each party is going to offer: the arbitrator's expectations of the union's wage offer is $\hat{W}_u$ and of management's wage offer is $\hat{W}_m$ and these may be expressed as follows:

$$\begin{cases} \hat{W}_u = \delta_u X + \eta_u Z + e_2 \\ \hat{W}_m = \delta_m X + \eta_m Z + e_3 \end{cases} \tag{5.7}$$

where X stands for the set of variables the arbitrator deems relevant to the wage offers, Z stands for variables the arbitrator deems irrelevant to the wage offers but that will enter each party's offers, and e_2 and e_3 are variables affecting the arbitrator's expectations but that are unobserved by the researcher. (X and Z are observed by the researcher.)

At this point, the arbitrator learns the two parties' actual wage offers, W_u and W_m, and he adjusts his initial estimate, W_I, on the assumption that each party has relevant information not available to the arbitrator. That is, if W_a is the arbitrator's wage award, then one representation of the updating of the arbitrator's initial wage estimate is the following quadratic approximation:

$$W_a = W_I + \mu_1 (W_u - \hat{W}_u) + \mu_2 (W_u - \hat{W}_u)^2 + \mu_3 (W_m - \hat{W}_m)$$
$$+ \mu_4 (W_m - \hat{W}_m)^2 \tag{5.8}$$

where $\mu_1 > 0$, $\mu_2 < 0$, $\mu_3 > 0$, and $\mu_4 > 0$.[30] To relate this model to previous work, suppose the quadratic terms in equation (5.8) are ignored for a moment and substitute equations (5.6) and (5.7) into (5.8):

$$W_a = \mu_1 W_u + \mu_2 W_m + b_1 X + b_2 Z + e_4 \tag{5.9}$$

where $b_1 = \lambda - \mu_1 \delta_u - \mu_3 \delta_m$, $b_2 = - (\mu_1 \eta_u + \mu_3 \eta_m)$, and $e_4 = e_1 - \mu_u e_2 - \mu_m e_3$. This equation (5.9) is close to equation (5.5), the equation routinely fitted in this literature. It is not precisely the same because equation (5.9) permits a role for variables, Z, that may affect the arbitrator's expectations of the wage offers but whose relevance the arbitrator discounts. Given the somewhat cavalier specification of the X variables in equation (5.5) in some studies, however, this difference between equations (5.5) and (5.9) is of slight importance.

Now, according to equation (5.9), what sign should we expect for b_1? If X is a variable such that larger values induce higher awards (that is, if $\lambda > 0$, $\delta_u > 0$, $\delta_m > 0$), then $b_1 \gtreqless 0$: in other words, *holding W_u and W_m constant*, the effect of the intrinsic circumstances of the case on W_a is ambiguous in sign. This is simply because W_u and W_m incorporate at least some of the effect of X on W_a and that the full effect of X on W_a is not b_1 but $b_1 + \mu_1 (\partial W_a / \partial X) + \mu_2 (\partial W_m / \partial X)$. Hence the apparent unimportance of the X variables in equation (5.5) is not surprising and it should not lead to the inference that arbitrators' wage awards are uninfluenced by the circumstances of the cases.[31]

If the model sketched in the previous paragraphs is at all appropriate as a description of arbitrator behavior,[32] then it suggests how unions and managements may optimize against it. Thus, if the union knows the arbitrator's algorithm for updating his initial award, then the union maximizes W_a in equation (5.8) when $\partial W_a / \partial W_u = 0$ and $\partial^2 W_a / \partial W_u^2 < 0$. The union's optimal W_u, call it W_u^*, is $W_u^* = \hat{W}_u - \mu_1 (2\mu_2)^{-1}$. Correspondingly, if the management know equation (5.8), they minimize W_a

---

[30] The narrative here is consciously Bayesian in spirit though the quantitative expression of it can only be interpreted as a very rough formalization of what a Bayesian analysis would imply.

[31] One of the few studies not drawing this inference was Farber and Bazerman's (1986), but this exception illustrates the point: by experimental design, W_a and W_m were independent of X.

[32] The model is fully operational. Suppose $\hat{W}_u$ and $\hat{W}_m$ may be expressed as least-squares combinations of the X and Z variables in which case $W_u - \hat{W}_u$ and $W_m - \hat{W}_m$ in equation (5.8) are the fitted residuals from equations (5.7).

when $\partial W_a / \partial W_m = 0$ and $\partial^2 W_a / \partial W_m^2 > 0$ and the optimal W_m, call it W_m^*, is $W_m^* = \hat{W}_m - \mu_3 (2\mu_4)^{-1}$. In time, with the same actors playing this strategy, ultimately the realization of W_u must equal $\hat{W}_u$ save for random error v_1 and similarly the realization of W_m must equal $\hat{W}_m$ except for random error v_2 in which case equation (5.8) reduces to

$$W_a = \lambda X + v$$

where v represents a convolution of random elements. If W_u and W_m meaningfully enter this equation, this must mean either that the situation has not yet reached an expectations equilibrium or that v is correlated with W_u and W_m.

If the recent literature is correct and uncertainty is the key element in understanding collective bargaining behavior under arbitration, then the prospects for the application of a structural model to describe actual arbitration cases (something currently lacking in research on these issues) are not encouraging in view of the very unsettled state of the literature on the economics of uncertainty. The expected utility hypothesis has taken a terrible beating in recent years and, indeed, the research on this topic would not lead us to believe that the union and management operate in pretty much the same way under CA as under FOA. This research emphasizes how individuals' behavior is affected by the particular framing of the uncertain prospects and how difficult it can be for individuals to calculate meaningful prior probability distributions over various outcomes. This should generate skepticism about the notion that the parties follow the same basic behavioral rules in making their offers under the two systems of arbitration. Under FOA, each party must be under no illusion that their final offer will come under the arbitrator's serious consideration and that the other party's offer may well be selected; the parties are forced to focus on two possible outcomes and on making an offer that affects that choice. By contrast, under CA, each party may regard the arbitrator's behavior as so difficult to foretell, the possibilities so diverse, and its own offer of so little relevance to the final outcome that it may not go through the same careful assessment of its options as it does under FOA.

More generally, the research on strikes and arbitration has not yet presented a compelling case that methods of dispute resolution are an essential ingredient in a behavioral model describing the outcomes of collective bargaining. There can be no doubt that a fully satisfactory understanding of bargaining needs to account for the convergence over time of a sequence of offers and counteroffers and for the role of strikes and arbitration. It is also the case that some insights into these issues can be claimed in research over the past decade or so. However, if an understanding of the pattern of wages, employment, and hours of work is being sought, then a convincing case has yet to be made that the methods of dispute resolution represent more than second-order considerations. Of course, this does not mean they should be ignored, but when our understanding of the first-order considerations remains quite incomplete, it is quite appropriate as a research strategy not to focus our efforts on how dispute resolution methods can be incorporated into our models.

5.5   Recursive Bargaining Models: Hours

In the exposition above, earnings was ordered first and employment second. How should hours of work be treated? Should work hours be characterized as subject to joint determination by the union and management or is it more appropriately treated as set unilaterally by the union or by management? The industrial relations literature does not provide a clear answer to this question in part because hours of work enter a collective bargaining agreement in several different ways.

There is first the length of the workday and the workweek together with starting and ending times. These establish "normal" or "standard" hours of work. For hours beyond these normal work hours, management is obliged typically to pay higher rates of wages, the rate itself varying with the particular day of the week the hours are worked and with the number of overtime hours. Then the length of the workyear will be affected by the number and length of holidays, vacations, and days absent through illness. In the 1950s US collective bargaining contracts in manufacturing industry rarely specified annual vacations longer than three weeks, but by the 1980s such vacations were common. Indeed, many senior blue-collar workers could enjoy six weeks or more. In Britain, over the past 30 years, there has been a marked increase in the length of paid vacations for those covered by collective bargaining agreements: in 1951, 97 percent of manual workers were entitled to two weeks or less annual paid vacation; in 1982, 93 percent were entitled to four weeks or more.[33]

If the contract calls for all employees to work the same number of weekly hours and yet they have different tastes for work and leisure, then at the negotiated wages some individuals are likely to find themselves working more hours on this job than they would like while others are working fewer hours. In this situation, some employees will discourage the union from negotiating a reduction in hours of work. By contrast, *all* employees will welcome higher wages. Presumably these differences in tastes for work help to explain why in many cases union pressure for reductions in the length of the normal workweek is less intensive

[33] These data are presented in table 1.13 of Pencavel (1986).

nowadays than was the case when hours of work were much longer. Bargaining agreements display considerable differences in the degree to which unions exert explicit control over work hours.[34] In some instances, the collective bargaining agreement explicitly prohibits any hours beyond a specified number or, even when not explicitly stated, the union may reserve the power to veto longer work schedules requested by management. In other cases, the union has been willing to grant management considerable discretion over changes in hours of work though only at the price of management paying higher premium rates for abnormal hours. In this case, the union's influence on hours is indirect: a complex premium pay structure is set up that penalizes for overtime hours. This is tantamount to the union and management jointly negotiating the wage and then management freely setting hours of work conditional on that wage. In other words, if management's profits are given by equation (4.4), its first-order condition for work hours is

$$WE - R_2 = 0$$

(where $R_2 \equiv \partial R/\partial h$). By comparison, with full contract efficiency, the first-order condition (4.3) may be written as $WE - R_2 = g_2 E/g_1 > 0$.

5.6 Hierarchy of Decision-Making

All the bargaining models considered in this section have a recursive structure: one or more variables are determined prior to the determination of the other variables.[35] In the descriptions above, wages have typically been determined at the first stage and employment and work hours subsequently. This may be because decisions about wages are made infrequently while the values of employment and work hours are reviewed habitually. Or decisions about wages may result from multi-plant or multi-firm bargaining while those regarding employment and work hours are decentralized. In one case, decisions are made at different times while, in the other case, decisions are made at a different level in the organization. In both cases, it would seem inappropriate to presume that each party's bargaining power or its no-trade point is the same for each decision.[36]

---

[34] For instance, see the account in Slichter, Healy and Livernash (1960).

[35] The importance of the ordering of decisions is stressed in Grout (1984), Johnson (1990), Manning (1987), and Earle and Pencavel (1990). The use of Nash's asymmetrical bargaining solution follows Grout and Manning.

[36] Manning (1987, pp. 124–5) catalogues the institutional and *a priori* reasons for expecting different values of these bargaining parameters at different stages of the bargaining problem. The exposition that follows is similar to Manning's particular characterization.

This is recognized in the following particular hierarchy of decision-making: at the first stage, the values of wages and of capital are determined; at the second stage, the level of employment is set; and, at the third stage, the level of work hours is determined. This ordering conforms to the notion that decisions about work hours are made most frequently and adjustments in work hours involve the least costs. Invoking Nash's asymmetrical bargaining solution, at the third stage, h is selected to maximize

$$\Psi_3(h; W, E, K) = [\Gamma(Wh, h, E) - \overline{\Gamma}_3]^{\alpha_3} [\pi(Wh, h, E, K) - \overline{\pi}_3]^{1-\alpha_3}$$

(5.10)

where α_3 is the union's relative bargaining power in this third-stage work hours decision. As in chapter 4, $\overline{\Gamma}_3$ and $\overline{\pi}_3$ are the values of the union's and firm's payoffs in the event of no agreement being reached over hours of work. The outcome of this round of bargaining is a solution for h expressed as a function of W, E, K, and other exogenous variables. In the second stage, the parties select E to maximize

$$\Psi_2(E; W, K) = [\Gamma(Wh, h, E) - \overline{\Gamma}_2]^{\alpha_2} [\pi(Wh, h, E, K) - \overline{\pi}_2]^{1-\alpha_2}$$

(5.11)

where α_2 is the union's relative bargaining power over employment. This round of bargaining results in E being expressed as a function of W, K, and other exogenous variables. In the first stage of bargaining over wages and capital, the parties choose W and K to maximize

$$\Psi_1(W, K) = [\Gamma(Wh, h, E) - \overline{\Gamma}_1]^{\alpha_1} [\pi(Wh, h, E, K) - \overline{\pi}_1]^{1-\alpha_1} \quad (5.12)$$

where α_1 is the union's relative power at this stage of the bargaining.

A special case of this recursive structure has been especially popular in the literature. This is the union monopoly model or labor demand curve equilibrium model according to which first the wage is set at the value that maximizes the union's objective function and then management follows by unilaterally determining the level of labor inputs, employment and hours of work. So, in negotiations over the wage, the union's bargaining power is preeminent though the union is restrained by the employment and hours implications of a high wage. This model is well suited, therefore, to Marshall's (1920) and Friedman's (1951) conjectures about the position and slope of the labor demand function determining the magnitudes of the relative wage effects of different types of unions. An institutional structure that might conform well to this bargaining representation is one where a powerful union negotiates a common wage with a number of relatively small firms, each of whom determines its employment and work hours independently. The US bituminous coal industry in the years immediately following the Second World War is an example.

The model is a special case of equations (5.10), (5.11), and (5.12) where $\alpha_1 = 1$ and $\alpha_2 = \alpha_3 = 0$. It implies that exogenous variables appearing exclusively in the union's objective function affect employment and hours only through their impact on the union's choice of the wage rate. Without further restrictions on the forms of the union's objective function and on the labor demand functions, the qualitative content of the model is meagre.[37] Nevertheless, the model has been popular for several reasons.

First, analytically it is familiar to economists insofar as it may be interpreted as the labor market analogy to Stackelberg's product market duopoly whereby one firm plays the role of leader and the other acts as follower.[38] Second, the model assigns to management exclusive control over employment and hours and, in the opinion of some, this characterization squares with the broad features of many collective bargaining contracts. Third, the model permits the derivation of convenient estimating equations in which the reduced form coefficients may be related explicitly to the structural parameters of the problem.

To illustrate this third point, consider the following form of the union's objective function:[39]

$$\Gamma(y, h, E; \bar{y}) = (\ln y - \rho \ln h - \ln \bar{y})^{\theta} (\ln E)^{1-\theta}. \tag{5.13}$$

This resembles the Stone–Geary function, equation (4.9), except that earnings, hours, and employment have been expressed in logarithms. If ρ is zero, the union attaches no weight to work hours (holding earnings constant) while if ρ is unity Γ may be written in terms of wage rates, not earnings. Suppose the firm's employment and hours demand functions have constant wage elasticities, $a_1 < 0$ and $b_1 < 0$ respectively:

$$\ln E = a_0 + a_1 \ln W + a_2 Z_1 \tag{5.14}$$

$$\ln h = b_0 + b_1 \ln W + b_2 Z_2 \tag{5.15}$$

where Z_1 and Z_2 represent other variables affecting employment and work hours. Z_1 and Z_2 are defined such that increases in each variable

---

[37] See Pencavel (1984a).

[38] Why the two parties should occupy the roles allotted to them is usually not examined and, indeed, problems arise if the parties reject their roles. See, for instance, Dowrick (1986).

[39] The model that follows was proposed by Pencavel and Holmlund (1988) as a description of the labor market for blue-collar workers in Sweden's manufacturing and mining industry. We also took account of taxes and unobserved variables in each of the following three equations to derive stochastic forms of equations (5.16), (5.17), and (5.18) where the disturbances are conveniently additive. These equations were fitted to annual observations on the variables over the period from 1950 to 1983.

induce increases in employment and hours (i.e., $a_2 > 0$ and $b_2 > 0$). Then maximizing equation (5.13) with respect to W subject to equations (5.14) and (5.15) yields the following equations for W, h, and E:[40]

$$\ln W = c_1 + \kappa(1 - \theta)\ln\bar{y} - \theta a_1^{-1}a_2 Z_1 - (1 - \theta)\kappa b_2(1 - \rho)Z_2 \quad (5.16)$$

$$\ln h = c_2 + \kappa(1 - \theta)b_1\ln\bar{y} - \theta a_2 a_1^{-1}b_1 Z_1 + [(1 - \theta)\kappa + \theta]b_2 Z_2$$
$$(5.17)$$

$$\ln E = c_3 + \kappa(1 - \theta)a_1\ln\bar{y} + (1 - \theta)a_2 Z_1 - (1 - \theta)\kappa b_2(1 - \rho)a_1 Z_2$$
$$(5.18)$$

where $\kappa = [1 + b_1(1 - \rho)]^{-1}$ and where c_1, c_2, and c_3 represent nonlinear configurations of the parameters. An increase in Z_1 (indicating a rightward shift in the employment demand function) raises wages and employment, but reduces hours of work. The more elastic the employment demand function (i.e., the larger the absolute magnitude of a_1), the smaller the wage impact of an increase in Z_1. The larger the value of θ, the greater the effect of an increase in Z_1 on wages and the smaller its effect on employment. Hence θ may be thought of as the union's aversion to variations in employment, a higher value of θ corresponding to relatively greater earnings response and relatively smaller employment response to exogenous shifts in the employment demand function.[41] Provided $\kappa > 0$,[42] an increase in alternative or comparison earnings, $\bar{y}$, raises wages, but (because the labor demand functions are unchanged) hours and employment fall. Note that, given the particular functional forms chosen, the qualitative implications for wages and employment of an increase in $\bar{y}$ in this union monopoly model are the same as those for the efficient contract model in section 4.7. In this instance, there is no opportunity to discriminate between the two bargaining models on the basis of their qualitative reduced form implications of $\bar{y}$. Given $\kappa > 0$, an increase in Z_2 will raise hours of work and, if $0 < \rho < 1$, employment will rise and wages fall.[43]

---

[40] The second-order conditions for a maximum are assumed to be satisfied. Their satisfaction is eased if $0 < \rho < 1$.

[41] The allusion here is to Arrow and Pratt's measure of relative risk aversion because $\theta = - (\ln E) [\partial^2\Gamma/\partial(\ln E)^2]/(\partial\Gamma/\partial(\ln E))$. The role of θ as distributing between wages and employment the greater opportunities for the union stemming from the effects of rightward shifts in the employment demand function is also discussed in Jackman (1985).

[42] $\kappa > 0$ implies $b_1(1 - \rho) < 1$. In fact, in Pencavel and Holmlund's (1988) estimates, $\hat{b}_1$ was about -0.10 and $\hat{\rho}$ was approximately 0.5 so that κ was not merely positive, but also close to unity.

[43] If equations (5.16), (5.17), and (5.18) are substituted into the union's objective function, equation (5.13), the maximized value of the objective function is derived. Clearly, this is increasing in Z_1 and Z_2 and decreasing in $\bar{y}$.

Of course, many (if not all) of the elements of Z_1 and Z_2 will be the same in which case a simultaneous rightward shift in both the hours and employment demand equations will definitely raise employment, but will have ambiguous implications for wages and hours. The reason for the ambiguity here is that a rightward shift in the demand for hours of work inclines management toward greater use of hours. However, the union opposes more work hours per employee and would prefer to take the greater opportunities afforded by an increase in the hours demand function in the form of higher wages. The union and management have opposing interests, therefore, and the particular values of the parameters determines the resolution of these interests.

In a particular application of this model to Swedish blue-collar workers in mining and manufacturing industry between 1950 and 1983, Bertil Holmlund and I (Pencavel and Holmlund, 1988) estimated ρ to be 0.48 and θ to be 0.15. As $\hat{\rho}$ is significantly different from both zero and unity by conventional criteria, hours appear to have a distinct role in union objectives quite separate from earnings. The value of $\hat{\theta}$ indicates that shifts in the labor demand function are reflected primarily in variations in employment and in hours of work and relatively little in earnings.

5.7 A Special Case: Producer Cooperatives and the Seniority Model

In the discussion in the preceding sections, it has been argued that it is with respect to the determination of employment (and perhaps of hours of work) that collective bargaining contracts are likely to diverge from efficiency. That is, whereas the union and management precisely specify wages and fringe benefits, employment is regulated only indirectly and many contracts appear to grant management considerable discretion over its determination. Indeed, employment may well lie on management's wage-taking labor demand curve. In this way, two polar cases have been identified, one where employment is on the labor demand curve and one where employment is on the contract curve.

There is one special case in which the distinction between these two cases disappears and this special case corresponds to that considered in the earlier literature on producer cooperatives. In order to link up with that research, suppose in our model the union were so powerful as to drive the firm's profits to zero and then suppose all revenues remaining after the payment of rents to capital were distributed to each employee per hour worked. In this case, set π to zero in equation (4.4) and solve for the implied payment, W^*, to each worker for each hour of work:

$$W^* = \frac{R(h, E, K; Z) - rK}{hE} \ .$$

In the literature on producer cooperatives W^* is often called the dividend rate. Ward's (1958) seminal paper conjectured that the producer cooperative would select its inputs, including labor, to maximize W^*. It is as if the union's objective function contains the wage rate as its only argument, employment and hours not being valued for their own sake but only insofar as they contribute to this maximum wage rate.

In terms of figure 5.1, the indifference curves for the union/producer cooperative are horizontal straight lines (a case explicitly considered by Fellner (1947) in his original contribution). If π_0 represents the isoprofit curve corresponding to zero profits, then clearly the highest (horizontal) indifference curve is attained at point e. In this special case, because $g_3 = 0$, both the conditions for employment under efficient contracts, equation (4.6), and for employment on the wage-taking labor demand curve, equation (5.1), are satisfied.

This particular outcome is also implied by what has been termed the "seniority model" of union–management bargaining (Oswald, 1985, 1987). This model equates the trade union's objectives with those of its typical (perhaps median) member who is presumed to have entirely selfish interests and, by virtue of his seniority, is insulated from all but the most drastic reductions in employment. Consequently the union's objectives contain wages as their only argument and, as is the case for Ward's producer cooperatives, in terms of figure 5.1, the union's indifference curves are horizontal straight lines.[44] Union–management bargaining over the wage will determine the particular isoprofit curve on which the firm operates, but because the union is supposed to be unconcerned with employment it is content to grant management unilateral determination of employment. As with Ward's producer cooperatives, the wage–employment combination is on the efficient contract curve and on the firm's labor demand curve.[45] I have already expressed the view that it is inappropriate to equate the objectives of the union with those of its typical member and that employment figures explicitly in the goals of most trade unions. This is also, without exception, what the analytical evidence on these issues indicates.

[44] To be specific, they are horizontal beyond the point at which the typical union member is confident of his employment. Uncertainty over the location of this point will impart some negative slope to the wage–employment trade-off.

[45] This will not be true if a very large decline in the firm's product demand threatens even the typical worker's employment. In this situation, a corner solution obtains in which wage cuts are accepted to retain the worker's job and the wage–employment contract moves off the firm's wage-taking labor demand curve. Of course, in this instance, after this negative shock to demand and the cut in employment, the typical worker is no longer typical but marginal and, by the logic of the seniority model, he will lose his job next period unless employment prospects improve.

Once it is recognized that Ward's producer cooperative is a special case of the behavioral models of trade unionism, it should be obvious how Ward's characterization of the producer cooperative may be generalized: define the producer cooperative's objectives over employment and hours of work as well as over wages so that its indifference curves resemble Γ_0, Γ_1, and Γ_2 in figure 5.1. Indeed, this is precisely how recent contributions to the literature on producer cooperatives may be understood.[46] Thus, Miyazaki and Neary (1983) endow the producer cooperative with an objective function equivalent to an expected utility formulation and they characterize the cooperative as selecting wages and employment to maximize this function subject to the constraint of earning just enough net revenue to pay for the cost of renting nonlabor inputs. In this way, the producer cooperative settles at a particular point on the same contract curve as that mapped out by the trade union and the capitalist firm.[47]

5.8   A Test Procedure

A distinguishing feature of the recursive models described in this chapter is that, for any wage, management's bargaining power over the determination of employment exceeds that corresponding to the efficient contract level. This is reflected in equation (5.3) which is repeated here for convenience:

$$R_3 = y - \chi(g_3 g_1^{-1})E , \qquad (5.3)$$

R_3 being the marginal revenue product of employment. For a fully efficient contract, $\chi = 1$ while employment on the wage-taking labor demand curve corresponds to $\chi = 0$. Johnson's model, whereby the union and management bargain over the wage and the capital–labor ratio and then management determines employment unilaterally, occupies an intermediate case where χ lies between zero and unity.

Equation (5.3) forms the basis of an empirical procedure for assessing whether the wage-taking labor demand function is the relevant construct for understanding the determination of employment in unionized markets. For the limiting case in which employment is on the labor demand curve is nested within equation (5.3): it represents the special case in which the term $-\chi(g_3 g_1^{-1})E$ is absent from equation (5.3). So by subjecting this exclusion restriction to conventional testing procedures,

---

[46] See, for instance, Brewer and Browning (1982), Miyazaki and Neary (1983), and Steinherr and Thisse (1979).

[47] Miyazaki and Neary also investigate the consequences for employment and wages for the producer cooperative when state-contingent contracts can be written.

equation (5.3) becomes potentially a very fruitful way of evaluating the relevance of a whole class of bargaining models, namely, those models implying that employment is on the firm's conventional wage-taking input demand function.[48]

Two limitations of this procedure need to be noted. First, this procedure does not discriminate among the employment implications of alternative bargaining models if the union is indifferent with respect to increases in employment (i.e., if $g_3 = 0$). As was described in the previous section on producer cooperatives and the seniority model, if in terms of figure 5.1 the union's earnings–employment indifference curves $(\Gamma_1, \Gamma_2, \Gamma_3$, etc.) are horizontal, then at least as far as employment is concerned, there is no meaningful distinction between efficient contracts and other contracts: an efficient contract is on the labor demand curve. Second, this procedure is attractive only insofar as the marginal revenue product of employment is measured accurately and with confidence. A misspecification in computing R_3 may give the appearance that $R_3 \neq y$ and that employment appears on the right-hand side of equation (5.3) whereas, in fact, management is on its labor demand curve. Hence, because a good deal of work needs to be undertaken to derive reliable estimates of R_3, this is not an empirically trivial task.[49]

This method for assessing the relevance of the conventional labor demand curve for the determination of employment was applied by MaCurdy and Pencavel (1986) to the labor market for typographers in 13

---

[48] Eberts and Stone (1986) present an empirical analysis which claims to distinguish between a situation in which employment is on a wage-taking labor demand function and one in which employment is on a contract curve. The distinguishing feature of their models of the labor market for public school teachers is the role played by employment security provisions (such as a tenure system, class-size limitations, or reduction-in-force procedures). The validity of their test rests crucially on a particular assumption about their production function $z = z(P, T)$ where z is the production of educational services, P the level of employment security provisions, and T the number of teachers. They write, "Restrictive employment provisions (P) are assumed to have no direct effect on output but may reduce the productivity of the explicit inputs." (In fact, P *must*, not "may," reduce the productivity of teachers for their argument to hold.) In other words, they assume $\partial z/\partial P = 0$, $\partial z/\partial T > 0$, and $\partial^2 z/\partial P \partial T < 0$. A production function with these properties is very unconventional and, as they provide no argument or evidence for these assumptions, it is difficult to know what to make of their results. (I am very grateful to Randall Eberts and Joe Stone for their helpful correspondence on these issues.)

[49] Because production function parameters appear in equation (5.3), one might envisage a procedure involving the estimation of this equation jointly with a production function. This might be adopted if the form of the production function were known, but if it is not known then it seems ill-advised to allow errors in specifying the production function to affect inferences about the determination of employment. In general, then, a sequential procedure is preferred whereby the production function is first discovered and then an empirical form of equation (5.3) is estimated.

US towns between 1945 and 1973.[50] An important shortcoming of the analysis is that, as with almost all the data relating to typographers, the observations on employment actually describe local union membership and reliable information on work hours is lacking. So first, using data on the number of typesetting machines, the number of teletypesetting machines, the number of typographers listed as members of the ITU local, and the amount of advertising linage sold annually, we fitted many different forms for the production function within a newspaper's composing room and decided on the Cobb–Douglas and translog as providing the most appropriate descriptions of the technology.[51] The first derivative of these production functions with respect to employment provided estimates of the marginal product of employment, $\hat{X}_E$.

Each firm's marginal revenue is equal to the ratio of the price of any other input, K, to that input's marginal product: r/X_K. Observations on X_K can be formed from the fitted production functions while observations on r are proportional (the factor of proportionality, γ, unknown) to an annual user cost of capital, r^*. Hence R_3 is estimated as equal to $\gamma r^* \hat{X}_E / \hat{X}_K$. If employment in these firms is on the corresponding labor demand functions, then variations in $r^* \hat{X}_E / \hat{X}_K$ will be proportional, γ^{-1}, to variations in earnings, y,[52] and no other variables contribute to explanations for the variations in $r^* \hat{X}_E / \hat{X}_K$.

To illustrate with perhaps the simplest of cases, suppose $g_3 g_1^{-1}$ is a stochastic linear function of y, E, and $\bar{y}$ so that equation (5.3) may be written:

$$\gamma \frac{r^* \hat{X}_E}{E \hat{X}_K} - \frac{y}{E} = a_0 + a_1 y + a_2 E + a_3 \bar{y} + \nu \qquad (5.19)$$

---

[50] A precursor was Thurow's (1968) analysis of the relevance of the marginal productivity theory of wages at the aggregate level. He fitted a production function to annual economy-wide data and calculated the derivative of this production function with respect to manhours. He called this the marginal product of labor and compared its values between 1929 and 1965 with the actual compensation of employees. He found that compensation represented about 60 percent of labor's estimated marginal product.

[51] Each firm was permitted to have its own intercept. To evaluate the estimated production functions, we determined whether the fitted values implied (a) diminishing marginal returns to successive applications of a single input (where other inputs are held fixed at their mean values) and (b) positive marginal products at the level of inputs actually used. The estimated Cobb–Douglas function satisfied these criteria for all observations and the estimated translog function met these criteria for almost all observations.

[52] In fact, the absence of reliable information on work hours implies that the annual contract wage rate was used in place of annual earnings. This creates no problems for the analysis provided typographers work the same number of hours across unions and over time (a highly unlikely event) in which case the parameters of the production function and of the union objective function implicitly hold work hours constant.

where ν represents an unobserved random disturbance. When employment is on the wage-taking labor demand curve, all the a_i coefficients are zero. Of course, the fact that observations on the marginal revenue product of employment are measured only up to an unknown factor of proportionality, γ, involves a notable weakening of the research hypothesis. That is, variations in $r^*\hat{X}_E/\hat{X}_K$ may be proportional to earnings and yet the observations on y and E need not be on the labor demand curve; conversely, if the firm is on its labor demand curve, then variations in $r^*\hat{X}_E/\hat{X}_K$ will be proportional to variations in y.

In fact, we found that consistently we could not reject hypotheses that expressions for $g_3 g_1^{-1} E$ helped towards accounting for variations in $r^*\hat{X}_E/\hat{X}_K$. For instance, when using the Cobb–Douglas production function and fitting equation (5.19) above, we derived the following parameter estimates of the a_i coefficients (with standard errors in parentheses):[53]

$$\hat{a}_1 = 0.042 \; , \qquad \hat{a}_2 = -0.0013 \; , \qquad \text{and} \quad \hat{a}_3 = -0.026 \; .$$
$$(0.008) \qquad\qquad (0.0006) \qquad\qquad\qquad\qquad (0.006)$$

The rejection of the labor demand curve equilibrium model does not imply that contracts are necessarily first-best efficient: in terms of figure 5.1, employment might be anywhere to the right of b and not necessarily at a.

A weak indication of whether the relationship between y and the calculated values of R_3 conform to an efficient contract is to fit equation (5.3) for particular assumed forms of $g_3 g_1^{-1}$ under the assumption that $\chi = 1$ and to assess whether the estimates imply a union objective function that is quasiconcave in earnings and employment. Once again we make the point that tests to determine whether contracts are efficient and tests of contract efficiency cannot be undertaken without assumptions about union objectives. Several different expressions for union objectives were posited including the rent maximand, the Stone–Geary function, a linear relationship as embodied in equation (5.19), and a quadratic specification. Note, however, that for the most part the parameters describing union objectives were assumed to be the same across different union locals, an assumption contrary to other empirical work on the International Typographical Union.[54] The results were somewhat mixed, the

---

[53] These are instrumental variable estimates using city dummies and city dummies interacted with time and time squared as instruments. The standard errors are adjusted to recognize that $r^*\hat{X}_E/\hat{X}_K$ is an estimated quantity. $\bar{y}$ is a wage index measured by the real average hourly earnings received by production workers in durable goods manufacturing.

[54] I write "for the most part" because one parameter was allowed to be different according to the size of the union local. See Dertouzos and Pencavel (1981) and Pencavel (1984a, b) for evidence of differences in union objectives across locals.

estimates of the Stone–Geary function not conforming to quasi-concavity while the linear and quadratic specifications did conform to quasi-concavity. A somewhat generous interpretation is needed for the results to be read as supportive of contract efficiency.

Two issues in this research need to be carefully distinguished: first, there are the tests of whether employment is on the firm's wage-taking labor demand curve; and, second, there are the inferences regarding contract efficiency. The former constitute the heart of this research and our results consistently and confidently reject the null hypothesis of the labor demand curve equilibrium model: the first-order condition for employment implied by firms being on their wage-taking labor demand curves seems not to be satisfied. The subsequent results regarding contract efficiency are considerably more ambiguous, different hypothesized union objective functions delivering contradictory results concerning their quasi-concavity.

5.9   Conclusions

This chapter has been concerned with labor contracts not satisfying conditions of full efficiency as described in chapter 4. There are many *a priori* reasons to doubt whether the contracts negotiated in unionized labor markets are efficient. Moreover, certain institutional practices at first sight seem to diverge from what one might expect from efficient contracts. For instance, procedures relating to the determination of employment in unionized markets appear to assign a greater weight to management's decisions than might be expected from joint bargaining. These observations give rise to models with recursive characteristics, wages being set prior to the determination of employment and (perhaps) hours of work. Indeed, such recursive contracts may well be the best type of arrangements where the parties bargain under conditions of mutual incomplete information. A popular special case is the union monopoly model where the union determines the wage rate taking into account the subsequent effects of this wage on management's choice of employment and hours of work.

Because it is with respect to the determination of employment that contracts are usually thought not to be efficient, a natural procedure for investigating whether unions cause employment to lie off management's conventional labor demand curve is to ascertain whether the marginal revenue product of employment diverges from wages. An application of this procedure was described in the previous section: for a sample of US typographers between 1945 and 1973, there was considerable evidence that the marginal revenue product of workers systematically differed from wages. Whether the particular conditions for contract efficiency were satisfied is more ambiguous.

The emphasis in the literature has been on two models of employment determination, one corresponding to employment on the contract curve and the other corresponding to employment on management's wage-taking labor demand curve. It would enrich our understanding of the issues if more research were directed to intermediate cases in which the union's effect on employment is less than that corresponding to the contract curve, but more than that corresponding to management's labor demand curve. One such model is Johnson's whereby the parties bargain over the wage and the capital–labor ratio. Other models can be envisaged in which through bargaining the union exercises some influence over procedures relating to management's determination of employment. As these models have yet to be articulated, let alone applied empirically, their appeal is difficult to assess.[55] However, my conjecture is that they will contribute a good deal to an understanding of employment determination in unionized markets.

---

[55] Andrew Clark's working papers (1989a, b) have embarked on this line of research.

6 Interactions among Markets

Previous chapters have been concerned with the determination of wages, hours, and employment in a single labor market. In this chapter, I address some issues relating to the interaction of wages and employment among several labor markets. Two types of wage interactions are considered: first, interactions among unionized markets; and, second, interactions between a unionized market on the one hand and a nonunionized market on the other hand. Both these topics have been the subject of considerable research, but much of it is not grounded in behavioral models of unionism. The selective review and exposition in this chapter concentrates on this aspect of the literature. I follow this discussion of wage interactions with an exposition of a simple three-sector model designed to shed light on how wages in the union sector affect the distribution of employment in the economy.

This chapter's discussion is particularly relevant to aggregate models of the labor market. That is, the single-market models outlined in earlier chapters would seem to have immediate application at the macroeconomic level in those economies where confederations of trade unions and managements arrive at agreements with respect to wages that are supposed to apply to all sectors. This is roughly the situation in Sweden, Norway, Denmark, Austria, and Spain where there may well be modifications of these basic wage settlements in particular sectors, but these modifications are supposed to be exceptions and abnormal.[1] In many

---

[1] In fact, as is well known, through "wage drift" the effective rate of pay increase in such economies often diverges from that negotiated in the centralized bargains and, it is sometimes conjectured, subsequent wage increases scheduled at the economy-wide level may

other countries pay determination is not so highly centralized.

In both the United States and Britain, wage determination is decentralized and there are important nonunion labor markets in addition to the unionized. Though aggregate models of wages neglecting the decentralization of pay and problems of interdependence among labor markets can generate equations that track the movement of aggregate wages over time, these equations are disturbingly fragile and their behavioral content is open to considerable debate. Many scholars would place more confidence in those macroeconomic models of wages derived explicitly from behavioral microeconomic models. The discussion in this chapter concerns issues required of a satisfactory aggregate model of a partially unionized economy.

In existing models of partially unionized economies, there is a real difference of opinion regarding the appropriate representation of the nonunion labor market. In some research, the nonunion market is modelled as perfectly competitive. In other research, nonunion wages are characterized as administered prices set by management with little regard for the availability of potential new employees. In my view, there is a good case to be made for both representations: some nonunion markets are highly competitive, particularly those for workers embodying general skills; in other nonunion markets, management view new hires as imperfect substitutes for existing employees and the wage serves as an instrument for discouraging the quits of specifically trained workers and for eliciting productive work effort from the existing body of workers. What this implies, therefore, is that a simple union–nonunion dichotomy of labor markets may be a misleading model of the economy and that, for some purposes, this two-sector model needs to give way to a three-sector model in which two quite different types of nonunion markets are identified.

Indeed, in many respects, the behavior of the nonunion, administered-wage, sector more closely resembles the union sector than the nonunion, competitive-wage, sector. Employees in the nonunion, administered-wage, sector and those in the unionized sector tend to embody firm-specific or job-specific skills and many workers remain with the same employer for a long time. In these sectors, the sizes of both firms and plants tend to be large and often product markets are not ruthlessly competitive. The prototype of such a nonunion, administered-wage, firm is in the public sector where, if wages are not the outcome of collective bargaining negotiations with unions or employee associations, they are set

---

do no more than ratify earnings increases that have already taken place on the factory floor. There is a danger, therefore, of exaggerating the importance of economy-wide bargains in such countries and of understating the relevance of decentralized wage determination.

by an administrative procedure that places heavy weight on wages paid to "comparable" employees and where little or no weight is attached to the supply of new employees for these jobs. Through explicit wage comparisons, unionized labor markets tend to interact more closely with the nonunion, administered-wage, sector than the nonunion, competitive-wage, sector. For this reason, in the discussion below, after examining interactions between different unionized markets, I turn to the inter-dependence of wages between those in the unionized sector and those in the nonunion, administered-wage, sector. The wages in both these sectors are, to a first order of approximation, independent of wages in the nonunion, competitive, sector. By contrast, wages and employment in the competitive sector are very much dependent on wage determination in the other two sectors and this is the subject of section 6.4 below.

6.2 Interactions among Unionized Markets

Wage interactions among unionized labor markets have long been recognized by industrial relations researchers. For example, within the US steel, automobile, and rubber industries, for many years a new agreement reached with a particular employer or group of employers set the "pattern" for agreements in the rest of the industry.[2] In other words, key bargains guided settlements for other bargaining units *in the same industry*. More controversially, it has been argued that wage increases negotiated in a few collective bargaining agreements set the standard for agreements *in other industries*. Perhaps the best known econometric expression of this argument was Eckstein and Wilson's (1962) work.

They identified five contracts or wage "rounds" between 1948 and 1962 and used these wage rounds as their observations to estimate two sets of regression equations: first, they regressed changes in hourly earnings in each of a "key group" of manufacturing industries[3] on the average level of profits and on the average unemployment rate in all the industries within this key group;[4] and, second, they regressed changes in hourly earnings for each of the manufacturing industries outside the key group on profits and unemployment in these industries and on wage changes within the key group industries. In this second set of regressions, changes

---

[2] See, for instance, Seltzer (1951) and Levinson (1960).

[3] The key group included rubber, stone, clay, and glass, primary metals, fabricated metals, non-electrical machinery, electrical machinery, transport equipment, and instruments.

[4] Of course, the models we have outlined in previous chapters would suggest that both the level of profits and the level of employment are determined within the bargaining process and cannot be treated as predetermined with respect to wages or the change in wages.

in wages in the key group industries were significantly associated with wage increases outside the key group for eight of the eleven non-key group industries. For these eight industries, Eckstein and Wilson conclude that wages "are largely determined by spillover effects of the key group wages and economic variables applicable to the industry" (p. 408).[5]

This line of work occasioned a good deal of research challenging these inferences and offering alternative explanations for the measured associations. In this literature, however, there was little attempt to derive the estimated wage equations from formal models of bargaining behavior. Such derivations can be provided, however, as I proceed to show using (as a simplification for expository purposes) interactions between merely two unionized markets. The models that follow explicitly draw on the literature of oligopolistic behavior in product markets. The analogies between unionized labor markets and oligopolistic product markets have frequently been alluded to and exploited in the construction of behavioral models.[6] Any originality here lies in the specific formulation of the models and their relation to empirical work.

Consider two unionized labor markets indexed by the subscripts 1 and 2. In market 1, the union maximizes $\Gamma_1 = g_1(y_1, h_1, E_1; y_2)$ and management maximizes $\pi_1 = R_1(h_1, E_1, K_1) - y_1 E_1 - r_1 K_1$ where, as before, $y_1 = W_1 h_1$ and $y_2 = W_2 h_2$. I assume $\partial g_1 / \partial W_2 < 0$ as illustrated in equations (4.9) and (5.13) above. In a second labor market, the union takes as its objective $\Gamma_2 = g_2(y_2, h_2, E_2; y_1)$ where $\partial g_2 / \partial W_1 < 0$ and management maximizes $\pi_2 = R_2(h_2, E_2, K_2) - y_2 E_2 - r_2 K_2$. Given these objectives, the interactions between these two markets originate in the unions' objective functions, not from managements' goals. Reasons why a management may not be indifferent to the wages paid in another firm are discussed in section 6.3.

To analyze the interactions between these markets requires some prior assumptions about the manner in which wages, hours, and employment are determined. Suppose the variables are determined recursively as described in section 5.6 above. That is, initially wages and the level of capital services are determined at Stage 1 according to some Nash bargaining formula and then at Stage 2, management (acting unilaterally) determines employment and hours of work. So, at Stage 1, in market

---

[5] Comparable regression equations based on similar reasoning were fitted by Hines (1969) to annual British industrial data between 1948 and 1962. In his work, there were 12 industrial groups and the key (or "lead") sector was presumed to be public utilities (gas, electricity, and water) and transport and communications. After accounting for movements in trade union membership, he reported a significant association between changes in wages in this key sector and changes in wages in seven industries. Also see Elliott (1976) and the literature cited there.

[6] See, for instance, Fellner (1949) and, more recently, Oswald (1979) and Dixon (1988).

1, $\Psi_1 = \Gamma_1^{\alpha_1} \pi_1^{1-\alpha_1}$ is maximized with respect to W_1 and in market 2, $\Psi_2 = \Gamma_2^{\alpha_2} \pi_2^{1-\alpha_2}$ is maximized with respect to W_2. The first-order conditions for the determination of wages in each market are

$$\frac{\partial \Psi_1}{\partial W_1} = \alpha_1 \Gamma_1^{\alpha_1 - 1} \pi_1^{1-\alpha_1} \left(\frac{\partial \Gamma_1}{\partial W_1} + \frac{\partial \Gamma_1}{\partial W_2} \frac{\partial c_2}{\partial W_1} \right)$$

$$+ (1 - \alpha_1) \Gamma_1^{\alpha_1} \pi_1^{-\alpha_1} \frac{\partial \pi_1}{\partial W_1} = 0 \tag{6.1}$$

$$\frac{\partial \Psi_2}{\partial W_2} = \alpha_2 \Gamma_2^{\alpha_2 - 1} \pi_2^{1-\alpha_2} \left(\frac{\partial \Gamma_2}{\partial W_2} + \frac{\partial \Gamma_2}{\partial W_1} \frac{\partial c_1}{\partial W_2} \right)$$

$$+ (1 - \alpha_2) \Gamma_2^{\alpha_2} \pi_2^{-\alpha_2} \frac{\partial \pi_2}{\partial W_2} = 0 \tag{6.2}$$

where $\partial c_i / \partial W_j$ is union j's estimate of how union i's wage-setting policies will be affected by a small increase in W_j. In other words, $\partial c_i / \partial W_j$ is the conjectural variation.

Now in some cases each union may well ignore the effects of its wage-setting behavior on the other union and set the conjectural variation to zero. This may arise when the effects have operated for only a relatively short period of time or when the unions may be poorly informed of the

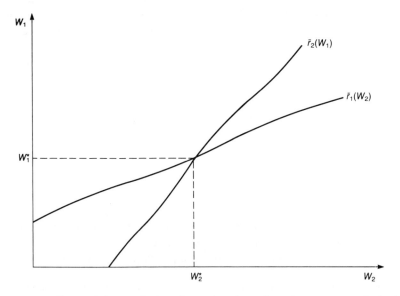

Figure 6.1 Bertrand characterization of wage interdependence between two unionized markets.

nature and magnitude of the interactions. This Bertrand characterization of interdependence between the wage-setting institutions may be represented through reaction functions according to which the optimal wage in each market is expressed as a function of the wage in the other market. In figure 6.1, $W_1 = \bar{r}_1(W_2)$ is the reaction function in market 1 and $W_2 = \bar{r}_2(W_1)$ is the reaction function in market 2: an increase in wages in sector i reduces union j's welfare and union j responds by pushing more on sector j's wages so that $\bar{r}_1' > 0$ and $\bar{r}_2' > 0$. When wages in each sector satisfy both reaction functions (that is, when the particular outcomes, W_1^* and W_2^*, satisfy $W_1^* = \bar{r}_1(W_2^*)$ and $W_2^* = \bar{r}_2(W_1^*)$), each sector's wages are consistent with those in the other sector and, other things being equal, there is no tendency for wages to change.

In the Bertrand model outlined in the previous paragraph, in negotiating wages, each union took wages in the other sector as given even though this was contradicted through wage interdependence. A model in which only one union, the "follower," behaves in this way may help to understand *pattern* or *key bargaining*. That is, suppose in labor market 2, the union ignores the effect of its wage on settlements in labor market 1 (so $\partial c_1/\partial W_2 = 0$). But, in market 1, the union behaves as a "leader" and in setting W_1 it takes into account the reaction function in market 2, $W_2 = \bar{r}_2(W_1)$. An asymmetrical situation exists in that the determination of W_2 assumes a fixed value of W_1, but the value at which W_1 is set recognizes the induced variation in W_2. In particular, the "leader" in market 1 recognizes that the induced increase in W_2 reduces Γ_1 and so W_1 will be lower (though union 1's welfare higher) than would be the case if these reactions were ignored.[7]

It will be instructive to illustrate the features of these models assuming particular expressions for the relevant functions. Suppose union 1's objective function takes the following form:

$$\Gamma_1 = \left[\ln(W_1 h_1) - \rho_1 \ln h_1 - \gamma_1 \ln(W_2 h_2)\right]^{\mu_1} \ln E_1 \qquad (6.3)$$

where $0 < \gamma_1 < 1$, an assumption implying that proportional increases in W_2 impair union 1's welfare less than the same proportional decreases in W_1. Correspondingly, union 2's objective function is as follows:

$$\Gamma_2 = \left[\ln(W_2 h_2) - \rho_2 \ln h_2 - \gamma_2 \ln(W_1 h_1)\right]^{\mu_2} \ln E_2.$$

As a solution to the bargaining problem, posit the special case of the recursive model described above where $\alpha_1 = \alpha_2 = 1$ in Ψ_1 and Ψ_2 (i.e., the union monopoly model). So the union first sets the wage to maximize

---

[7] A third solution, of course, occurs when the unions collude. The situation would then correspond to the case of a single union bargaining with two firms.

its objective function and then management responds by determining employment. Also, to facilitate exposition, assume hours of work are fixed at $\bar{h}_1$ in market 1 and at $\bar{h}_2$ in market 2. The employment demand functions in each market are assumed to be

$$\ln E_i = \alpha_{0i} + \alpha_{1i}\ln W_i + \alpha_{2i}X_i + \alpha_{3i}\ln\bar{h}_i, \quad i = 1, 2 \qquad (6.4)$$

where $\alpha_{1i} < 0$. Let X_i be a sector specific exogenous variable defined such that increases in X_i increase employment (i.e., $\alpha_{2i} > 0$). So X_i might be the price of a substitute input or the price of a substitute product. Then the reaction function in, say, market 2 is as follows:

$$\ln W_2 = - \left[\frac{\alpha_{02}\,\mu_2}{\alpha_{12}(1 + \mu_2)}\right] - \left[\frac{\alpha_{22}\,\mu_2}{\alpha_{12}(1 + \mu_2)}\right]X_2$$

$$+ \left[\frac{\alpha_{12}(\rho_2 - 1) - \alpha_{23}\mu_2}{\alpha_{12}(1 + \mu_2)}\right]\ln\bar{h}_2 + \left(\frac{\gamma_2}{1 + \mu_2}\right)\ln(W_1\bar{h}_1). \qquad (6.5)$$

The reaction function in market 1 is defined analogously. The full Bertrand equilibrium pair of wages satisfies both reaction functions and, for W_1, this is given by

$$\ln W_1^* = k_1 - \alpha_{12}^{-1}\delta_1\gamma_1\alpha_{22}\mu_2 X_1 - \alpha_{11}^{-1}\delta_1(1 + \mu_2)\alpha_{21}\mu_1 X_2$$

$$+ \delta_1[\gamma_1\gamma_2 + (\rho_1 - 1)(1 + \mu_2) - \alpha_{12}^{-1}\gamma_1\alpha_{23}\mu_2]\ln\bar{h}_1$$

$$+ \delta_1\gamma_1(\mu_2 + \rho_1)\ln\bar{h}_2 \qquad (6.6)$$

where $\delta_1 = [(1 + \mu_1)(1 + \mu_2) - \gamma_1\gamma_2]^{-1} > 0$ and k_1 is a congeries of parameters. Equation (6.6) is an example of the equilibrium wage W_1^* graphed in figure 6.1. An increase in X_1 induces a rightward shift in the employment demand curve, equation (6.4), and the union exploits this by setting a higher wage so $\partial\ln W_1^*/\partial X_1 > 0$. This increase in X_1 induces a rightward shift in the reaction function $\bar{r}_2(W_1)$ in figure 6.1 and this causes wages in the second market, W_2^*, to rise. With hours set exogenously in this example, an increase in $\ln h_2$ reduces Γ_1 and the union responds by increasing W_1^*: $\partial\ln W_1^*/\partial\ln\bar{h}_2 > 0$. An increase in X_2 induces union 2 to push for a higher W_2^* and this causes union 1 to raise its wage correspondingly; in other words, the reaction function $\bar{r}_1(W_2)$ shifts upwards.

With a Stackelberg equilibrium, while equation (6.5) describes the determination of the wage in sector 2 (the sector that follows), the leading sector union 1 selects W_1 to maximize Γ_1 and in so doing recognizes that W_2 will change according to the reaction function specified in equation (6.5). This results in the following equation for W_1:

$$\ln W_1 = k_2 - \alpha_{11}^{-1}(1 + \mu_1)^{-1}\alpha_{21}\mu_1 X_1 - \alpha_{12}^{-1}\delta_2\gamma_1\alpha_{22}\mu_2 X_2$$

$$+ [\delta_2\rho_1(1 + \mu_2) - \alpha_{11}^{-1}(1 + \mu_1)^{-1}(\alpha_{31}\mu_1 + \alpha_{11})]\ln\bar{h}_1$$

$$+ \delta_2\gamma_1(\mu_2 + \rho_2)\ln\bar{h}_2 \tag{6.7}$$

where $\delta_2 = [(1 + \mu_1)(1 + \mu_2 - \gamma_1\gamma_2)]^{-1} > 0$ and k_2 is another constant. Together equations (6.5) and (6.7) imply an equilibrium wage
differential of the form

$$\ln(W_1/W_2) = \tilde{a}_0 + \tilde{a}_1 X_1 + \tilde{a}_2 X_2 + \tilde{a}_3\ln\bar{h}_1 + \tilde{a}_4\ln\bar{h}_2 \tag{6.8}$$

where the coefficients are functions of the parameters of equations (6.5)
and (6.7). It may be verified that, though the magnitudes of the responses
of $\ln W_1$ to changes in the exogenous variables are different in equations
(6.6) and (6.7), qualitatively the comparative static implications are the
same.[8] In other words, the Bertrand model of wage-setting behavior and
the Stackelberg model of behavior do not imply simple inclusion or
exclusion restrictions that effectively discriminate between them. Any
empirical attempt to differentiate between the two characterizations of
interdependence among unionized markets needs to resort to the estimation of structural parameters of the behavioral functions.

I know of no study that has addressed this. Usually, the empirical
research is motivated not by the goal of discriminating among alternative
behavioral models, but by the more modest goal of ascertaining whether
such interdependence exists among union contracts. For instance, using
the multi-year contract as the unit of observation, Flanagan (1976)
selected seven major contracts and related the annual percentage change
in the wage over the life of contract i negotiated at time t, $\Delta\ln W_i(t)$, to
the proportional difference in wages between sectors i and j just prior to
t. Holding constant the effects of changes in consumer prices and lagged
changes in industry-wide employment, he reported negative effects of
relative wages on $\Delta\ln W_i(t)$ though in less than one-fifth of instances
would this effect be judged as significant by conventional criteria.

Flanagan's study has the distinct attraction over most other empirical
work of using observations that relate precisely to unionized contracts

---

[8] The effect of changes in $\bar{h}_1$ on wages in market 1 is ambiguous in sign even if the effect
of work hours on employment is ignored (i.e., even if $\alpha_{31} = 0$). With this assumption, an
increase in $\ln\bar{h}_1$ has an immediate effect of raising Γ_1 by $(1 - \rho_1)$. If $(1 - \rho_1) > 0$, the
increase in $\ln\bar{h}_1$ allows union 1 to opt for a lower wage, W_1, to enhance Γ_1 through an
increase in employment. At the same time, an increase in $\ln\bar{h}_1$ reduces Γ_2 by the amount γ_2
which induces union 2 to press for a higher value of W_2. In turn, this reduces Γ_1 by the
amount $-\gamma_1$ so the first union will be inclined towards a higher value of W_1. The net effect
on W_1 will depend upon the particular magnitudes of the parameters so $\partial\ln W_1^*/\partial\ln\bar{h}_1$ is
ambiguous in sign.

rather than to some industry aggregates, but it leaves quite unsettled whether wage interactions across unionized labor markets are of empirical importance. No doubt, instances can be cited strongly suggesting the relevance of such wage interactions, but what is at issue is how extensive these instances are and whether these wage interactions are merely surrogates for other variables.[9]

These issues are difficult to address because industrial relations research leads one to believe that, though wage interactions may be operative at all times, some interactions persist for a long period of time while others are quite changeable. For instance, in studying manual workers employed in London newspapers during the 1960s, Brown and Sisson (1975) maintained that, early in the decade, the dominant wage interactions were among workers in different London newspapers whereas after about 1964 interactions among different grades of workers in the same newspaper assumed greater importance. Comparable changes in the sources of wage interactions were identified among engineering workers in Coventry: before 1964 and after 1971, wage interactions among workers in the same plant were dominant, but between 1964 and 1971 the effects of wages in other plants assumed greater importance. These inferences were drawn from a careful study of the ways in which employers' associations and trade unions collected and disseminated information on wages. If the authors are correct and the nature of wage interactions is constantly shifting,[10] then empirical research that presumes stability in these interactions will deliver unsatisfactory results.

In order to focus on alternative models describing the interdependence of wages in different unionized markets, the exposition in the previous paragraphs was undertaken in a "timeless" framework where the dating of each collective bargaining contract was deliberately ignored. In fact, of course, this interdependence proceeds in a time dimension with wages in one contract negotiated at a different moment from wages in another contract. If both contracts have the same duration, then the nonsynchronization of collective bargaining agreements implies overlapping

---

[9] Mehra (1976) pursued an unconventional line to determine the presence of wage interdependence. After relating each industry's wage to a vector of regressors, he examined the structure of the covariance matrix of the cross-industry residuals. He argued that different models of wage interaction implied different forms for the off-diagonal terms in the residual matrix. The defect with this procedure is that, by construction, the estimated residuals are orthogonal with respect to the regressors and yet there seems no reason why the interaction effects should be uncorrelated with other effects on wages.

[10] As another example, when Eckstein (1968) extended his and Wilson's earlier study (Eckstein and Wilson, 1962) to the 1960s, he found the composition of his "leading" sector had changed. Evidence of these effects for public sector workers in Britain is provided in Elliott (1977).

contracts, a feature that has been assigned a central role by some macro-economists in explaining the persistence of business cycles.[11] In the earlier literature, wage interdependence was essentially backward-looking: that is, if $W_j(t)$ is the wage negotiated at time t in period j, then the earlier literature emphasized the dependence of $W_1(t)$ on $W_2(t-1)$. The modern literature[12] provides a forward-looking component: $W_1(t)$ depends on $W_2(t+s)$ where $W_2(t+s)$ is sector 2's wage expected to prevail during 1's contract period, the duration of which is s periods. The empirical work quantifying wage interactions across labor markets pays scant attention to such forward-looking components of wages.

6.3 Interactions between Unionized and Nonunionized Markets

The previous section was concerned with interactions among unionized labor markets. These interactions arose because each union's objectives were assumed to depend upon the wage negotiated by some other union. This section is concerned with interactions between unionized and nonunionized labor markets and, in particular, with the dependence of each sector's wage on that prevailing in the other sector.

There are at least two reasons to expect unions to negotiate a higher wage, W^u, in response to an increase in the nonunion wage, W^m. First, an increase in W^m will raise the prices of products produced by nonunion workers and, assuming these products are substitutes for those produced by union workers, this will tend to raise the derived demand for union labor. Indirectly through the product market, therefore, a rise in W^m induces an increase in W^u. Second, union members may gauge their welfare in terms of the wage prevailing in the nonunion sector in much the same way as was discussed in the previous section with respect to wage interactions among unionized markets. In the second case, W^m affects W^u directly whereas in the first case W^m affects W^u through its effect on product prices. In either case, increases in the nonunion wage, W^m, effect an increase in the union wage, W^u. This may be expressed as follows:

[11] See Akerlof (1969), Fischer (1977), Taylor (1980), and Blanchard (1986). Immediate questions prompted by this literature are why are contracts not synchronized and why does the degree of synchronization vary across countries? One explanation runs in terms of the degree to which shocks are sector-specific: where all firms and unions experience the same shocks at the same time, full synchronization is conjectured to be more likely. A different argument stresses the effects of incomplete information: where management and unions can acquire useful information by observing the contractual terms negotiated by others, there is an incentive for each collective bargain to be negotiated after others have been settled.

[12] See Taylor (1980, 1983).

$$W^u = \varphi^u(W^m; X_1) \tag{6.9}$$

where $\partial\varphi^u/\partial W^m > 0$ and where X_1 represents exogenous variables affecting union wages. X_1 includes variables from the product and factor markets (such as the prices of substitute products and inputs), variables that affect the union's relative bargaining power and no-trade opportunities, and variables from the union's objective function. A particular example of equation (6.9) is equation (5.16) (with W^n replacing $\bar{y}$).

There are several reasons to believe that a higher union wage will induce a higher nonunion wage. The first reason goes under the name of the "threat effect" of unionism and the second arises from the desire of nonunion employers to maintain a given level of labor quality, to prevent the quits of specifically trained workers, and to bolster work effort. I shall call this second effect the "effort effect." Let us consider these two effects in turn.

The threat effect of unionism refers to the likelihood of a nonunion employer's work force becoming unionized in the future: other things being equal, a firm is more susceptible to unionization, the greater the differential between nonunion wages and those wages negotiated under collective bargaining. Raising nonunion wages to reduce the threat of unionization is a well-documented practice of nonunion employers. In his study of the pay policies of large, nonunion companies, Foulkes (1980) found that they "work hard to ensure that they are not vulnerable to a union organizational drive on the basis of pay or related issues. . . . It would be acceptable to say that the activities of many unions in the United States are benefiting many nonmembers; in other words, unions are doing much good for many people who do not pay them any dues. . . . [I]n all the companies studied union settlements, particularly those of competitors, are closely monitored" (pp. 141–54). As another example, in their study of the Chicago labor market, Rees and Shultz (1970) reported that some nonunion employers volunteered that their wage policies were largely affected by the possibility of their establishments being organized and the authors attributed the absence of a union–nonunion wage differential for most of their sample of workers to this threat effect.[13]

---

[13] "At least half the nonunion employers were conscious enough of union activity to bring it explicitly into our interviews. In many of these cases, recent attempts at organization had failed or further attempts were expected. . . . The methods used to keep informed about employee needs included plant grievance committees of various sorts. In one case, to forestall threatened unionization of skilled model makers, the employer shifted them from an hourly wage to a monthly salary basis of pay" (Rees and Shultz, 1970, pp. 45–6). As another example, in a survey of 24 nonunion firms in a Mid-West community where unions were well represented, Conant (1959) concluded, "It would not be accurate to say the union-forestalling motive was the sole consideration in compensation determination in these firms.

Of course, a higher wage may not be the nonunion employer's most effective method of forestalling the organization of his employees. Indeed, until they were effectively declared illegal by a Supreme Court decision in 1937 that ruled the 1935 National Labor Relations Act constitutional, the promotion of company unions was a common tactic for a nonunion employer to deter the unionization of his workers. Thus a Bureau of Labor Statistics survey (US Department of Labor, 1937) of company unions just before their demise indicates that, of those in existence in April 1935, most had been formed in the years 1915-19 and 1933-5, both periods when unions were rapidly expanding their membership. Furthermore, in their enquiries, the BLS staff found that the unionization of workers in neighboring establishments represented the single most important factor preceding the formation of the company union.[14] Along the same lines, Lewis (1963, p. 24) reasoned that the threat effect is most likely to be of consequence at times when unions have succeeded in organizing comparable or neighboring workers, that is, times when their threats of organizing nonunion employees have been carried out, and for this reason he conjectured that the late 1930s and early 1940s was the period when the threat effect is likely to have been most widespread.

The fact is that, while there may be a good deal of evidence of a qualitative kind to support the notion that the presence of trade unions affects the wages paid to nonunion workers, good, solid, evidence on the direction, size, and variations of these effects does not exist. It is suggestive that in many cases the wages of nonunion workers seem to be correlated with the extent of unionism in their industry, their occupation, or their locality, but the direction and magnitude of this correlation is disturbingly fickle.[15] This is not surprising because the threat effect of

---

Obviously, supply and demand factors in the local labor market exercised an influence. However, the union-forestalling motive was expressed so frequently and definitively that the conclusion is warranted that this factor alone and in isolation would have been sufficient to cause firms to make these adjustments" (p. 103).

[14] "Examination of a representative group of 126 company unions indicates that their establishment was most frequently due to the pressure of trade union activity either in the form of organization drives or strikes in the trade or vicinity. . . . Since in so many instances the presence of a trade union had inspired the movement to organize a company union, one phase of the work of setting up a company union was to attack the trade union or to hamper it by delay and manipulation" (US Department of Labor, 1937, p. 199).

[15] This is very well documented in Lewis (1986, pp. 146-53) who provides most of the references on this issue. Kahn (1978) tries to infer the effects of unions on nonunion wages by comparing the annual earnings of workers in predominantly unorganized occupations in a "union town," San Francisco, with those in a nonunion location, Los Angeles. On average, those in San Francisco are almost 25 percent below those in Los Angeles, other things being

unionism surely varies a good deal across firms depending upon management's distastes for collective bargaining and its assessment of the likelihood of being organized,[16] neither being closely correlated with the fraction unionized in the industry, occupation, or region.

The second reason why a nonunion firm's wage policies will be affected by the wage paid to comparable unionized workers arises from the effect of the firm's relative wage on its labor turnover which, in turn, affects the productivity and work effort of its employees. This is the "effort effect" according to which a reduction in wages does not imply the same reduction in labor costs if other firms' wages remain unchanged for, in this instance, a decline in the firm's relative wage will increase the costs of turnover and will impair work performance. The argument here is closely related to Marshall's notion (1920, pp. 456–7) that, among firms whose nonpecuniary conditions of employment are the same, competition in the labor market tends to equalize earnings per unit of work performed, not equalize actual pay. Hence, among workers with the same training and experience, variations in earnings across firms are consistent with competition in the labor market if these earnings differences correspond to differences in the effort and efficiency with which employees work.

Detailed labor market studies have documented the relevance of *relative* wages to a firm's personnel policies and of the effect of relative wages on the efficiency with which its employees work. For instance, on the basis of a careful study of a New England city in the late 1940s, Reynolds concluded:

A relatively high wage level has many advantages to the firm. It simplifies the recruitment problem. Even though the company might be able to get enough workers at a lower wage level, it can get them faster and with less persuasion at higher wages. It can also establish strict hiring specifications. . . . The company may also be able to insist on better-than-average efficiency. . . . It is not too easy for a firm to slip down substantially from its customary position in the area wage structure, even if it wishes to do so. . . . Even if there is no union, a company which lags behind a general wage movement risks disaffection among its employees. . . . A high-wage company thus tends to maintain its position as long as it can afford to because

---

equal. Is this the effect of unions or does it reflect other differences between the cities? Kahn entertains other explanations, but prefers that involving unions. Is a 25 percent higher wage sufficient compensation for choosing Los Angeles over San Francisco?

[16] See, for instance, the framework for the issue suggested by Rosen (1969).

the position confers positive advantages, because the possible gains from a lower wage level are quite uncertain, and because the transition to a lower wage level would be difficult and unpleasant. (Reynolds, 1951, pp. 232-3)[17]

According to this argument, then, a firm's wage policies are directed toward maintaining a particular position in the interfirm wage distribution. If this distribution is itself not shifting, then any single firm will be reluctant to alter its position in the wage hierarchy even if there are other factors that suggest the firm change its wages. This reasoning is revealed in an interesting survey of personnel managers in 26 British firms in the summer of 1982 (Kaufman, 1984). Most of the firms were small, nonunion, enterprises whose management would be expected to exercise greater discretion over wages than unionized firms that may be subsidiaries of larger corporations. Moreover, with a national unemployment rate of 13.2 percent, one might expect some downward pressure on wages. In fact, Kaufman

found that non-union wages responded very slowly and incompletely to the current slackness in the labour market. Among the sixteen non-union firms which gave a definite answer, exactly half believed they could find qualified workers at lower wages. . . . [T]here appeared to be a substantial amount of specific training in most firms, even the small retail establishments. Because of the investment in both formal and informal job specific training, the employers in these "competitive" sectors also tried to establish long-term employment relationships and rejected the possibility of turning over their entire labour force if the latter refused to accept wage cuts. . . . Employers invariably felt that work effort was endogenous and depended upon worker motivation and satisfaction. As a result, they believed that there was substantial potential variation in both the quantity and quality of output for a constant input of labour hours. (Kaufman, 1984, pp. 106-7).

This and other research provides support for the characterization of wages appearing not only as a cost item in a firm's statement of its profits, but also as a factor in gross revenues through its effect on work effort. And, according to these labor market studies, what is relevant to turnover and work effort is the *relative* wage, the firm's wage relative to some norm or to a market average or to a wage paid by a comparison firm. One

---

[17] Also see Reynolds (1951, pp. 156-69), Rees and Shultz (1970, p. 219), Slichter (1954), and MacKay et al. (1971, pp. 93, 390-1).

formalization of the nonunion firm's wage decisions and one which expresses its sensitivity to the wages paid by a comparable unionized firm is to define the nonunionized firm's relative wage position as

$$v = \frac{W^n - W^u}{W^u},$$

where W^n is the nonunion firm's wage rate and W^u the going union wage rate. v is likely to be negative. The firm's choice of W^n (and, therefore, given W^u, its choice of v) affects its net revenues in three ways. First, conventionally, an increase in W^n raises the firm's wage bill. Second, an increase in W^n reduces the firm's quits which, in turn, reduces the firm's costs of hiring and training new workers. In other words, the firm's turnover costs tend to fall with an increase in W^n. Suppose each period's turnover costs per employee are proportionate, c, to a component that varies with relative wages: $c\tau(v)$ where $\tau'(v) < 0$ and, assuming the responsiveness of turnover costs to higher wages diminishes with v, $\tau''(v) > 0$. Third, an increase in W^n raises the efficiency of the labor input both by increasing the quality of the work force and by increasing cooperative team effort or morale. If e denotes an index of labor efficiency, then this argument suggests $e(v)$ where $e'(v) > 0$. Again, a "diminishing returns" type of argument would suggest that eventually $e''(v) < 0$.

The firm's effective labor input may be represented as $L = ehE$ where h is hours of work per employee and E is the number of employees. The production function is $X = X(L)$ with $X'(L) > 0$ and $X''(L) < 0$. The nonunion firm's profits are given by

$$\pi(E, v) = pX[e(v)\bar{h}E] - (1 + v)W^u \bar{h}E - c\tau(v)E \qquad (6.10)$$

where, for convenience, hours of work are assumed given at $\bar{h}$ and p is the firm's fixed price per unit of output. The firm chooses employment, E, and its relative wage, v, to maximize π given $\bar{h}$, p, W^u, c, and the form of the production function. The first-order condition[18] for employment is a familiar requirement that the marginal revenue product of employment equal its marginal cost:

$$pX'e\bar{h} = (1 + v)W^u\bar{h} + c\tau, \qquad (6.11)$$

the marginal cost (on the right-hand side of equation (6.11)) consisting of one part wage costs and the other part turnover costs. There is also a less

---

[18] Our assumptions regarding the second derivatives of the functions (in particular, $X''(L) < 0$, $e''(v) < 0$, and $\tau''(v) > 0$) ensure that the first-order conditions do, indeed, describe a maximum of profits.

familiar "marginal-benefit-equals-marginal-cost" type of condition regarding the determination of v:

$$pX'\bar{h}e' = W^u\bar{h} + c\tau' \ . \tag{6.12}$$

The marginal contribution to gross revenue from a small increase in v is the term on the left-hand side of equation (6.12), e' being the increase in work performance induced by a rise in v. A small increase in v reduces turnover costs by $c\tau'$, but increases wage costs by $W^u\bar{h}$, the sum of these two terms being the effect on total costs of a small increase in v. A pair of decision functions is implied:

$$E = E(p, W^u, \bar{h}, c) \tag{6.13}$$

$$v = v(p, W^u, \bar{h}, c) \tag{6.14}$$

Our particular interest is in determining the effect on the nonunion firm's employment and wage of changes in the union wage rate.[19] It can be shown that an increase in W^u induces the nonunion firm to reduce v: the higher wage costs that would result from increasing W^n to match exactly the increase in W^u are greater than the savings in turnover costs and the greater production efficiency that follow from allowing the union–nonunion wage differential to rise and so an increase in the union wage induces the nonunion firm to allow the shortfall of W^n below W^u to widen. The fact that v falls when W^u rises does not mean that W^n falls. Indeed, it is more likely that W^n rises though not enough to maintain v unchanged.[20]

An increase in W^u induces a fall in the nonunion firm's total effective labor input, $e\bar{h}E$, in accordance with conventional reasoning. However, it does not necessarily follow that a higher W^u reduces employment, E. The higher wage costs induced by a higher W^u discourages employment, but the reduction in v accompanying a higher W^u causes e to fall. This reduction in e means a drop in the firm's effective labor input which may be so large that the firm would like to offset it by increases in employment.

---

[19] A brief appendix lays out the comparative statics more fully.

[20] The effect of W^u on W^n is given by

$$\frac{\partial W^u}{\partial W^n} = (1 + v) + W^u\frac{\partial v}{\partial W^u},$$

where $\partial v / \partial W^u < 0$. Suppose initially $W^u = \$10$ and $W^n = \$8$ implying $v = -0.2$. Now let W^u increase by 10 percent to $\$11$. If v declines to -0.25, a relatively large change in the union–nonunion wage differential as measured by its average annual movements, then W^n rises to $\$8.25$, a 3 percent increase in W^n. In this example, v will decline to -0.273 if W^n is unchanged.

The net effect on the change in employment is uncertain.

Together the threat and effort effects call for the dependence of W^n on W^u:

$$W^n = \varphi^n(W^u; X_2) \tag{6.15}$$

with $\partial \varphi^n / \partial W^u$ likely to be positive. Here X_2 represents exogenous variables affecting the impact of W^u on W^n. The threat effect suggested X_2 might include the extent of union organization in a locality or industry while the effort effect identified X_2 with product prices and turnover costs. Together the union and nonunion sectors of the labor market may be said to be in equilibrium when there is no tendency for their wages to change and an equilibrium union–nonunion wage differential emerges. That is, denoting the union–nonunion wage differential by $r = (W^u - W^n)/W^n$ as in chapter 2, then the joint satisfaction of equations (6.9) and (6.15) yields an equation for r:

$$r = r(X_1, X_2).$$

As an illustration, suppose equations (6.9) and (6.15) are linear in the logarithms of the variables:[21]

$$\ln W^u = \alpha_0^u + \alpha_1^u \ln W^n + \alpha_2^u X_1, \quad 0 < \alpha_1^u < 1 \tag{6.16}$$

$$\ln W^n = \alpha_0^n + \alpha_1^n \ln W^u + \alpha_2^n X_2, \quad 0 < \alpha_1^n < 1. \tag{6.17}$$

The α_i^u coefficients embody parameters from the union objective function and the firm's production function as illustrated by equation (5.16) and their values will reflect the particular resolution of the bargaining problem between the union and management. The α_i^n coefficients will be related to the parameters determining the nature of unionism's threat effect and to the relation between work effort and wages as given by the effort effect. Then the union–nonunion wage differential is approximately

$$r = \bar{\alpha}[(\alpha_0^u - \alpha_0^n) + (\alpha_1^u \alpha_0^n - \alpha_1^n \alpha_0^u)] + \bar{\alpha}\alpha_2^u(1 - \alpha_1^n)X_1$$
$$+ \bar{\alpha}\alpha_2^n(\alpha_1^u - 1)X_2 \tag{6.18}$$

where $\bar{\alpha} = (1 - \alpha_1^u \alpha_1^n)^{-1} > 1$. Presumably it is an equation such as this that may be called upon to understand the pattern of union–nonunion wage differentials described in chapter 2. Suppose X_1 and X_2 are each defined such that increases in X_1 raise $\ln W^u$ and increases in X_2

---

[21] Recall that equation (5.16) was a particular example of equation (6.9) and equation (5.16) is, indeed, linear in the logarithms of the variables.

raise $\ln W^n$. Then the equilibrium union–nonunion wage differential increases with X_1 and decreases with X_2.[22] Note though that, under the stated assumptions, the effect of an increase in (say) X_1 on the union–nonunion wage differential is less than its direct impact on the union wage.[23]

In fact, few studies have made efforts to explain the pattern of union–nonunion wage differentials in this way. The research described in chapter 2 has been focused on deriving estimates of the magnitudes of the union–nonunion wage differential, the definition of an advance in this literature being work that offers a more precise or more defensible estimate or that extends estimates to a different group of workers or to a different time. Usually researchers have eschewed interpretation and they have not derived equations such as (6.18) in order to provide a structural explanation for their results. Yet, without such a framework, conjectures advanced to account for differences or variations in union–nonunion wage differentials are inherently ambiguous. For instance, consider the empirical regularity that, in the United States, in the 1970s, the union–nonunion wage differential was greater in private than in public employment. Is this because of the effect of private–public employment on union wages or its effect on nonunion wages? If the former, is this because union objectives are different between the two sectors or because the production technologies constraining the attainment of these objectives are different? Without a structural model, these questions are difficult to answer.

6.4   The Distribution of Employment

The previous section has examined wage interactions between a unionized and a nonunionized market. Because of the operation of threat and effort effects, the nonunion wage was an administered price; it did not equate the demand for and the supply of labor in a conventional, textbook-like, fashion. This is an apt description of nonunion markets for many types of skilled labor especially those where skills are firm-specific or job-specific. However, there are also labor markets in the United States and Britain where such administered wage-setting is not a useful characterization and where wages are determined by conventional competitive forces. The purpose of this section is to add a competitive sector to the union

---

[22] Rosen (1969) conjectured that the extent of unionism is an element of both X_1 and X_2 and its effect on r is theoretically indeterminant.

[23] In other words, the direct effect of X_1 on $\ln W^u$ is α_2^u while the effect of X_1 on r is $\alpha_2 \alpha^*$ where $\alpha^* = [\,(1 - \alpha_1^n)/(1 - \alpha_1^u \alpha_1^n)\,] < 1$.

labor market and nonunion market described in the previous section and examine employment interactions among these three markets.

Recall that the argument in section 6.3 above distinguishes two sectors, a unionized labor market and a nonunion labor market whose wages are directly affected by those in the union market. In this nonunion labor market, the wage rate is an administered price: first, as a union avoidance strategy, management pay rents to their employees in the form of higher wages; and, second, to reduce costly turnover and enhance productivity, management maintain a particular position in the frequency distribution of wages across firms. As a result, for given values of exogenous variables X, union wages bear a given relation to administered nonunion wages:

$$W^u = \lambda(X)W^n. \qquad (6.19)$$

It would be wrong, however, to think that all nonunion firms behave in this fashion. On the contrary, for some firms, the threat of being unionized is virtually nonexistent while their employees have few specific skills that are lost through turnover so there is little reason to pay wage premiums. I shall call this the "competitive" sector. In many respects it bears the features of Doeringer and Piore's (1971) secondary labor market.[24] It is characterized by relatively low wages and high labor turnover. This sector is exempt from statutory wage regulation either *de jure* or (because of enforcement costs) *de facto*. Jobs are not difficult to get, but they offer little opportunity for advancement. The firms are often in industries the demand for whose output is volatile so employment in a given firm fluctuates considerably. The competitive sector absorbs workers unable to find employment either in the unionized or in the nonunion, administered-wage, labor markets.

Hence three sectors are distinguished: a unionized sector, a nonunion, administered-wage, sector, and a competitive sector. Wages in the first two sectors are determined in relation to one another in accordance with the arguments in section 6.3; their wages are uninfluenced by the competitive sector. Employment in these two sectors is determined without reference to the labor market in the competitive sector. By contrast, employment and wages in the competitive sector are set by conventional market demand and supply functions.

The demand for workers in the nonunion, administered-wage, sector may be expressed as

[24] Perhaps a more appropriate reference for the model in this section is to Edwards's (1979) taxonomy of secondary, subordinate primary, and independent primary labor markets. I depart from Edwards in his claim that, "Labor markets are segmented because they express a historical segmentation of the labor process; specifically, a distinct system of control inside the firm underlies each of the three market segments" (Edwards, 1979, p. 178).

$$E^n = A_1 (W^n)^{-\eta_1}$$

where, for convenience, I assume (here and below) a constant-elasticity specification and where the A_is are parameters. In the union sector, if employment is determined unilaterally by management, an analogous employment equation is

$$E^u = \tilde{A}_2 (W^u)^{-\tilde{\eta}_2}. \tag{6.20}$$

If, on the other hand, employment is determined jointly with wages in the union sector, then we might specify an equation for employment such as

$$E^u = A_2 (W^n)^{-\eta_2}. \tag{6.21}$$

This is precisely analogous to equation (4.21) in chapter 4 where, for a particular representation of union and management objectives, such a constant-elasticity equation resulted. Whether equation (6.20) or (6.21) holds is not particularly important here in view of our assumption that W^n bears a fixed relation to W^u, equation (6.19). In the competitive sector, c, the demand for labor is given by

$$E^c = A_0 (W^c)^{-\eta_0}. \tag{6.22}$$

If the supply of labor to the economy as a whole is expressed by the equation $E = BW^\sigma$, where B is a parameter, the issue becomes one of allocating these workers among the three sectors.

The most tractable assumption is that employment in the union and nonunion, administered-wage, sectors is allocated randomly among the supply. In an analysis that acknowledged the varying characteristics of workers and that recognized the claims of job occupancy, this random allocation assumption would be quite inappropriate, but here where such factors are neglected it is less objectionable especially as other formulations such as queues quickly lead to complexities that conceal rather than reveal the basic forces. So, with the random allocation assumption, the probability of employment in the union and nonunion, administered-wage, sectors is q^u and q^n respectively:

$$q^u = (A_2 B^{-1} \lambda^{-\sigma})(W^n)^{-(\sigma + \eta_2)}$$

$$q^n = A_1 B^{-1} (W^n)^{-(\sigma + \eta_1)}.$$

In this event, the supply of workers to the competitive sector is

$$S = (1 - q^u - q^n)B(W^c)^\sigma = Z(W^c)^\sigma \tag{6.23}$$

where $Z = B - A_2 \lambda^{-\sigma} (W^n)^{-(\sigma + \eta_2)} - A_1 (W^n)^{-(\sigma + \eta_1)}$. The wage in the competitive sector, W^c, equates demand, equation (6.22), and supply, equation (6.23):

$$W^c = (A_0^{-1}Z)^\gamma \qquad\qquad (6.24)$$

where $\gamma = -(\sigma + \eta_0)^{-1} < 0$. Employment in the competitive sector is given by

$$E^c = A_0^{-\sigma\gamma} Z^{-\gamma\eta_0}.$$

This model differs from a number of other sectoral, labor market, models in which some workers who are unable to find employment in the high wage sectors do not obtain employment in the competitive sector, but wait for jobs that periodically become available in the high wage sectors.[25] These models adopt the equilibrium condition used by Todaro (1969) and by Harris and Todaro (1970) in their analysis of migration and unemployment in less developed economies: wages in the rural sector are equated with expected wages in the urban sector where the expectation takes account of the probability of being employed at the urban sector's wage rate. In their model, the two sectors are spatially distinct from one another and so there is good reason for their tacit assumption that a worker has to choose between certain employment in the rural sector and uncertain employment in the urban sector.

However, in the labor markets of the United States and Britain, the three sectors identified do not have a clear spatial dimension such that a worker must forego the chance of employment in the competitive sector if he searches for work in the union or nonunion, administered-wage, sector. Frequent inquiries about job vacancies in high wage firms can be made without sacrificing the individual's employment in the competitive sector. Indeed, it is sometimes argued that an individual stands a better chance of being hired in the union sector or in the nonunion, administered-wage, sector if he is *not* stigmatized by being unemployed and if he already has a job. The Harris–Todaro characterization may well be quite appropriate in spatially separated markets and in the context of migration in less developed economies, but its relevance is doubtful for the analysis of different labor market sectors in the United States and Britain. So, although there is an understandable temptation to say something about unemployment and to adopt a formulation that gives the appearance of doing so, I find the common characterization quite unconvincing and artificial. In short, although it would be straightforward to introduce the Harris–Todaro equilibrium condition and to claim the amended model provides an explanation for unemployment, I believe the claim is largely unconvincing and I eschew it.

What this model does provide is a description of how the competitive sector's wages and employment are affected by forces emanating from the

---

[25] See, for instance, Hall (1975), Mincer (1976), and McDonald and Solow (1985).

union and nonunion, administered-wage, sectors. As an illustration, suppose increases in X are associated with greater union bargaining power that raises the union–nonunion wage differential (i.e., increases λ). Employment in the union and nonunion, administered-wage, sectors falls while that in the competitive sector rises driving competitive wages down. More formally,

$$\frac{\partial W^c}{\partial X}\frac{X}{W^c} = \frac{\gamma \sigma q^u}{q^c}\epsilon \text{ and } \frac{\partial E^c}{\partial X}\frac{X}{E^c} = -\frac{\eta_0 \gamma \sigma q^u}{q^c}\epsilon$$

where $\epsilon = \partial \log \lambda / \partial \log X$ and $q^c = 1 - q^u - q^n$. In this illustration, $\epsilon > 0$, $\partial \log W^c / \partial \log X < 0$, and $\partial \log E^c / \partial \log X > 0$: increases in the union–nonunion wage differential are associated with less employment in the union and nonunion, administered-wage, sectors and with greater employment in the competitive sector. Higher union wages tend to raise wages in the nonunion, administered-wage, sector, but depress wages in the competitive sector. Insofar as wages in the nonunion, administered-wage, sector are higher than those in the competitive sector, increases in the union–nonunion wage differential are associated with a wider dispersion of earnings among all nonunion workers.

6.5 Implications for Aggregate Models of Employment

The previous sections have considered wage interactions between markets within unionized economies. Wages in each market are not independent of wages in other markets. An equilibrium wage distribution obtains when, in the absence of changes in the environment, relative wages are unchanged. Equation (6.8) is an illustration of such an equilibrium wage distribution in the case of two unionized markets and equation (6.18) is an example in the case of one unionized and one nonunionized labor market. Equation (6.24) relates equilibrium wages in a competitive labor market to the union–nonunion wage differential, λ, in other noncompetitive markets.

Consider now the movements in aggregate labor market variables in an economy where wage and employment determination is decentralized. For purposes of illustration, suppose there are merely two sectors, 1 and 2. They may be two unionized markets or one unionized and the other nonunion. In each sector, suppose wages are a convenient linear function of exogenous variables X_1 and X_2:

$$W_j = \gamma_{0j} + \gamma_{1j} X_1 + \gamma_{2j} X_2, \quad j = 1, 2.$$

This is the wage equation in sector j after the dependence of wages in j

on wages in i has been substituted out. The aggregate wage, W^a, may be expressed as an arithmetic weighted average of wages in the two sectors:

$$W^a = (E_1/E^a)W_1 + [1 - (E_1/E^a)]W_2 \qquad (6.25)$$

where E_1 is employment in sector 1 and $E^a(=E_1 + E_2)$ is aggregate employment. By straightforward substitution, the aggregate wage may be written as

$$W^a = \gamma_{02} + \gamma_{12}X_1 + \gamma_{22}X_2 + [(\gamma_{01} - \gamma_{02}) + (\gamma_{11} - \gamma_{12})X_1$$
$$+ (\gamma_{21} - \gamma_{22})X_2](E_1/E^a) . \qquad (6.26)$$

Now what is needed is an expression for employment because it is highly improbable that the distribution of employment should be independent of the same exogenous variables determining wages. Perhaps the most convenient assumption would be one relating the employment share linearly to X_1 and X_2:

$$(E_1/E^a) = c_0 + c_1X_1 + c_2X_2.$$

By substituting this equation into (6.26), it is immediately apparent that, even with these simple assumptions, wage equations that are linear in the variables within each sector typically require higher order terms when aggregate equations are specified.

It has become fashionable to estimate aggregate employment equations in which total employment is expressed as a function of average wages. Again, it is unusual for these macro equations to be derived explicitly from their sector-specific components. If they are, additional problems arise if employment in sector j depends upon the wage in sector i holding constant wages in sector i:

$$E_j = a_{0j} + a_{1j}W_1 + a_{2j}W_2 + a_{3j}X_j, \quad j = 1, 2, \qquad (6.27)$$

in the simple case of merely two sectors, 1 and 2. Not all the models discussed in this chapter have this implication. When sector j's wage rate affects sector i's employment *through* sector i's wage, then direct cross-sector employment–wage effects can be ignored. However, when sector j's wage rate affects sector i's employment directly as in the effort model described in section 6.3, it becomes more difficult to justify equations in which aggregate employment may be expressed as an exclusive function of average wages. Thus, given total employment $E^a = E_1 + E_2$, equation (6.27) may be aggregated across sectors to yield

$$E^a = a_0 + a_1W_1 + a_2W_2 + a_{31}X_1 + a_{32}X_2$$

where $a_i = a_{i1} + a_{i2}$ for $i = 0, 1, 2$. Using equation (6.25), a relationship between aggregate employment and average wages may be obtained:

$$E^a = a_0 + \bar{a}W^a + (a_1 - \bar{a}k) W_1 + [a_2 - \bar{a}(1 - k)] W_2 + a_{31}X_1 + a_{32}X_2$$

where $k = E_1/E^a$ and $\bar{a} = 0.5 \ (a_1 + a_2)$. But note that this equation requires the presence of sector-specific wages in addition to the average wage level, a problem not resolved if the employment–wage slopes (that is, a_1 and a_2) are the same.

6.6 Conclusions

Conventional, auction-type, models of labor markets imply that wage interactions among markets operate through labor supply functions: an increase in wages in one sector reduces the supply of labor to another sector and this puts upward pressure on wages in this other sector. The models in this chapter have sketched wage interactions among markets that operate not indirectly through the supply of labor, but directly through wage-setting procedures. These models imply that variations in the wage premiums negotiated by unions will depend upon (union and nonunion) wages elsewhere in the economy. They imply also that some nonunion wages respond directly to union wages. Although certain descriptive labor market studies (e.g., Reynolds, 1951; MacKay et al., 1971; Kaufman, 1984) provide evidence of such interactions, analytical work has largely ignored the issues. However, if a satisfactory explanation is to be provided for the movement of wages among various unionized labor markets and for variations in union–nonunion wages, some structural specification and estimation would seem to be necessary.

A major hurdle in this empirical work is to identify the relevant market interdependencies. I have argued that some nonunion markets are best characterized as competitive and for those the direction of causation runs primarily from the union to the competitive sector: competitive sector wages and employment are affected by wage and employment outcomes in the union sector, but union wages are barely affected by the competitive sector's wages and employment. Union wages are more closely linked to those in the nonunion, administered-wage, sector where the specific skills of the workers induce management through threat and effort effects to set wages at levels above the workers' supply prices. Many public sector employees and some of those working in the nonprofit sector are likely to be employed in the nonunion, administered-wage, sector. However, though there may be indicators of specific skills that help in distinguishing between these two types of nonunion labor markets, the task of classifying workers into these two sectors is formidable.

The issues discussed in this chapter are relevant to the enduring question of whether trade unions can exercise an independent influence on the aggregate wage level. There is surely little doubt that unions have the capacity to exercise such an influence when all or virtually all workers are unionized even if collective bargaining is decentralized. For instance, suppose wages rise for whatever reason in one sector and, in order to maintain a particular wage differential, unions in another sector negotiate a higher wage. As outlined in section 6.2, according to this wage transfer mechanism (Bowen, 1960, pp. 209–21), the attempt to maintain a certain wage structure transmits a sector-specific shock to other sectors and causes all wages to rise.

However, in a partially unionized economy such as that of the United States and of Britain, a convincing case for unions to affect aggregate wages requires an explanation for how the effects of unions on wages in the unionized sector are conveyed to wages in the nonunion sector. The discussion in this chapter suggested that a rise in the union sector tends to cause wages to rise in the nonunion, administered-wage, sector, but to induce wages to fall in the nonunion, competitive-wage, sector. The independent effect of unions on the aggregate wage level is quite ambiguous, therefore, as is well known. Because the influence of unions on wages in the nonunion sector depends on factors such as the magnitude of the threat and effort effects and the relative size of the competitive-wage to the administered-wage sectors, factors that have varied over time and from place to place, it is probable that the effect of unions on aggregate wages has been of importance on some occasions and has been negligible at other times. For instance, unionism may well have exercised an important independent role in the United States during the 1930s and in Britain in the late 1960s and in the 1970s. In the United States, these issues were once the subject of animated research and they will surely be so again, but in the past decade they have been out of fashion. Appropriately enough, unions have been recognized as an active agent in studies of wage inflation in Britain though here it has been unusual for economists to specify and estimate the structural parameters of a behavioral model.

Appendix to Chapter 6

The purpose of this appendix is simply to provide a more formal statement of the model in chapter 6 of the nonunion firm's employment and wage behavior. The firm's objective is to choose E and v to maximize profit as expressed in equation (6.10). The first-order conditions for E and v, respectively, are

$$pX'e\bar{h} - (1 + v)W^u\bar{h} - c_T = 0$$

$$(pX'e'\bar{h} - W^u\bar{h} - c_T')E = 0 .$$

The second-order conditions are as follows:

$$\frac{\partial^2 \pi}{\partial E^2} = p(e\bar{h})^2 X'' < 0$$

$$\frac{\partial^2 \pi}{\partial v^2} = \left[p\bar{h}^2 E X''(e')^2 + p\bar{h}X'e'' - c\tau'' \right] E < 0$$

$$\Delta = \frac{\partial^2 \pi}{\partial E^2} \frac{\partial^2 \pi}{\partial v^2} - \left(\frac{\partial^2 \pi}{\partial E \partial v} \right)^2 = pe^2 \bar{h}^2 X'' E (p\bar{h}X'e'' - c\tau'') > 0.$$

From differentiation of the first-order conditions,

$$\frac{\partial v}{\partial W^u} = \frac{\bar{h}[e - e'(1 + v)]}{e(p\bar{h}X'e'' - c\tau'')} < 0$$

and

$$\frac{\partial E}{\partial W^u} = \frac{(1 + v)}{pe^2 \bar{h}X''} - \frac{\bar{h}Ee'[e - e'(1 + v)]}{e^2(p\bar{h}X'e'' - \tau'')} \gtreqless 0.$$

This previous equation may be written

$$\frac{\partial E}{\partial W^u} = \left(\frac{\partial E}{\partial W^u} \right)^* - \frac{E}{e} e' \frac{\partial v}{\partial W^u}$$

where $(\partial E / \partial W^u)^*$ is the change in employment induced by a higher W^u assuming $\tau' = e' = 0$. This term is unambiguously negative. The second term on the right-hand side is positive: an increase in W^u reduces v which causes e to fall and the firm may offset this decline in work effort by increasing employment. The effect of an increase in W^u on the firm's total effective labor input is as follows:

$$\frac{\partial(e\bar{h}E)}{\partial W^u} = \frac{(1 + v)}{peX''} < 0.$$

Other qualitative implications are as follows:

$$\frac{\partial v}{\partial p} = 0; \quad \frac{\partial E}{\partial p} > 0; \quad \frac{\partial v}{\partial c} > 0; \quad \text{and} \quad \frac{\partial E}{\partial c} < 0.$$

7 Conclusions

A large literature has been described and evaluated in the preceding chapters. Though I have not been reticent to express judgements about particular aspects of this research, some general assessment of this entire line of thinking and investigation is called for. This assessment should also indicate where future research energies are profitably directed.

There is very good reason to believe that the presence of trade unions should normally make a difference in the way labor markets operate. As argued in chapter 1, upon unionization, the structure of property rights within a firm changes: the rules, procedures, and institutions regulating the input of labor services are altered such that the representatives of the unionized work force participate explicitly in determining their environment. These property rights changes are likely to manifest themselves in the values of the variables closely associated with a worker's welfare – his pay, hours of work, and employment. As indicated in chapter 2, a large volume of evidence shows that unionized workers enjoy a premium in wages over nonunion workers and there are persuasive arguments suggesting that at least some of this premium is the product of bargaining by unions. There is reason to expect differences in employment and hours of work between unionized and nonunion workers and also differences in the manner in which unionized markets respond to cyclical shocks, but at present there is little firm evidence to buttress these expectations.

Notwithstanding the considerable volume of empirical research on unionism, there remains a number of quite basic questions we need answered. The paucity of research on the employment and hours of work effects of unionism has already been noted. This is an area where the issues have barely been the subject of modern methods of empirical inquiry. Confident statements of the type "unionism . . .

reduces employment in the organized sector . . . and in many settings it is associated with increased productivity" (Freeman and Medoff, 1984, p. 247) are simply not warranted. As we saw in chapter 2, little work has been directed to the effects of unionism on employment while that on the productivity effects of unionism has been, for the most part, cavalier and unconvincing.

There is also the important question of whether the measured correlations between wages (or employment or hours of work) and the incidence of unionism may appropriately be interpreted as the wage *effects* of unionism. The union status of firms and workers is not randomly distributed in the population so that variables omitted from wage equations and relegated to the residual in least-squares regression equations may well be correlated with the incidence of unionism. There is the danger of attributing to unionism what is, in fact, the consequence of other variables that are correlated with the pattern of unionism. This issue remains very much unsettled at present and will remain so, I believe, until economists treat the incidence of unionism in a more systematic and less perfunctory fashion. Ultimately, the goal is an explanation for the *joint* distribution of wages and unionism.

One of the tasks of economics should be to account for the empirical regularities observed. By the current standards that the discipline of economics sets for itself, this involves the specification and corroboration of *behavioral* models; that is, models in which the actors are not aimless but have some sort of purpose though the satisfaction of their ends is frustrated by resource and other limitations. A number of these models were outlined in chapters 3 through 6. They are useful only insofar as the objectives of a union and management are stable and can be characterized in a compact manner. Whether this is the case (or, more accurately, when and where this is the case) is impossible to determine at present. To date, the research on this topic raises the hope that this is a useful way of understanding the wage, hours, and employment aspects of unionism, but it would be inappropriate to believe that much more has been achieved beyond raising hopes. A similar judgement is in order regarding the literature on bargaining: though encouraging steps have been taken toward specifying and estimating behavioral models, their empirical relevance is still very much in question.

The problem for research on these topics is not the paucity of plausible models. On the contrary, the economics literature is replete with plausible (and a good many implausible) characterizations of trade union behavior – the ability of economists to conjure up models that can claim some correspondence to the world seems almost boundless. In fact, most of these models are not prompted by some empirical phenomenon, but by a previous theoretical model that in turn was a response to a prior paper.

In this way, research has an internal momentum that is sometimes difficult to explain to those not party to it.

There is, for instance, a voluminous literature in game theory on bargaining, but it has contributed very little indeed to an understanding of issues such as the pattern of union–nonunion wage differentials or the movements over time in wages or employment for a single union. Instead, researchers have been attracted to the solution of often quite subtle and complicated theoretical puzzles. The task of directing these models to the more prosaic task of understanding empirical phenomena has attracted far less attention. There are, no doubt, reasons for this emphasis in research energies. The empirical applications often involve resolving a whole host of auxiliary issues and, as a result, they lack the pristine definition and clarity of theoretical problems. By the same logic, research success is less easily discerned in empirical work so the profession's honors tend to be awarded disproportionately to theorists. These patterns within the discipline have been evident for several decades now so it should not occasion much surprise that the empirical literature on behavioral models of unionism should not have attracted the attention and the distinction accorded to the theory. Models of union behavior are not scarce, but quality empirical research applying and discriminating among them is.

The theoretical research has furnished us with many models ripe for empirical implementation and applied economists have some remarkable opportunities to exploit them. The next decade could be an exciting and productive time for research on these issues. With a little work, data from a number of firms and industries can be found with which to apply the union–management models discussed here. There is an extensive industrial relations literature upon which the analytical models can be built. This literature cautions us from expecting that all union–management situations can be successfully described in terms of a single model: the model relevant to the craft unions in the newspaper and printing industries in the United States and Britain may well not be that applicable to the coal mining unions or to the unions of school teachers. The understandable partiality for *one* model to describe union–management bargaining will probably have to give way to the reality that varied institutional settings and histories call for different models and different solutions of the same model. Some may lament the fact that a good understanding of labor markets requires the use of more than one model. However, for the empirical researcher, this variety implies a bountiful research agenda.

It also holds out the prospect of a relaxation in the long-standing tension between the work of labor economists and that of industrial relations researchers. Thirty or so years ago, the dominant line of thinking among most labor economists held that the appropriate way to characterize the primary features of labor markets was through the use of competitive market models. Even in studying the effects of collective bargaining – bargaining – the principal research study, Gregg Lewis's *Unionism and Relative Wages in the United States*, used the language of and claimed to have estimated competitive labor supply and demand functions. The emphasis in research was on the use of the competitive model to account for differences in wages and employment across industries and occupations and over time. There is no doubt that this research strategy yielded considerable success in explaining some basic patterns in wages and employment and, with less success, in hours of work.

By contrast, industrial relations scholars typically eschewed this framework. They tended to concentrate on explaining wage and employment structures *within* firms and industries and they claimed economists' competitive market models were, at best, of little assistance and, at worst, plain wrong. They offered explanations in which notions of "custom," "equity," and "power" figured prominently, concepts that economists often found vague and difficult to operationalize. Industrial relations lacked the clear analytic vision that economics had with its constrained optimizing actors and perhaps this explains why economists found industrial relations research unsatisfactory. The strength of industrial relations research was that it explicitly addressed questions of institutional structures. Whereas most economists regarded labor market institutions as mere ciphers, industrial relations scholars sought explanations for the different types of institutions, rules, and conventions.

There has been a significant change in economists' vision of labor markets. Bargaining figures much more in labor market models than it used to. In part, this is because the concept of specific human capital provides a clear and unambiguous role for bargaining even in markets without unions. Also, the literature on internal labor markets, implicit contracts, and transaction costs has motivated economists to look for employer–employee arrangements that facilitate exchanges in long-lasting employment relationships. This has brought the subject of the structure of institutions within the purview of economists' analytical thinking. In fact, it harks back to the writings of John R. Commons (1934), an economist whose industrial relations pedigree is without peer: he interpreted the rules and conventions of economic organizations in terms of the interests of the transacting parties and, in this way, he was very much in the spirit of the modern economic analysis of organizations and institutions.

As a consequence of these innovations in economics, labor economists are better equipped to address those issues central to industrial relations researchers. This does not mean that economists and industrial relations scholars talk the same language and that their perceptions are the same. The influence of the external labor market usually figures more prominently in economists' bargaining models and their explanations of institutional structures place greater emphasis on the role of resource costs in effecting exchanges than is the case in the industrial relations literature. Nevertheless, the chasm between economics and industrial relations has narrowed. I believe that progress on the union–management models described in this book would bring the two disciplines still further together. Each discipline has something distinctive to bring to the study of unionism and an understanding of the issues will be enhanced by greater intellectual cooperation.

Not only will progress on the models described in this book help bring economists and industrial relations researchers together in their shared interest in collective bargaining, but there is also the prospect that bargaining models will occupy a more conspicuous role in the study of nonunion labor markets. As already mentioned, today it is much more common than it was 30 or so years ago for economists to characterize the operation of (nonunion) labor markets in terms of a bargaining relationship. I suspect that this trend toward the use of bargaining models to help an understanding of certain features of labor markets, whether unionized or not, will continue and, perhaps, accelerate. Then researchers will be induced to go beyond the rather facile distinction between unionized and nonunionized labor markets and get down to determining what particular features of the institutions, rules, and conventions give rise to different bargaining relationships and outcomes.

Indeed, I believe the most unsatisfactory aspect of this book and the literature discussed within it is that it too readily accepts the union–nonunion distinction as a way of categorizing information and too frequently it poses as meaningful the comparison between the operation of unionized and nonunionized markets. When I have argued that different models are likely to be appropriate for different unionized labor markets, I am merely expressing the same point that I am registering in the previous paragraph, namely, it is not the fact of unionism that gives rise to different models of wages, employment, and hours, but the particular characteristics of these unions and of collective bargaining that are relevant. There is, indeed, a literature on these topics in industrial relations where, for instance, issues associated with different union governance structures and different types of management organizations are standard fare. However, this literature is primarily discursive and taxonomic and it lacks the sort of analytical foundations that economic models of hierarchy and organization might be able to provide. I expect that, in time, bargaining models and outcomes will be related less to the presence or absence of unions and more to the characteristics of the organization of work, characteristics present in all firms.

Given, then, our scant knowledge currently of the way in which unionized markets work, it would seem unwarranted to make confident statements about the appropriate posture for economic policy with respect to unions and collective bargaining. That is, the models of unionism discussed in this book have diverse implications for the operation of labor markets. For instance, according to one model, unions simply reallocate firm- or industry-specific rents from owners or managers to production workers and the effects on the efficient allocation of resources in the economy may be of negligible importance. According to another version, union wage increases are made at the expense of employment in the unionized sector and these displaced workers bid down wages in nonunion markets so that some workers gain while others lose. Yet another version suggests that, in some nonunion markets, management seek to maintain a certain relative wage differential over those paid to unionized workers so that wage increases secured by unions are extended to some nonunion workers.

In each of these cases, unions have different effects on resource allocation. If the empirical relevance of various models of unionism are not known at present, the appropriate stance by economists with respect to policy issues on unionism would seem to be a modest and guarded one. Informed judgements and speculation may be offered, but they need to be buffeted with clear qualifications. Moreover, even if the wage, employment, and hours effects of unionism were known, an evaluation of the contribution to society made by unions and collective bargaining would also involve assessing the many other activities in which unions are engaged. This book has been largely silent on these other activities.

For the particular goal of providing more relevant information for economic policy, what is required is not simply more empirical work. The computation of more and more correlations will not resolve some of the modelling questions raised in this literature. Simply knowing that wages are higher in unionized establishments than in comparable nonunion establishments does not necessarily imply that resource allocation has been affected in a particular way; higher wages may imply no more than a redistribution of rents in the economy. The relevant policy would seem to depend on how unions behave and how the allocation of resources is affected. These issues have only started being resolved.

References

Abowd, John M. 1989: The effect of wage bargains on the stock market value of the firm. *American Economic Review*, 79 (4), 774–809.

Akerlof, George A. 1969: Relative wages and the rate of inflation. *Quarterly Journal of Economics*, 83 (3), 353–74.

Akerlof, G.A. and Miyazaki, H. 1980: The implicit contract theory of unemployment meets the wage bill argument. *Review of Economic Studies*, 47 (2), 321–38.

Alchian, Armen A. and Demsetz, Harold 1972: Production, information costs, and economic organization. *American Economic Review*, 62 (5), 777–95.

Alogoskoufis, G. and Manning, A. 1987: Tests of alternative wage–employment bargaining models with an application to the UK aggregate labour market. London: Birkbeck College.

Aoki, Masahiko 1984: *The Co-operative Game Theory of the Firm*. Oxford: Clarendon Press.

Aoki, Masahiko 1988: The participatory generation of information rents and the theory of the firm. Unpublished manuscript.

Arrow, Kenneth J. 1971: *Essays in the Theory of Risk-bearing*. Amsterdam/London: North-Holland.

Ashenfelter, Orley 1978: Union relative wage effects: new evidence and a survey of their implications for wage inflation. In Richard Stone and William Peterson (eds), *Econometric Contributions to Public Policy*. New York: International Economic Association, 31–60.

Ashenfelter, Orley 1985: Evidence on US experiences with dispute resolution systems. Industrial Relations Section Working Paper No. 185, Princeton, NJ: Princeton University.

Ashenfelter, Orley and Bloom, David E. 1984: Models of arbitrator behavior: theory and evidence. *American Economic Review*, 74 (1), 111–24.

Ashenfelter, Orley and Johnson, George E. 1969: Bargaining theory, trade unions, and industrial strike activity. *American Economic Review*, 59 (1), 35–49.

Ashenfelter, Orley and Layard, Richard 1983: Incomes policy and wage differentials. *Economica*, 50 (198), 127–43.

Ashenfelter, Orley and Pencavel, John 1969: American trade union growth: 1900–1960. *Quarterly Journal of Economics*, 83 (3), 434–48.

Atherton, Wallace N. 1973: *Theory of Union Bargaining Goals*. Princeton, NJ: Princeton University Press.

Azariadis, Costas 1975: Implicit contracts and underemployment equilibria. *Journal of Political Economy*, 83 (6), 1183–1202.

Baily, Martin N. 1974: Wages and employment under uncertain demand. *Review of Economic Studies*, 41 (1), 37–50.

Barker, Allan, Lewis, Paul and McCann, Michael 1984: Trades unions and the organization of the unemployed. *British Journal of Industrial Relations*, 22 (3), 391–404.

Bean, C.R. and Turnbull, P.J. 1987: Employment in the British coal industry: a test of the labour demand model. Centre for Labour Economics, Discussion Paper No. 274, London School of Economics.

Becker, Gary S. 1964: *Human Capital: a Theoretical and Empirical Analysis with Special Reference to Education*. National Bureau of Economic Research. New York: Columbia Press.

Ben-Ner, Avner and Estrin, Saul 1988: Union bargaining with firms and union management of firms: the impact on wages, employment, and productivity. Centre for Labour Economics, Working Paper No. 1053, London School of Economics.

Berkowitz, Monroe 1954: The economics of trade union organization and administration. *Industrial and Labor Relations Review*, 7 (4), 537–49.

Binmore, K. 1987: Nash bargaining theory II. In Ken Binmore and Partha Dasgupta (eds), *The Economics of Bargaining*. Oxford: Basil Blackwell, 61–76.

Binmore, Ken, Rubinstein, Ariel and Wolinsky, Asher 1986: The Nash bargaining solution in economic modelling. *Rand Journal of Economics*, 17 (2), 176–88.

Bishop, Robert L. 1964: A Zeuthen–Hicks theory of bargaining. *Econometrica*, 32 (3), 410–17.

Blair, Douglas H. and Crawford, David L. 1984: Labor union objectives and collective bargaining. *Quarterly Journal of Economics*, 99 (3), 547–66.

Blanchard, Olivier J. 1986: The wage price spiral. *Quarterly Journal of Economics*, 101 (3), 543–65.

Blanchard, Olivier J. and Summers, Lawrence H. 1986: Hysteresis and the European unemployment problem. *NBER Macroeconomics Annual*, National Bureau of Economic Research, 15–78.

Blanchflower, David 1984: Union relative wage effects: a cross-section analysis using establishment data. *British Journal of Industrial Relations*, 22 (3), 311–32.

Blanchflower, D., Millward, N. and Oswald, A. 1989: Unionization and employ-ment behaviour. Centre for Labour Economics Discussion Paper No. 339, London School of Economics.

Bloom, David E. 1979: The effect of final offer arbitration on the salaries of municipal police officers in New Jersey. Industrial Relations Section Working

Paper No. 129, Princeton, NJ: Princeton University.

Bloom, David E. 1986: Empirical models of arbitrator behavior under conventional arbitration. *Review of Economics and Statistics*, 68 (4), 578-85.

Boal, William March 1985: Unionism and productivity in West Virginia coal mining. Unpublished PhD dissertation, Department of Economics, Stanford University, California, 135 pp.

Booth, Alison 1984: A public choice model of trade union behaviour and membership. *Economic Journal*, 94 (376), 883-98.

Borch, Karl 1962: Equilibrium in a reinsurance market. *Econometrica*, 30 (3), 424-44.

Bowen, William G. 1960: *The Wage-Price Issue*. Princeton, NJ: Princeton University Press.

Brewer, A.A. and Browning, M.J. 1982: On the "employment" decision of a labor-managed firm. *Economica*, 49 (194), 141-6.

Brown, Charles and Medoff, James 1978: Trade unions in the production process. *Journal of Political Economy*, 86 (3), 355-78.

Brown, James N. and Ashenfelter, Orley 1986: Testing the efficiency of employment contracts. *Journal of Political Economy*, 94 (3, suppl. 2), S40-87.

Brown, William and Sisson, Keith 1975: The use of comparisons in workplace wage determination. *British Journal of Industrial Relations*, 13 (1), 23-53.

Bureau of National Affairs 1986: *Basic Patterns in Union Contracts*, 11th edn. Washington, DC.

Cahill, Marion C. 1932: *Shorter Hours: A Study of the Movement since the Civil War*. New York: Columbia University Press.

Calmfors, Lars 1982: Employment policies, wage formation and trade unions in a small open economy. *Scandinavian Journal of Economics*, 84 (2), 345-73.

Calmfors, Lars and Horn, Henrik 1985: Classical unemployment, accommodation policies and the adjustment of real wages. *Scandinavian Journal of Economics*, 87 (2), 234-61.

Calvo, Guillermo A. 1978: Urban unemployment and wage determination in ldc's: trade unions in the Harris-Todaro model. *International Economic Review*, 19 (1), 65-81.

Card, David 1983: Cost-of-living escalators in major union contracts. *Industrial and Labor Relations Review*, 37 (1), 34-48.

Card, David 1986: Efficient contracts with costly adjustment: short-run employment determination for airline mechanics. *American Economic Review*, 76 (5), 1045-71.

Card, David 1987: An empirical study of strikes and wages. Industrial Relations Section Working Paper No. 221, Princeton, NJ: Princeton University.

Carruth, Alan A. and Oswald, Andrew J. 1985: Miners' wages in post-war Britain: an application of a model of trade union behaviour. *Economic Journal*, 95 (380), 1003-20.

Carruth, Alan A. and Oswald, Andrew J. 1987: On union preferences and labour market models: insiders and outsiders. *Economic Journal*, 97 (386), 431-45.

Carruth, Alan, Oswald, Andrew J. and Findlay, Lewis 1986: A test of a model of trade union behaviour: the coal and steel industries in Britain. *Oxford Bulletin of Economics and Statistics*, 48 (1), 1-18.

Cartter, Allan M. 1959: *Theory of Wages and Employment*. Homewood, IL: Irwin.

Chamberlain, Neil W. and Kuhn, James W. 1965: *Collective Bargaining*, 2nd edn. New York: McGraw-Hill.

Chen, Paul 1987: Wage changes in long-term labor contracts. Unpublished PhD dissertation, Department of Economics, Stanford University, California.

Clark, Andrew 1989a: An expanded union utility function and a discussion of some possible firm–union bargains. Centre for Labour Economics Working Paper No. 1099, London School of Economics.

Clark, Andrew 1989b: Strategy vs. survival in flexibility bargaining: theory and evidence. Centre for Labour Economics Working Paper No. 1157, London School of Economics.

Clark, Kim B. 1980: The impact of unionization on productivity: a case study. *Industrial and Labor Relations Review*, 33 (4), 451–69.

Coase, Ronald H. 1937: The nature of the firm. *Economica*, 4 (16), 386–405.

Commons, John R. 1909: American shoemakers, 1648–1895: a sketch of industrial evolution. *Quarterly Journal of Economics*, 24, 39–84.

Commons, John R. 1934: *Institutional Economics*. Madison, WI: University of Wisconsin Press.

Conant, Eaton B. 1959: Defenses of nonunion employers: a study from company sources. *Labor Law Journal*, 10 (2), 100–9 and 132.

Cooper, Russell W. 1987: *Wage and Employment Patterns in Labor Contracts: Microfoundations and Macroeconomic Implications*. Chur, Switzerland: Harwood Academic Publishers.

Cross, John G. 1965: A theory of the bargaining process. *American Economic Review*, 55 (1), 67–94.

Davidson, Carl 1988: Multiunit bargaining in oligopolistic industries. *Journal of Labor Economics*, 6 (3), 397–422.

de Menil, George 1971: *Bargaining: Monopoly Power versus Union Power*. Cambridge, MA: MIT Press.

Dertouzos, James N. 1979: Union objectives, wage determination, and the international typographical union. Unpublished PhD dissertation, Stanford University, California.

Dertouzos, James N. and Pencavel, John 1981: Wage and employment determination under trade unionism: the International Typographical Union. *Journal of Political Economy*, 89 (6), 1162–81.

Dix, Keith 1988: *What's a Coal Miner to Do? The Mechanization of Coal Mining*. Pittsburgh, PA: University of Pittsburgh Press.

Dixon, Huw 1988: Unions, oligopoly, and the natural range of employment. *Economic Journal*, 98 (393), 1127–47.

Doeringer, Peter B. and Piore, Michael J. 1971: *Internal Labor Markets and Manpower Analysis*. Lexington, MA: D.C. Heath and Company.

Dowrick, Steve 1986: Von Stackelberg and Cournot duopoly: choosing roles. *Rand Journal of Economics*, 17 (2), 251–60.

Duncan, Greg J. and Stafford, Frank P. 1980: Do union members receive compensating wage differentials. *American Economic Review*, 70 (3), 355–71.

Dunlop, John T. 1944: *Wage Determination Under Trade Unions*. New York: Macmillan.

Earle, John S. 1988: Empirical studies of cyclical labor market fluctuations in the postwar United States. Unpublished PhD dissertation, Stanford University, California.

Earle, John S. and Pencavel, John 1990: Hours of work and trade unionism. *Journal of Labor Economics*, 8 (1, suppl. 2), S150–74.

Eberts, Randall W. and Stone, Joe A. 1986: On the contract curve: a test of alternative models of collective bargaining. *Journal of Labor Economics*, 4 (1), 66–81.

Eckstein, Otto 1968: Money wage determination revisited. *Review of Economic Studies*, 35 (102), 133–43.

Eckstein, O. and Wilson, T. 1962: The determination of money wages in American industry. *Quarterly Journal of Economics*, 76, 379–414.

Edwards, Richard 1979: *Contested Terrain: the Transformation of the Workplace in the Twentieth Century*. New York: Basic Books.

Edwards, Richard and Swaim, Paul 1986: Union–nonunion earnings differentials and the decline of private-sector unionism. *American Economic Review Papers and Proceedings*, 76 (2), 97–102.

Ehrenberg, Ronald G. 1979: *The Regulatory Process and Labor Earnings*. New York: Academic Press.

Elliott, Robert F. 1976: The national wage round in the United Kingdom: a sceptical view. *Oxford Bulletin of Economics and Statistics*, 38 (3), 179–201.

Elliott, Robert F. 1977: Public sector wage movements: 1950–1973. *Scottish Journal of Political Economy*, 24 (2), 133–51.

Elliott, Robert F. 1980: Union wage policy, inflation, and skill differentials: an example of the impact of labour market institutions on pay structure. Unpublished manuscript.

Epstein, E. and Monat, J. 1973: Labor contracting and its regulation: I. *International Labour Review*, 107 (5), 451–70.

Erickson, Christopher and Ichino, Andrea 1989: Lump sum bonuses in union contracts: semantic change or step toward a new wage determination system. Unpublished manuscript.

Faith, Roger L. and Reid, Joseph D. Jr 1983: The labor union as its members' agent. In Joseph D. Reid Jr (ed.), *New Approaches to Labor Unions: Research in Labor Economics*, Supplement 2. Greenwich, CT: JAI Press, 3–25.

Farber, Henry S. 1977: The united mine workers and the demand for coal: an econometric analysis of union behavior. PhD dissertation, Princeton University.

Farber, Henry S. 1980: An analysis of final-offer arbitration. *Journal of Conflict Resolution*, 24 (4), 683–705.

Farber, Henry S. 1981: Splitting-the-difference in interest arbitration. *Industrial and Labor Relations Review*, 35 (1), 70–7.

Farber, Henry S. 1983: The determination of the union status of workers. *Econometrica*, 51 (5), 1417–38.

Farber, Henry S. 1986: The analysis of union behavior. In O. Ashenfelter and

R. Layard (eds), *Handbook of Labor Economics, Volume 2.* Amsterdam/
London: North-Holland, 1039–89.

Farber, Henry S. and Bazerman, Max H. 1986: The general basis of arbitrator
behavior: an empirical analysis of conventional and final-offer arbitration.
Econometrica, 54 (4), 819–44.

Farber, Henry S. and Bazerman, Max H. 1989: Divergent expectations as a cause
of disagreement in bargaining: evidence from a comparison of arbitration
schemes. *Quarterly Journal of Economics*, 104 (1), 99–120.

Farber, Henry S. and Katz, Harry C. 1979: Interest arbitration, outcomes, and
the incentive to bargain. *Industrial and Labor Relations Review*, 33 (1), 55–63.

Fellner, William 1947: Prices and wages under bilateral monopoly. *Quarterly
Journal of Economics*, 61 (4), 503–32.

Fellner, William 1949: *Competition Among the Few*, New York: Alfred A.
Knopf.

Fischer, Stanley 1977: Long-term contracts, rational expectations, and the
optimal money supply rule. *Journal of Political Economy*, 85 (1), 191–205.

Fisher, Lloyd H. 1953: *The Harvest Labor Market in California.* Cambridge,
MA: Harvard University Press.

Flanagan, Robert J. 1976: Wage interdependence in unionized labor markets.
Brookings Papers in Economic Activity, 3, 635–73.

Flanagan, Robert J. 1983: Workplace public goods and union organizations.
Industrial Relations, 22 (2), 224–37.

Flanagan, Robert J. 1984: Wage concessions and long-term union wage
flexibility. *Brookings Papers on Economic Activity*, 1, 183–216.

Foldes, Lucien 1964: A determinate model of bilateral monopoly. *Economica*, 31
(122), 117–31.

Foulkes, Fred K. 1980: *Personnel Policies in Large Nonunion Companies.*
Englewood Cliffs, NJ: Prentice-Hall.

Frank, Jeff 1985: Trade union efficiency and overemployment with seniority
wage scales. *Economic Journal*, 95 (380), 1021–34.

Freeman, Richard B. 1980: The exit-voice tradeoff in the labor market: unionism,
job tenure, quits, and separations. *Quarterly Journal of Economics*, 94 (4),
643–74.

Freeman, Richard B. 1981: The effect of trade unionism on fringe benefits.
Industrial and Labor Relations Review, 34 (4), 489–509.

Freeman, Richard B. 1982: Union wage practices and wage dispersion within
establishments. *Industrial and Labor Relations Review*, 36 (1), 3–21.

Freeman, Richard B. 1986a: The effect of the union wage differential on management opposition and union organizing success. *American Economic Review
Papers and Proceedings*, 76 (2), 92–6.

Freeman, Richard B. 1986b: In search of union wage concessions in standard data
sets. *Industrial Relations*, 25 (2), 131–45.

Freeman, Richard B. and Medoff, James L. 1982: Substitution between production labor and other inputs in unionized and nonunionized manufacturing.
Review of Economics and Statistics, 64 (2), 220–33.

Freeman, Richard B. and Medoff, James L. 1984: *What Do Unions Do?* New
York: Basic Books.

Friedman, Milton 1951: Some comments on the significance of labor unions for economic policy. In David McCord Wright (ed.), *The Impact of the Union: Eight Economic Theorists Evaluate the Labor Union Movement*. New York: Harcourt Brace, 204–34.

Fudenberg, Drew, Levine, David and Ruud, Paul 1983: Strike activity and wage settlements. Department of Economics Working Paper No. 249, Los Angeles: University of California.

Geroski, Paul A. and Stewart, Mark B. 1986: Specification-induced uncertainty in the estimation of trade union wage differentials from industry-level data. *Economica*, 53 (209), 29–40.

Gottfries, Nils and Horn, Henrik 1987: Wage formation and the persistence of unemployment. *Economic Journal*, 97 (388), 877–84.

Greenberg, David H. 1968: Deviations from wage-fringe standards. *Industrial and Labor Relations Review*, 21 (2), 197–209.

Grossman, Gene M. 1983: Union wages, temporary layoffs, and seniority. *American Economic Review*, 73 (3), 277–90.

Grout, Paul A. 1984: Investment and wages in the absence of binding contracts: a Nash bargaining approach. *Econometrica*, 52 (2), 449–60.

Hall, Robert E. 1975: The rigidity of wages and the persistence of unemployment. *Brookings Papers in Economic Activity*, 2, 301–35.

Hall, Robert E. and Lilien, David M. 1979: Efficient wage bargains under uncertain supply and demand. *American Economic Review*, 69 (5), 868–79.

Handy, L.J. 1981: *Wages Policy in the British Coalmining Industry*, Department of Applied Economics Monographs 27. Cambridge, England: Cambridge University Press.

Harris, J. and Todaro, M. 1970: Migration, unemployment, and development: a two-sector analysis. *American Economic Review*, 60 (1), 126–42.

Harsanyi, John C. 1956: Approaches to the bargaining problem before and after the theory of games. *Econometrica*, 24 (2), 144–57.

Harsanyi, John C. 1977: *Rational Behavior and Bargaining Equilibrium in Games and Social Situations*. Cambridge, England: Cambridge University Press.

Harsanyi, J.C. and Selten, R. 1972: A generalized Nash solution for two-person bargaining games with incomplete information. *Management Science*, 18 (5), 80–106.

Hart, Oliver 1989: Bargaining and strikes. *Quarterly Journal of Economics*, 104 (1), 25–44.

Hart, Oliver and Holmstrom, Bengt 1987: The theory of contracts. In *Advances in Economic Theory, Fifth World Congress*, Econometric Society Monographs No. 12. Cambridge, England: Cambridge University Press, 71–155.

Hayes, Beth 1984: Unions and strikes with asymmetric information. *Journal of Labor Economics*, 2 (1), 57–83.

Hendricks, Wallace 1977: Regulation and labor earnings. *Bell Journal of Economics*, 8 (2), 483–96.

Hendricks, Wallace, and Kahn, Lawrence M. 1984: The demand for labor market structure: an economic approach. *Journal of Labor Economics*, 2 (3), 412–38.

Henle, Peter 1973: Reverse collective bargaining? A look at some concession situations. *Industrial and Labor Relations Review*, 26 (3), 956–68.

Henle, P. 1976: *Work-sharing as an Alternative to Layoffs*. Washington, DC: Congressional Research Service.

Herrington, Douglas J. 1988: The effect of private information on wage settlements and strike activity. Industrial Relations Section Working Paper No. 231, Princeton, NJ: Princeton University.

Hicks, John R. 1963: *The Theory of Wages*, 2nd edn. London: Macmillan.

Hines, A.G. 1969: Wage inflation in the United Kingdom 1948–62: a disaggregated study. *Economic Journal*, 79 (313), 66–89.

Hirsch, Barry T. 1982: The interindustry structure of unionism, earnings, and earnings dispersion. *Industrial and Labor Relations Review*, 36 (1), 22–39.

Hirsch, Barry T. 1988: Trucking regulation, unionization, and labor earnings: 1973–85. *Journal of Human Resources*, 23 (3), 296–319.

Hirtle, Beverly 1985: Interfirm information, strikes, and union bargaining behavior. Unpublished manuscript.

Hobsbawm, E.J. 1964: British gas-workers 1873–1914. In E.J. Hobsbawm (ed.), *Labouring Men: Studies in the History of Labour*. New York: Basic Books, 158–78.

Holmlund, Betil 1989: Wages and employment in unionized economies: theory and evidence. In Bertil Holmlund, Karl-Gustaf Lofgren and Lars Engstrom, *Trade Unions, Employment, and Unemployment Duration*. Oxford: Clarendon Press, 5–104.

Holmstrom, B. and Myerson, R. 1983: Efficient and durable decision rules with incomplete information. *Econometrica*, 51 (6), 1799–1819.

Horn, Henrik and Wolinsky, Asher 1988: Worker substitutability and patterns of unionisation. *Economic Journal*, 98 (391), 484–97.

Ichniowski, Casey 1986: The effects of grievance activity on productivity. *Industrial and Labor Relations Review*, 40 (1), 75–89.

Jackman, Richard 1985: Counterinflationary policy in a unionised economy with nonsynchronised wage setting. *Scandinavian Journal of Economics*, 87 (2), 357–78.

James, Ralph C. and James, Estelle D. 1965: *Hoffa and the Teamsters*. Princeton, NJ: Van Nostrand.

Jensen, Michael C. and Meckling, William H. 1979: Rights and production functions: an application to labor-managed firms and codetermination. *Journal of Business*, 52 (4), 469–506.

Johnson, George E. 1984: Changes over time in the union–nonunion wage differential in the United States. In J.-J. Rosa (ed.), *The Economics of Trade Unions: New Directions*. Boston: Kluwer-Nijhoff Publishing, 3–19.

Johnson, George E. 1990: Work rules, featherbedding, and Pareto-optimal union–management bargaining. *Journal of Labor Economics*, 8 (1, suppl. 2), S237–59.

Kahn, Lawrence M. 1978: The effect of unions on the earnings of nonunion workers. *Industrial and Labor Relations Review*, 31 (2), 205–16.

Kahn, Lawrence M. and Morimune, Kimio 1979: Unions and employment stability: a sequential logic approach. *International Economic Review*, 20 (1), 217–35.

Kahneman, Daniel, Knetsch, Jack L. and Thaler, Richard 1986: Fairness as a constraint on profit seeking: entitlements in the market. *American Economic Review*, 76 (4), 728–41.

Kahneman, Daniel, Knetsch, Jack L. and Thaler, Richard 1987: Fairness and the assumptions of economics. In Robin M. Hogarth and Melvin W. Reder (eds), *Rational Choice: the Contrast between Economics and Psychology*. Chicago, IL: University of Chicago, 101–16.

Kahneman, Daniel and Tversky, Amos 1979: Prospect theory: an analysis of decision under risk. *Econometrica*, 47 (2), 263–92.

Kalai, E. 1977: Proportional solutions to bargaining situations: interpersonal utility comparisons. *Econometrica*, 45 (7), 1623–30.

Kalai, E. and Smorodinsky, M. 1975: Other solutions to Nash's bargaining problem. *Econometrica*, 43 (3), 513–18.

Kaufman, Bruce E. and Martinez-Vazquez, Jorge 1988: Voting for wage concessions: the case of the 1982 GM-UAW negotiations. *Industrial and Labor Relations Review*, 41 (2), 183–94.

Kaufman, Roger T. 1984: On wage stickiness in Britain's competitive sector. *British Journal of Industrial Relations*, 22 (1), 101–12.

Kennan, John 1986: The economics of strikes. In Orley Ashenfelter and Richard Layard (eds), *Handbook of Labor Economics Volume 2*. Amsterdam/ London: North-Holland, 1091–1137.

Kidd, David P. and Oswald, Andrew J. 1987: A dynamic model of trade union behavior. *Economica*, 54 (215), 355–65.

Knowles, K.G.J.C. and Robertson, D.J. 1951: Earnings in engineering, 1926–1948. *Bulletin of the Oxford University Institute of Statistics*, 13 (6), 179-200.

Kochan, Thomas A., Katz, Harry C. and McKersie, Robert B. 1986: *The Transformation of American Industrial Relations*. New York: Basic Books.

Kramer, G.H. 1973: On a class of equilibrium conditions for majority rule. *Econometrica*, 41 (2), 285–97.

Lawrence, Colin and Lawrence, Robert Z. 1985: Manufacturing wage dispersion: an end game interpretation. *Brookings Papers in Economic Activity*, 1, 47–106.

Layard, R., Metcalf, D. and Nickell, S. 1978: The effect of collective bargaining on relative and absolute wages. *British Journal of Industrial Relations*, 16 (3), 287–302.

Lazear, Edward P. 1983: A competitive theory of monopoly unionism. *American Economic Review*, 73 (4), 631–43.

Leonard, Jonathan S. 1986: Employment variation and wage rigidity: a comparison of union and non-union plants. Unpublished manuscript.

Leontief, Wassily 1946: The pure theory of the guaranteed annual wage contract. *Journal of Political Economy*, 54 (1), 76–9.

Levinson, Harold M. 1960: Pattern bargaining: a case study of the automobile workers. *Quarterly Journal of Economics*, 74 (2), 296–317.

Lewis, H. Gregg 1959: Competitive and monopoly unionism. In Philip D. Bradley (ed.), *The Public Stake in Union Power*. Charlottesville, VA: University of Virginia Press, 181–208.

Lewis, H. Gregg 1963: *Unionism and Relative Wages in the United States: an*

Empirical Inquiry. Chicago, IL: University of Chicago Press.

Lewis, H. Gregg 1964: Relative employment effects of unionism. In Gerald G. Somers (ed.), *Proceedings of the Sixtieth Annual Meeting*, Industrial Relations Research Association, Boston, MA, December 27 and 28, 1963, 104–15.

Lewis, H. Gregg 1969: Employer interests in employee hours of work. Unpublished paper, University of Chicago.

Lewis, H. Gregg 1970: Unionism, wages, and employment in US coal mining, 1945–68. Mimeograph.

Lewis, H. Gregg 1986: *Union Relative Wage Effects: a Survey*. Chicago, IL: University of Chicago Press.

Lindbeck, Assar and Snower, Dennis J. 1986: Wage rigidity, union activity and unemployment. In Wilfred Beckerman (ed.), *Wage Rigidity and Unemployment*. Baltimore, MD: Johns Hopkins University Press, 97–125.

Linneman, Peter and Wachter, Michael L. 1986: Rising union premiums and the declining boundaries among noncompeting groups. *American Economic Review Papers and Proceedings*, 76 (2), 103–8.

Lipset, S.M., Trow, M.A. and Coleman, J.S. 1956: *Union Democracy: the Internal Politics of the International Typographical Union*, Glencoe, IL: Free Press.

Lockwood, Ben and Manning, Alan 1987: Dynamic wage and employment determination with endogenous union membership. Mimeograph, Department of Economics, Birkbeck College, London.

Loomes, G. and Sugden, R. 1982: Regret theory: an alternative theory of rational choice under uncertainty. *Economic Journal*, 92 (368), 805–24.

Lundberg, Erik 1957: *Business Cycles and Economic Policy*. Cambridge, MA: Harvard University Press.

Lunt, Richard D. 1979: *Law and Order vs. the Miners: West Virginia, 1907–1933*. Hamden, CT: Archon Books.

Lupton, Tom 1963: *On the Shop Floor: Two Studies of Workshop Organization and Output*. Elmsford, NY: Pergamon Press.

Machina, Mark J. 1983: The economic theory of individual behavior toward risk: theory, evidence, and new directions. Institute for Mathematical Studies in the Social Sciences (IMSSS), Technical Report No. 433, Stanford University, California.

McConnell, Sheena 1989: Strikes, wages, and private information. *American Economic Review*, 79 (4), 801–15.

McDonald, Ian M. and Solow, Robert M. 1981: Wage bargaining and employment. *American Economic Review*, 71 (5), 896–908.

McDonald, Ian M. and Solow, Robert M. 1985: Wages and employment in a segmented labor market. *Quarterly Journal of Economics*, 100 (4), 1115–41.

McGuire, Timothy W. and Rapping, Leonard A. 1968: The role of market variables and key bargains in the manufacturing wage determination process. *Journal of Political Economy*, 76 (5), 1015–36.

MacKay, D.I., Boddy, D., Brack, J., Diack, J.A. and Jones, N. 1971: *Labor Markets under Different Employment Conditions*. London: George Allen and Unwin.

MaCurdy, Thomas E. and Pencavel, John H. 1986: Testing between competing models of wage and employment determination in unionized markets. *Journal of Political Economy*, 94 (3, suppl. 2), S3-39.

Manning, Alan 1987: An integration of trade union models in a sequential bargaining framework. *Economic Journal*, 97 (385), 121-39.

Marshall, Alfred 1920: *Principles of Economics*, 8th edn. London: Macmillan.

Mathewson, Stanley B. 1931: *Restriction of Output among Unorganized Workers*. New York: Viking Press.

Medoff, James L. 1979: Layoffs and alternatives under trade unions in US manufacturing. *American Economic Review*, 69 (3), 380-95.

Mefford, Robert N. 1986: The effect of unions on productivity in a multinational manufacturing firm. *Industrial and Labor Relations Review*, 40 (1), 105-14.

Mehra, Y.P. 1976: Spillovers in wage determination in US manufacturing industries. *Review of Economics and Statistics*, 58 (3), 300-12.

Mellow, Wesley 1983: Employer size, unionism, and wages. In Joseph D. Reid Jr, *New Approaches to Labor Unions*, Supplement 2 to *Research in Labor Economics, a Research Annual*. Connecticut: JAI Press, 253-82.

Miernyk, William H. 1980: Coal. In Gerald G. Somers (ed.), *Collective Bargaining: Contemporary American Experience*. Madison, WI: Industrial Relations Research Association.

Millward, Neil and Stevens, Mark 1986: *British Workplace Industrial Relations 1980-1984: the DE/ESRC/PSI/ACAS Surveys*. Aldershot, England: Gower Publishing Company.

Mincer, Jacob 1976: Unemployment effects of minimum wages. *Journal of Political Economy*, 84 (4, suppl. 2), S87-104.

Miyazaki, H. and Neary, H.M. 1983: The Illyrian firm revisited. *Bell Journal of Economics*, 14 (1), 259-70.

Montgomery, David 1967: *Beyond Equality: Labor and the Radical Republicans 1862-1872*. New York: Knopf.

Montgomery, Edward 1989: Employment and unemployment effects of unions. *Journal of Labor Economics*, 7 (2), 170-90.

Moore, William J. and Raisian, John 1980: Cyclical sensitivity of union/nonunion relative wage effects. *Journal of Labor Research*, 1 (1), 115-32.

Moore, William J. and Raisian, John 1987: Union-nonunion wage differentials in the public administration, educational, and private sectors: 1970-1983, *Review of Economics and Statistics*, 69 (4), 608-16.

Nash, John F. 1950: The bargaining problem. *Econometrica*, 18 (2), 155-62.

Navarro, Peter 1983: Union bargaining power in the coal industry, 1945-1981. *Industrial and Labor Relations Review*, 36 (2), 214-29.

Nelson, Phillip 1970: Information and consumer behavior. *Journal of Political Economy*, 78 (2), 311-29.

Nickell, S. and Wadhwani, S. 1987: Financial factors, efficiency wages and employment: investigations using US micro-data. Centre for Labour Economics, Discussion Paper No. 295, London School of Economics.

Norsworthy, J.R. and Zabalza, Craig A. 1985: Worker attitudes, worker behavior, and productivity in the U.S. automobile industry, 1959-1976. *Industrial and Labor Relations Review*, 38 (4), 544-57.

Ochs, Jack and Roth, Alvin E. 1989: An experimental study of sequential bargaining. *American Economic Review*, 79 (3), 355–84.

Olmstead, Alan L. and Rhode, Paul 1985: Rationing without government: the West Coast gas famine of 1920. *American Economic Review*, 75 (5), 1044–55.

Olson, Craig A. 1988: Dispute resolution in the public sector. In Benjamin Aaron, Joyne M. Najita and James L. Stern (eds), *Public-Sector Bargaining*, Industrial Relations Research Association Series, 2nd edn. Washington, DC: Bureau of National Affairs, 160–88.

Olson, Mancur 1965: *The Logic of Collective Action*. Cambridge, MA: Harvard University Press.

Oswald, Andrew J. 1979: Wage determination in an economy with many trade unions. *Oxford Economic Papers*, 31 (3), 369–85.

Oswald, Andrew 1985: The economic theory of trade unions: an introductory survey. *Scandinavian Journal of Economics*, 87 (2), 160–93.

Oswald, Andrew 1987: Efficient contracts are on the labour demand curve: theory and facts. Centre for Labour Economics, Discussion Paper No. 284, London School of Economics.

Pemberton, James 1988: A 'managerial' model of the trade union. *Economic Journal*, 98, 392, 755–71.

Pencavel, John 1971: The demand for union services: an exercise. *Industrial and Labor Relations Review*, 24 (2), 180–90.

Pencavel, John 1977: Industrial morale. In Orley Ashenfelter and Wallace E. Oates (eds), *Essays in Labor Market Analysis in Memory of Yochanan Peter Comay*. New York: John Wiley, 129–46.

Pencavel, John 1984a: The empirical performance of a model of trade union behavior. In Jean-Jacques Rosa (ed.), *The Economics of Trade Unions: New Directions*. Boston: Kluwer-Nijhoff Publishing, 221–76.

Pencavel, John 1984b: The tradeoff between wages and employment in trade union objectives. *Quarterly Journal of Economics*, 99 (2), 215–31.

Pencavel, John 1986: Labor supply of men: a survey. In Orley Ashenfelter and Richard Layard (eds), *Handbook of Labor Economics*. Amsterdam/London: North-Holland, 3–102.

Pencavel, John and Hartsog, Catherine E. 1984: A reconsideration of the effects of unionism on relative wages and employment in the United States, 1920–1980. *Journal of Labor Economics*, 2 (2), 193–232.

Pencavel, John and Holmlund, Bertil 1988: The determination of wages, employment, and work hours in an economy with centralized wage-setting: Sweden, 1950–83. *Economic Journal*, 98 (393), 1105–26.

Perry, Charles R. 1984: *Collective Bargaining and the Decline of the United Mine Workers*. Industrial Research Unit Studies No. 60, The Wharton School, University of Pennsylvania.

Petridis, Anastasios 1973: Alfred Marshall's attitudes to an economic analysis of trade unions: a case of anomalies in a competitive system. *History of Political Economy*, 5 (1), 165–98.

Pettengill, John S. 1980: *Labor Unions and the Inequality of Earned Income*, Contributions to Economic Analysis, 129. Amsterdam/London: North-Holland.

Phelps Brown, Henry 1983: *The Origins of Trade Union Power*. Oxford: Clarendon Press.

Phelps Brown, E.H. and Hart, P.E. 1952: The share of wages in national income. *Economic Journal*, 62 (246), 253-77.

Plott, Charles R. 1967: A notion of equilibrium and its possibility under majority rule. *American Economic Review*, 57 (4), 787-806.

Pratt, John W. 1964: Risk aversion in the small and in the large. *Econometrica*, 32 (1/2), 122-36.

Raiffa, Howard 1953: Arbitration schemes for generalized two-person games. In H.W. Kuhn and A.W. Tucker (eds), *Contributions to the Theory of Games, 2*. Princeton, NJ: Princeton University Press, 361-87.

Raisian, John 1983: Contracts, job experience, and cyclical labor market adjustments. *Journal of Labor Economics*, 1 (2), 152-70.

Rayack, Elton 1958: The impact of unionism on wages in the men's clothing industry, 1911-1956. *Labor Law Journal*, 9 (9), 674-88.

Reder, Melvin W. 1955: The theory of occupational wage differentials. *American Economic Review*, 45 (5), 833-52.

Rees, Albert 1962: *The Economics of Trade Unions*. Chicago, IL: University of Chicago Press.

Rees, Albert 1963: The effects of unions on resource allocation. *Journal of Law and Economics*, 6, 69-78.

Rees, Albert 1977: *The Economics of Trade Unions*, 2nd edn. Chicago, IL: University of Chicago Press.

Rees, Albert and Shultz, George P. 1970: *Workers and Wages in an Urban Labor Market*. Chicago, IL: University of Chicago Press.

Reynolds, Lloyd G. 1951: *The Structure of Labor Markets*. New York: Harper.

Riordan, Michael 1984: Uncertainty, asymmetric information, and bilateral contracts. *Review of Economic Studies*, 51 (1), 83-93.

Robinson, Chris 1989: The joint determination of union status and union wage effects: some tests of alternative models. *Journal of Political Economy*, 97 (3), 639-67.

Roethlisberger, F.J. and Dickson, W.J. 1939: *Management and the Worker*. Cambridge, MA: Harvard University Press.

Rose, Nancy L. 1987: Labor rent sharing and regulation: evidence from the trucking industry. *Journal of Political Economy*, 95 (6), 1146-78.

Rosen, Sherwin 1969: Trade union power, threat effects and the extent of organization. *Review of Economic Studies*, 36 (106), 185-96.

Rosen, Sherwin 1970: Unionism and the occupational wage structure in the United States. *International Economic Review*, 11 (2), 269-86.

Rosen, Sherwin 1985: Implicit contracts: a survey. *Journal of Economic Literature*, 23 (3), 1144-75.

Ross, Arthur M. 1948: *Trade Union Wage Policy*. Berkeley/Los Angeles: University of California Press.

Roth, Alvin E. 1987: Bargaining phenomena and bargaining theory. In Alvin E. Roth (ed.), *Laboratory Experimentation in Economics: Six Points of View*. Cambridge, England: Cambridge University Press, 14-41.

Roth, Alvin E. and Malouf, Michael W.K. 1979: Game-theoretic models and the role of information in bargaining. *Psychological Review*, 86 (6), 574–94.

Roth, Alvin E. and Schoumaker, Françoise 1983: Expectations and reputations in bargaining: an experimental study. *American Economic Review*, 73 (3), 362–72.

Roy, Donald 1952: Quota restriction and goldbricking in a machine shop. *American Journal of Sociology*, 67 (2), 427–42.

Rubinstein, Ariel 1982: Perfect equilibrium in a bargaining model. *Econometrica*, 50 (1), 97–109.

Schoemaker, Paul J.H. 1982: The expected utility model: its variants, purposes, evidence and limitations. *Journal of Economic Literature*, 20 (2), 529–63.

Seltzer, George 1951: Pattern bargaining and the United Steelworkers. *Journal of Political Economy*, 59 (4), 319–31.

Sen, A.K. 1977: On weights and measures: informational constraints in social welfare analysis. *Econometrica*, 45 (7), 1539–72.

Shultz, George P. and Myers, Charles A. 1950: Union wage decisions and employment. *American Economic Review*, 40 (3), 362–80.

Simons, Henry C. 1944: Some reflections on syndicalism. *Journal of Political Economy*, 52 (1), 1–25.

Slichter, Sumner H. 1941: *Union Policies and Industrial Management*. Washington, DC: The Brookings Institution.

Slichter, Sumner H. 1954: Do the wage-fixing arrangements in the American labor market have an inflationary bias? *American Economic Review, Proceedings*, 44 (2), 322–46.

Slichter, Sumner H., Healy, James J. and Livernash, E. Robert 1960: *The Impact of Collective Bargaining on Management*. Washington, DC: The Brookings Institution.

Solow, Robert M. 1985: Insiders and outsiders in wage determination. *Scandinavian Journal of Economics*, 87 (2), 411–28.

Stahl, Ingolf 1972: *Bargaining Theory*. Stockholm: The Economic Research Institute, Stockholm School of Economics.

Steinherr, A. and Thisse, J.F. 1979: Are labor-managers really perverse? *Economics Letters*, 2 (2), 137–42.

Stevens, Carl M. 1966: Is compulsory arbitration compatible with bargaining? *Industrial Relations*, 5 (2), 38–52.

Stewart, Mark B. 1983: Relative earnings and individual union membership in the United Kingdom. *Economica*, 50 (198), 111–26.

Stewart, Mark B. 1987: Collective bargaining agreements, closed shops and relative pay. *Economic Journal*, 97 (385), 140–56.

Svejnar, Jan 1986: Bargaining power, fear of disagreement, and wage settlements: theory and evidence from US industry. *Econometrica*, 54 (5), 1055–78.

Taylor, John B. 1980: Aggregate dynamics and staggered contracts. *Journal of Political Economy*, 88 (1), 1–23.

Taylor, John B. 1983: Union wage settlements during a disinflation. *American Economic Review*, 73 (5), 981–93.

Throop, Adrian W. 1968: The union–nonunion wage differential and cost-push inflation. *American Economic Review*, 58 (1), 79–99.

Thurow, Lester C. 1968: Disequilibrium and the marginal productivity of capital and labor. *The Review of Economics and Statistics*, 50 (1), 23-31.

Todaro, Michael 1969: A model of labor migration and urban unemployment in less developed countries. *American Economic Review*, 59 (1), 138-48.

Tracy, Joseph S. 1987: An empirical test of an asymmetric information model of strikes. *Journal of Labor Economics*, 5 (2), 149-73.

Turner, H.A. 1957: Inflation and wage differentials in Great Britain. In J.T. Dunlop (ed.), *The Theory of Wage Determination*. International Economic Association, London: Macmillan, 123-35.

US Department of Labor 1937: *Characteristics of Company Unions 1935*. Bureau of Labor Statistics, BLS Bulletin No. 634.

US Department of Labor 1972: *Major Collective Bargaining Agreements: Layoff, Recall, and Worksharing Procedures*. Bureau of Labor Statistics, BLS Bulletin 1425-13.

US Department of Labor 1981: *Characteristics of Major Collective Bargaining Agreements, January 1, 1980*. Bureau of Labor Statistics, BLS Bulletin 2095, May.

Ulman, Lloyd 1955: *The Rise of the National Trade Union*. Cambridge, Massachusetts: Harvard University Press.

von Weizsacker, Carl Christian 1978: A small contribution to the theory of wage structure in collective bargaining. In Z. Griliches et al. (eds), *Income Distribution and Economic Inequality*. Frankfurt/Main: Campus Verlag, 155-59.

Ward, Ben 1958: The firm in Illyria: market syndicalism. *American Economic Review*, 48 (4), 566-89.

Webb, Sidney and Webb, Beatrice 1902: *Industry Democracy*. London: Longmans.

Weiss, Yoram 1985: The effect of labor unions on investment in training: a dynamic model. *Journal of Political Economy*, 93 (5), October, 994-1007.

Wessels, Walter J. 1985: The effects of unions on employment and productivity: an unresolved conflict. *Journal of Labor Economics*, 3 (1, suppl. 1), 101-8.

Williamson, Oliver E. 1975: *Markets and Hierarchies: Analysis and Antitrust Implications*. New York: Free Press.

Williamson, Oliver E. 1985: *The Economic Institutions of Capitalism: Firms, Markets, and Relational Contracting*. New York: Free Press.

Zeuthen, F. 1930: *Problems of Monopoly and Economic Warfare*. London: G. Routledge and Sons.

Index

Labor Markets under Trade Unionism
Employment, Wages, and Hours
John Pencavel

In recent years the study of contracts, bargaining, transaction costs, and internal labor markets has considerably extended the theoretical base of labor economics and research on unionism. At the same time, there has been a noticeable split between theoretical model-building and the empirical study of the effects of unions on contracts.

The essential aim of John Pencavel's important new book is to relate and bring a little closer these two strands. Professor Pencavel provides a selective survey and synthesis of the extensive literature on the subject but relates this throughout to the empirical evidence. The analysis is further extended by a comparative study of US and British labor markets.

This book will unquestionably push forward the study of labor markets, unionization, and wage bargaining. In setting out an agenda for future research John Pencavel both draws out the importance of the empirical implementation of theory and stresses the need for a closer understanding by economists of the industrial relations literature.